TRUST • RESILIENCE • TEAMWORK

Success: Fully Charged

Making of a SUPER AUTO

Binu Nair

INDIA • SINGAPORE • MALAYSIA

ISBN
Paperback 979-8-89699-516-6
Hardcase 979-8-89699-791-7

Contents

Author's Note

The story of **Success: Fully Charged** has its roots in the transformative journey of TI Cycles of India, a division of Tube Investments of India (TII), part of the illustrious Murugappa Group. For decades, TI Cycles had been a stalwart in India's mobility landscape, but the Indian cycling industry had stagnated, as consumers increasingly turned to motorized two-wheelers. As a business division, we were with the question that haunted us all: how do we grow? If not, how do we remain profitable as a business?

In 2018, the arrival of Mr. Kalyan Kumar Paul as President of TI Cycles marked a turning point. A seasoned leader with over three decades of experience in TII, Mr. Paul brought with him both a deep understanding of the cycling industry and an unflinching mandate to turn the business around. Under his leadership, we embarked on a series of bold initiatives. One of the most pivotal projects he entrusted to me was the restructuring of the organization itself. This "clean-sheet" restructuring, termed as Zero-Based Organisation (ZBO), became a benchmark within TII. It allowed us to align the workforce to our strategic objectives, unlocking agility, reducing overheads, and ensuring on-time delivery of products. The results were transformative—in 2021, TI Cycles achieved its second-highest profit-before-tax (PBT) since its inception 75 years ago.

Beyond restructuring, I had the privilege of leading a large-scale visioning exercise to redefine our collective aspiration for TI Cycles. Through a large-scale interactive process, we co-created the vision:

"Improving quality of life through Eco-Friendly Mobility Solutions." This vision became the guiding star for our business, shaping not just our strategic decisions but also our sense of purpose as an organization.

Having stabilized the core business and reignited confidence, we turned our attention to the future. While electrification of bicycles was a logical first step, it soon became clear that scaling profitably in this space was challenging. Exploring electric two-wheelers revealed a crowded and competitive market dominated by incumbents and a flood of new entrants. However, our foray into the electric three-wheeler space opened up a new horizon. At the time, three-wheeler electrification was still nascent, offering us an opportunity to create something meaningful and impactful.

The project began modestly, with a small team drawn from our existing workforce at TI Cycles. None of us had experience in the automobile industry, but we were brimming with the spirit to take on this challenge. Our guiding principle was simple yet ambitious: we would not create another run-of-the-mill product. Instead, we sought to design an electric auto-rickshaw that would genuinely address customer pain points—offering reliability, affordability, and innovation. Along the way, we collaborated with a South Korean design firm to develop a proof of concept and initial technical specifications. As the project gained momentum, the management decided to establish a dedicated subsidiary, TI Clean Mobility Pvt. Ltd., which now oversees a diverse portfolio under the Montra Electric brand.

This book is inspired by that remarkable journey, blending real experiences with fictional storytelling. It captures the technical challenges, organizational dynamics, and personal struggles faced by a team of professionals tasked with creating something extraordinary under immense pressure. It shines a light on the moments of doubt, the hard-fought consensus, and the exhilaration of small victories. At its heart, this story is about transformation—of an organization, a team, and the individuals within it.

Through the characters, readers will see the realities of cross-functional collaboration, the balancing act of meeting deadlines without compromising quality, and the human challenges of leading through uncertainty. The narrative highlights how a team of determined individuals, tackled seemingly insurmountable odds with creativity, resilience, and trust in each other. It shows the power of an aligned vision and the courage to pursue it.

Success: Fully Charged is more than just a story about building a product. It's about the lessons we learn when we embrace challenges head-on—about what happens when we decide to innovate and disrupt, even when the odds are against us. For readers, this book provides a behind-the-scenes glimpse into the complex, often messy process of turning an idea into reality. Whether you're an industry professional, an entrepreneur, or simply someone who loves a story of grit and innovation, I hope you'll find something relatable in these pages.

Above all, this book is a celebration of the human spirit—the willingness to experiment, the drive to solve real-world problems, and the belief that with the right people and the right vision, no challenge is insurmountable. I hope it inspires you, as it inspired us, to dream boldly and work tirelessly to make those dreams come true.

– Binu Nair

Foreword

It is rare to come across a novel that captures not only the emotional dynamics of a corporate journey but also dives deeply into the technical, strategic, and human elements of what it takes to bring a product to life. This book, centered around the development of an Electric Passenger Auto, does exactly that. The author has woven together a story that is both gripping and realistic, taking readers on a journey that many of us in the corporate world can deeply relate to.

At its core, this novel is not just about launching a product—it is about the relentless pursuit of excellence under intense pressure, the discipline required to succeed, and the teamwork that is essential in overcoming obstacles. The characters come to life through their interactions, their struggles, and their triumphs. They face the kinds of challenges that are all too familiar in the real world—delays, financial constraints, technical setbacks—and yet, they push through with resilience and focus.

What stands out most about this novel is how authentic the portrayal of corporate life is. The detailed descriptions of meetings, decision-making processes, and the politics of pricing, cost management, and market strategy are spot on. The author has clearly spent time in the trenches of corporate life, and it shows. Every conversation between the characters feels real, whether it's about negotiating with suppliers, managing cash flow, or balancing the demands of leadership with the personal sacrifices required to achieve something great.

The novel's technical depth is another element that makes it stand out. Whether discussing Battery Management Systems (BMS), powertrains, chassis integration, or the intricacies of supply chain management, the story does not shy away from the details. Instead, it embraces them, adding layers of complexity to the narrative that make it as informative as it is entertaining. Readers who appreciate the engineering side of product development will find themselves captivated by the author's command of the subject matter, while those unfamiliar with the technical aspects will appreciate how seamlessly the technical jargon is explained within the context of the story.

The corporate landscape in the novel feels incredibly real— complete with tense boardroom discussions, high-stakes investor meetings, and the balancing act of managing team dynamics under pressure. Each character is fully realized, from Amit, the project manager who holds the team together, to Nisha, the seasoned CEO whose leadership steers the company through treacherous waters. These are not just characters in a book—they feel like colleagues you've worked with, leaders you've looked up to, and teammates who've had your back during the most challenging projects.

Beyond the technical and corporate aspects, what truly resonates is the human story at the heart of the novel. The way the team forms, storms, and ultimately gels into a cohesive unit is both inspiring and relatable. Their personal sacrifices, late nights, and shared triumphs remind us that behind every great product is a dedicated group of individuals working together to make it happen.

The lucid style of writing makes even the most complex concepts easy to understand, yet the narrative never loses its intensity. The pacing is steady, building suspense as the team navigates each obstacle on their path to the final launch. The dialogue is sharp, the characters' motivations clear and the story flows naturally, all of which keeps readers engaged from start to finish.

For anyone who has ever been part of a major project or worked in a corporate setting, this novel will strike a chord. It is a celebration of discipline, leadership, and teamwork—qualities that are not only relevant in business but in life as well. It is a story that highlights the importance of staying the course, no matter how challenging the road may be.

This novel will undoubtedly inspire readers, not only by showing them what goes into creating a successful product but by illustrating that with the right mindset, a strong team, and unwavering discipline, anything is possible.

I congratulate the author on creating such a compelling narrative, one that feels both timely and timeless in its relevance. This novel is a must-read for anyone who wants to understand the inner workings of corporate success, and it will leave a lasting impression on all who pick it up.

- Mukesh Ahuja

Managing Director

Tube Investments of India,

Chennai

Introduction

The Rise of Electric Vehicles in India

The world is on the brink of a transportation revolution, and India—one of the fastest-growing economies—is no exception. As urbanization intensifies, the country's roads are teeming with an ever-increasing number of vehicles. The resulting pollution, coupled with the rising cost of fuel, has spurred the Indian government and industries to search for sustainable alternatives. Electric Vehicles (EVs), once considered a distant possibility, are now at the forefront of India's transportation strategy.

This novel is set against the backdrop of India's rapidly evolving electric vehicle industry, where the intersection of innovation, regulation, and market forces creates both immense opportunities and formidable challenges. At the heart of this industry is Volt Motors, an ambitious new player, and its efforts to launch a series of electric vehicles—starting with the Electric Passenger Auto. The company's success or failure mirrors the challenges that the broader EV industry in India faces.

India's Push for Electric Vehicles

India's commitment to reducing its carbon footprint is driving significant momentum toward EV adoption. The government has set aggressive goals to transition to electric mobility, particularly in urban areas, to reduce air pollution and decrease reliance on imported oil. Incentives like tax breaks, subsidies, and the Faster Adoption and Manufacturing of Electric Vehicles

(FAME) scheme have made the EV space attractive to both established manufacturers and start-ups.

While traditional automotive giants have been slow to pivot, several new players—including start-ups like Volt Motors—are stepping up to the challenge. These new entrants bring fresh energy and innovative thinking, seeing electric vehicles as a way to disrupt the industry. They believe that EVs represent the future of transportation, particularly in densely populated cities where affordable, eco-friendly transport options are critical.

Why New Players Are Interested

Volt Motors, founded by forward-thinking entrepreneurs, is determined to carve out a niche in the electric vehicle market. Unlike established auto manufacturers that are burdened by legacy technology and slower to innovate, new entrants like Volt Motors are agile, unencumbered by decades of internal combustion engine (ICE) development. Their goal is to design vehicles specifically for the electric age, from the ground up, which gives them an edge in terms of cost, innovation, and adaptability.

India, with its vast population and growing urban infrastructure, presents a huge untapped market for electric autos, buses, and commercial vehicles. The potential to dominate this space is attracting global attention, as well as significant investment from both domestic and international venture capital firms. Start-ups like Volt Motors are positioning themselves to be the first movers in a rapidly expanding market, with the hope of capturing early market share before larger players fully commit to EV technology.

Technology Challenges

Despite the enthusiasm, developing and launching electric vehicles in India is fraught with technological challenges. The core components of any electric vehicle are its battery and powertrain— both of which are complex, expensive, and heavily reliant on cutting-edge technology. This presents a major hurdle for Indian EV manufacturers, including Volt Motors.

1. **Battery Technology:** The battery is the most critical component of an EV, and its performance determines the range, speed, and cost of the vehicle. However, India currently lacks the domestic capacity to manufacture advanced lithium-ion batteries at scale. Most of the battery cells are imported, particularly from China, which has a near-monopoly on the global lithium-ion battery supply chain. This dependence on foreign suppliers introduces significant supply chain risks and cost fluctuations. For companies like Volt Motors, securing reliable and affordable battery supplies is a constant challenge.

2. **Powertrain and Electric Motors:** The powertrain—the system that drives the vehicle using electrical power—is another critical piece of EV technology. Developing efficient and cost-effective powertrains requires significant R&D investment, something that many Indian companies are just beginning to tackle. While Volt Motors is working with both domestic and international partners to source powertrain components, they still rely on technology from countries like Germany and Japan for high-performance motors and control systems.

3. **Charging Infrastructure:** A major technological challenge for EVs in India is the lack of a widespread charging infrastructure. While the government is promoting the establishment of charging stations, the pace of implementation is slow. Many prospective buyers are hesitant to switch to electric vehicles due to concerns about range and the availability of charging stations. This puts additional pressure on companies like Volt Motors to ensure their vehicles have a competitive range and energy efficiency, even in the absence of a robust charging network.

4. **Battery Recycling and Sustainability:** Beyond the immediate challenges of manufacturing, there's the issue of sustainability. As the industry scales up, dealing with end-of-life battery disposal and recycling will become a critical issue. While Volt Motors is committed to sustainability, the lack of established battery recycling infrastructure in India adds complexity to their long-term plans.

People Challenges

The EV revolution is not just about technology; it's also about the people driving the change. One of the major challenges facing companies like Volt Motors is the talent gap. The automotive industry has traditionally been centered around internal combustion engines, and many engineers, designers, and technicians are still catching up on the nuances of electric vehicle technology.

1. **Talent Shortage:** Skilled engineers who specialize in electric drivetrains, battery systems, and power electronics are in high demand but short supply. Volt Motors must compete not only with

other Indian startups but also with global automakers and tech giants for top talent. Attracting, retaining, and training engineers who understand the intricacies of electric vehicles is one of the company's biggest challenges.

2. **Workplace Dynamics:** In addition to technical expertise, the cultural shift within the workplace is another hurdle. Employees at Volt Motors are working in a high-pressure, high-stakes environment, where innovation must be balanced with execution. Navigating office politics, team dynamics, and maintaining morale are constant struggles for Amit Gupta and his leadership team. As a project manager, Amit must ensure his team stays motivated and focused while dealing with the intense pressures of deadlines, cost constraints, and external competition.
3. **Resistance to Change:** Within the broader industry, there is resistance to change. Many automotive workers are deeply rooted in the traditional manufacturing processes of ICE vehicles. Convincing the workforce that EVs are the future, and that their skill sets need to evolve, is a challenge that Volt Motors faces internally and within the larger supply chain.

Regulatory Environment

India's regulatory environment for electric vehicles is evolving rapidly. The government, recognizing the environmental benefits and the need to reduce oil imports, has implemented a range of incentives to accelerate EV adoption. However, these regulations are still a work in progress, and there is uncertainty about how policies might shift in the coming years.

1. **Government Incentives:** The **FAME** (Faster Adoption and Manufacturing of Hybrid and Electric Vehicles) & PM eDrive schemes have been instrumental in reducing the cost of electric vehicles for consumers. Subsidies for EV buyers, tax exemptions, and grants for charging infrastructure are key components of the government's plan to increase EV penetration. Companies like Volt Motors rely on these incentives to make their products competitive in the market.

2. **Import Duties:** One significant regulatory challenge is India's high import duties on electric vehicle components, especially those related to batteries and powertrains. This makes it expensive for companies like Volt Motors, which import key components from countries like China. The government is gradually encouraging local manufacturing but building a domestic supply chain will take time.

3. **Environmental Regulations:** India's growing focus on environmental regulations is a double-edged sword for the EV industry. On one hand, stricter emission norms are pushing traditional automakers to shift toward cleaner technologies. On the other hand, companies like Volt Motors must navigate complex rules around the recycling of batteries and ensuring that their manufacturing processes meet sustainability standards.

Dependence on Foreign Technology

One of the most critical issues facing the Indian EV industry is its dependence on foreign technology, particularly from China. This dependence is most evident in the battery supply chain, where China controls a significant portion of the world's lithium-ion battery production. Volt Motors, like many other companies, is acutely aware of the risks this dependency presents—ranging from price volatility to potential supply chain disruptions due to geopolitical tensions.

Battery Supply Chain: China's dominance in the battery market means that Indian manufacturers have little choice but to source their components from Chinese suppliers. This dependency not only affects cost structures but also exposes companies to supply chain risks. The Indian government has announced plans to encourage domestic battery production, but it will take years for India to reduce its reliance on imports.

1. **Powertrain Components:** While China leads in battery technology, other countries such as Germany, Japan, and the U.S. are leaders in electric powertrain development. Volt Motors imports many of its key components, such as motors and control systems, from foreign suppliers. This dependence makes Volt vulnerable to global supply chain disruptions, especially in the current climate of trade tensions and protectionist policies.

2. **Local Manufacturing Push:** In response to these challenges, Volt Motors is working on long-term strategies to localize its supply chain. However, building local capacity—particularly in advanced

technology areas like battery cell production and high-efficiency powertrains—will require significant investment and time.

Conclusion

In this novel, we will follow Amit Gupta and his team at Volt Motors as they navigate the complexities of launching their first Electric Passenger Auto in a rapidly evolving and highly competitive market. The challenges they face—technological constraints, regulatory pressures, people dynamics, and international dependencies—are reflective of the broader struggles that all new players in India's electric vehicle industry must confront. Their success or failure will not only define their own futures but also shape the future of the Indian automotive landscape, as the country races toward a greener, more sustainable tomorrow

Chapter 1

What is the DNA You Want to Build to Differentiate in the Market?

Part 1: Introduction to Volt Motors

Amit Gupta stepped into the spacious, climate-controlled lobby of Volt Motors, his stride confident but his mind brimming with anticipation and the enormity of the task ahead. Today wasn't just a regular day at the office—it was the beginning of a defining journey, one that could shape Volt Motors' future in the electric vehicle market. The tall, gleaming glass windows framed the lobby, allowing the bright morning sunlight to flood in and bounce off polished concrete floors, filling the space with an energizing light that was as bold and sharp as Volt's ambitions. Designed with sleek, minimalist lines, the building itself was a physical manifestation of Volt's ethos of sustainability and transparency, a structure meant to reflect Volt's forward-thinking mission. Solar panels spanned the entire rooftop, powering the building with clean energy, while a row of modern electric charging stations lined the parking lot just outside, ready to serve not only employees but visiting EV owners as well.

The open-plan design, with glass walls and collaborative workspaces, was intended to foster openness and teamwork among employees—a reminder that the company valued new ideas and embraced innovation. But Amit knew all too well that this open environment also had its share of underlying competition and power struggles, where individual agendas sometimes clashed despite the outward unity. As he crossed the lobby, he felt the intensity of the day gathering around him, his usual calm laced with a thrill of pressure and anticipation. This project—the development and launch of Volt's first Electric Passenger Auto—wasn't just another line on his resume. It was the most critical endeavor of his career, an initiative that would either cement Volt's reputation as an industry leader or leave them trailing behind competitors in an increasingly crowded space.

Today was the formal kickoff for a project that would either propel Volt into the next phase of its evolution or leave it struggling to catch up. The stakes were sky-high; this wasn't just about designing a reliable, affordable electric vehicle. It was about defining a product that would embody Volt's brand and promise. The Electric Passenger Auto was Volt's opportunity to carve out a unique space in the market—a space where affordability, innovation, and sustainability were not just ideals but essentials, seamlessly blended into a product that Indian urban commuters could truly rely on. Amit had always thrived under pressure, but even he could feel the weight of this project pressing down on him as he walked through the polished lobby.

As he headed to the Strategy Room on the top floor, Amit noticed the heightened energy coursing through the building. Employees moved with a sense of purpose and urgency that matched his own. They understood the importance of this project and what it meant for Volt's future. Everyone knew that the Electric Passenger Auto was the company's most ambitious project to date, and failure was not an option. The anticipation and anxiety in the air were palpable, a mix of hope and nervous excitement that Amit felt mirrored within himself. This wasn't just another product—it was a landmark initiative with the power to redefine the market, to show what Volt could achieve under intense competition.

Entering the Strategy Room, a modern, glass-enclosed space perched on the top floor with expansive views of the bustling city skyline, Amit took a moment to appreciate the setting. The room, with its panoramic view of the city and open layout, represented Volt's mission to bring a new vision to urban India. The skyline beyond was a constant reminder of the sprawling urban landscape their vehicle would serve—a market filled with complex needs and high expectations. Seated at the head of the long, polished conference table was Nisha Mehta, Volt Motors' dynamic and formidable CEO. Known for her intense focus and visionary leadership, Nisha had driven Volt's push into the electric vehicle market with an uncompromising determination that made her both respected and feared. She had an uncanny ability to see through any façade, a sharpness in her gaze that measured not only people's words but their intentions. Today, that gaze was fixed on Amit as he entered, her expression unyielding yet with a spark of excitement that matched his own.

"Morning, Amit," she said, her tone brisk and direct, as if every second of the meeting was already accounted for.

"Good morning, Nisha," Amit replied, taking a seat across from her. He nodded to Raghav, the head of strategy, who sat beside her. Raghav was a study in contrast to Nisha's fierce drive. Calm, methodical, and always grounded, Raghav brought balance to Nisha's fiery leadership, often serving as the voice of reason in the room. His strategic mind was razor-sharp, and his approach deliberate; where Nisha dreamed of disrupting entire markets, Raghav made sure those dreams were feasible, backing every plan with careful data analysis. Today, his focus was fully trained on Amit, his steely gaze assessing every movement, every word.

"Let's get right into it," Nisha said, wasting no time as she slid a thick market analysis report across the table toward Amit. "The Electric Passenger Auto. Competitors are moving fast—some established, others new, but all eager to grab market share. We can't afford to lag behind. Speed is essential, yes, but we need to be strategic. This can't just be another product launch. This has to be something that redefines what an affordable, eco-friendly vehicle means for the average commuter in India."

Amit nodded, already familiar with the stakes of the project. He had spent hours reviewing the same market analysis and customer data, getting a sense of the intense competition they were up against. "I've been analyzing customer insights and the market landscape. It's clear that while there's demand for affordability, customers aren't willing to compromise on quality or innovation. The market is fragmented—people want low costs, but they also want reliability and cutting-edge features. The challenge will be to bring all these elements together in a way that makes sense financially and appeals to the consumer."

Raghav leaned forward, his fingers steepled thoughtfully, his gaze sharp but encouraging. "Amit let's cut to the heart of it. What's the DNA of this vehicle? What is going to make it stand out in the market? We need something specific—performance, design, price point. What's the story we're telling with this product?"

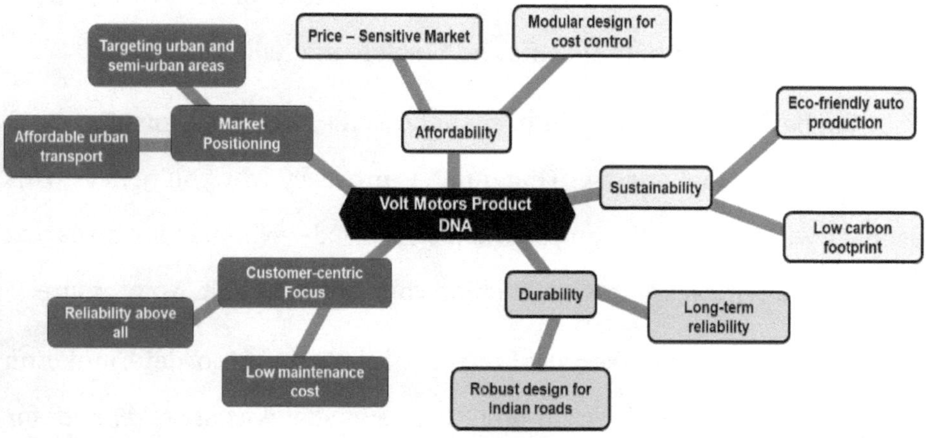

Fig 1.1

Amit paused, choosing his words carefully as he considered the high expectations surrounding the project. "It's about creating a product that balances all aspects. We're not just designing an electric vehicle; we're providing a solution. A solution to urban congestion, pollution, and the rising costs of fuel. This Electric Auto has to resonate with the average Indian commuter, someone who needs affordability but also values durability and low maintenance. It has to appeal to a broader, eco-conscious audience as well. Affordability, durability, and sustainability are our non-negotiables here."

Nisha's critical gaze softened slightly, though the intensity remained. "We don't just need to compete, Amit. We need to disrupt. This vehicle must be a game-changer. Otherwise, we're just another voice in a crowded field."

"That's exactly what I'm thinking," Amit said, the excitement of the challenge tempered by the weight of responsibility. "But we have to be mindful of overpromising. We can't build the perfect vehicle overnight. We need a focus—something specific and tangible that will set us apart."

Raghav's lips curved into a slight smile, his tone turning both supportive and challenging. "That, Amit, is precisely why you're here. This product will carry your name. How it's received—whether it's a roaring success or a critical failure—will define your future at Volt. No pressure."

Amit let a slight smirk cross his face, masking the mix of determination and anxiety that stirred within him. He knew what was at stake, both for the company and for his own career. This project was more than just a product launch; it was a chance to create something lasting, something that would redefine both Volt's reputation and his own. Failure wasn't just a setback—it was a path to irrelevance.

Part 2: Market Research

Later that afternoon, Amit convened the key members of his team in Volt Motors' Design Lab, a spacious, open area filled with the spirit of innovation and ambition. The lab, with its sleek interactive whiteboards and prototypes of past models suspended from the ceiling, was where Volt's boldest ideas took form, a physical representation of the company's vision for the future. Rows of screens displayed the latest market research and customer insights, along with charts tracking the evolving trends in electric vehicle technology. For Amit, this room was more than just a workspace; it was the nerve centre of Volt Motors' potential, the birthplace of products that could shape the future of urban transportation in India.

Standing at the head of the oval-shaped glass table, Amit watched as his team filtered in. They were a formidable group of specialists, each of them bringing unique expertise and a fiercely individual perspective. He knew that aligning them on a single vision for the Electric Passenger Auto would be no easy task. Each member had their own priorities, and the intense focus each brought to their area of responsibility often led to friction. As they took their seats, Amit could sense the anticipation and tension in the room, an energy that mirrored his own excitement tempered with responsibility.

Vivek, the head of engineering, was the first to break the silence. He placed a stack of technical reports on the table with a solid thud and crossed his arms, his gaze steady and uncompromising. Vivek's tall, serious frame and no-nonsense approach gave him an air of authority that few questioned. He was known for his meticulousness and his insistence on engineering precision, a trait that ensured his designs were of the highest quality but often brought him into conflict when budgets or timelines conflicted with his ideals.

"Amit, we need to focus on performance metrics if we're going to make this a success," Vivek said, his tone matter of fact. "The market is flooded with cheap electric autos that run on lead-acid batteries—they're unreliable and give the entire segment a bad name. If we're going to distinguish ourselves, we need something that delivers consistent range, dependable torque, and, most importantly, durability. No shortcuts on the powertrain, not if we want this to last."

Amit gave a slight nod, unsurprised by Vivek's stance. He knew Vivek's commitment to quality was unwavering, and while this assured that his engineering standards were high, it often clashed with the practical realities of budget constraints and customer needs. "I hear you, Vivek. We've all seen the impact that compromised engineering can have on a product's reputation. But remember, performance isn't the only thing driving this market."

At that, Kiran, the head of marketing, leaned forward, his face lighting up with the enthusiasm that was his trademark. Kiran's energy was infectious, and his customer-centred mindset kept the team grounded in the realities of consumer expectations. He was skilled at getting to the heart of what Volt's customers wanted and reminding the team that technical specifications alone wouldn't sell a product. However, Amit had learned that Kiran's optimism sometimes led him to oversimplify challenges, a trait that Amit balanced with a pragmatic approach.

"Exactly, Amit! If we focus only on performance, we're going to lose sight of what our customers actually care about," Kiran said, his voice laced with conviction. "Let's not forget who we're building this for—urban and semi-urban commuters who depend on these autos day in and day out. For them, it's not about a premium experience; it's about affordability and reliability. If we don't meet them where they are, we're going to lose market share to every small player who can offer a cheaper product. They're not just buying a vehicle; they're investing in something that affects their livelihood."

Amit absorbed Kiran's words, knowing that he was right in many ways. This was a market defined by a unique blend of needs and limitations, a demographic that couldn't afford to experiment with a high-end product but still valued quality and consistency. Balancing these priorities without sacrificing the integrity of the product was the challenge. Kiran's enthusiasm for connecting with the market was invaluable, yet Amit knew they couldn't ignore the technical and financial realities the project faced.

As Kiran finished, Suhani, the head of finance, who had been listening intently, tapped a few figures into her tablet before looking up. Her tone was cool and pragmatic, a voice that constantly reminded the team of Volt's financial boundaries. Suhani's approach was rooted in a meticulous understanding of cost structures and margins, and while her firm control over finances kept the project grounded, her emphasis on budget constraints often put her at odds with Vivek's commitment to technical excellence.

"Kiran's absolutely right about the price-sensitive market," she said, her voice calm but firm. "I've been running projections, and if we price this auto even slightly higher than the competition, we'll start bleeding potential buyers. We need to control costs from day one. Every element—batteries, motors, chassis materials—needs to be scrutinized. We can't afford to blow the budget if we're going to make this vehicle accessible to the masses."

Suhani's practicality was indispensable, and Amit respected her clear-eyed view of Volt's financial capabilities. However, he could also sense the tension brewing between her and Vivek. Both were right in their concerns, but he knew that finding common ground would be crucial to the project's success. Vivek's dedication to quality clashed with Suhani's financial caution, and Kiran's focus on customer value added a third dimension to the equation.

"Pooja," Amit said, turning to their head designer, who had been quietly sketching ideas in her notebook. Known for her unorthodox approach and creative flair, Pooja was often the wild card in the room. Her design ideas had a way of challenging conventions, pushing the boundaries of what was considered possible or practical. Yet her designs, once refined, often brought a unique edge to Volt's products, adding an element of innovation that resonated with customers.

Pooja looked up, her black-framed glasses reflecting the soft light in the lab, her hair pulled back in a loose bun. She was someone who rarely held back her ideas, and her out-of-the-box thinking often brought a fresh perspective to the team. "I've been listening, and here's my take," she began, tapping her pencil thoughtfully on her sketchbook. "We're looking at this too rigidly. Yes, cost and performance are essential, but design can bridge gaps that engineering, and finance can't. If we create a design that feels premium, we can enhance customer perception without necessarily relying on high-end materials."

Vivek raised an eyebrow, scepticism plain on his face. "Design isn't going to make the battery last longer, Pooja. It's the performance that makes or breaks a product, not how sleek it looks."

"True," Pooja replied without missing a beat, her tone confident. "But design can enhance perception. If our auto looks modern and well-built, customers will associate it with quality, even if we're using cost-effective materials where we can. We can leverage textured plastics and lightweight metals that feel durable without driving up costs. It's about creating a cohesive experience—one where form and function work together to make the vehicle feel valuable."

She flipped open her sketchbook, revealing a series of rough designs. The auto she had envisioned was sleek yet practical, with clean lines and an aerodynamic silhouette that felt contemporary without being extravagant. Her design emphasized both style and utility, with durable materials in critical areas and an aesthetic that communicated reliability and innovation.

Kiran leaned forward; his interest piqued. "I like where this is going, Pooja. If we market it as the 'future of urban transport,' we can appeal to a younger demographic—people who want to feel like they're part of something innovative, even if they're not paying top dollar."

Suhani, however, looked less convinced, her gaze steady on her tablet as she calculated potential costs. "Let's not get carried away with aesthetics. Design is important, yes, but it's not going to save us if the performance falls short or if our costs spiral out of control."

Amit could feel the fractures forming in the conversation. Each person brought their own expertise to the table, but their perspectives were still siloed, focused on individual goals rather than the collective vision. To succeed, they would need to unify these viewpoints, to find a balance that respected engineering standards, financial limitations, and customer expectations.

"All right let's take a step back," Amit said, pulling up a chart on the interactive screen behind him. The screen displayed data from customer surveys, highlighting common concerns and preferences. "We've collected insights from prospective customers, and here's what they're saying. Price is definitely a major factor, but it's not the only thing. They also care about reliability, low maintenance costs, and a reasonable range. They want something that doesn't feel cheap, something that won't break down or require constant repairs."

He pointed to a section of the data that showed customer pain points with current electric autos. "A large percentage of current auto drivers complain about high maintenance costs—batteries that degrade too quickly, motors that fail, constant repairs. If we want to capture this market, we need to create something they can depend on."

Vivek, now more engaged, leaned forward, a hint of enthusiasm in his voice. "Exactly, Amit. This is why we can't compromise on the powertrain. We need a robust battery that provides good range without degrading after a year of use. I've been researching solid-state battery technology—it offers better energy density and longer life cycles, but it's costly."

Amit nodded thoughtfully. "I'm with you on the potential of solid-state tech, but it might be out of our budget for now. Can we look at optimizing our current lithium-ion options to find a balance between cost and performance?"

Vivek's expression shifted, conceding the point. "We could explore more efficient cells from suppliers in South Korea or Japan. It would increase the initial costs, but over time, it could reduce total ownership costs for the user, which aligns with our value proposition."

Suhani looked up from her tablet, her mind already turning to the logistics. "It's a potential solution, but we need to be careful with our import dependencies. China dominates the global lithium-ion market, and any disruption there could jeopardize our entire plan."

The room fell silent for a moment as the weight of Suhani's words settled. The team was well aware of the risks associated with import dependencies, particularly in such a volatile sector. Any shift in trade policies or supply chain disruptions could upend their carefully laid plans.

Amit broke the silence, his tone steady but determined. "Then we need to start diversifying our supplier base. Let's look at partnerships in South Korea, Japan, or even potential domestic suppliers. Suhani, can you take the lead on researching these options and see where we can secure favourable pricing?"

She nodded, already jotting down notes. "I'll get on it and compile a list of viable suppliers."

Kiran, ever the optimist, jumped in with renewed enthusiasm. "If we play this right, the story practically writes itself. 'Volt Motors delivers reliability in uncertain times,' or 'Affordable, dependable, and futuristic.' We market this as something that's built for the future—something that holds up when things get tough."

Amit allowed himself a small smile at Kiran's unflagging enthusiasm, though he quickly redirected the focus. "Our message must be grounded in reality. If we overpromise and underdeliver, we'll lose the trust we're working so hard to build."

Turning to Vivek, he continued, "What about the powertrain? Can we achieve something durable and cost-effective without compromising on quality?"

Vivek exhaled deeply, his tone contemplative but resolute. "We're exploring lightweight alloys for the chassis to reduce weight and improve range. I've also been in talks with a few suppliers specializing in high-efficiency motors. They're not cheap, but they could give us the extra torque and longevity we need without pushing us over budget."

Pooja interjected, her voice carrying a note of excitement. "If we go with the lightweight alloys, I can adjust the design to complement it. We'll keep the auto sleek but rugged, something that can handle the daily grind on tough roads without looking clunky."

The discussion gained momentum as ideas bounced around the room. Amit felt a sense of progress, a feeling that they were moving toward a cohesive strategy. The initial resistance was melting away, replaced by a shared purpose that aligned their individual priorities into a unified direction.

"Good," Amit said, stepping back from the table to address the group. "We're making progress, but there's a long road ahead. Vivek, I want you to refine the engineering specs to maximize both durability and cost-efficiency. Suhani, keep an eye on cost projections with a focus on long-term sustainability. Kiran, work on a marketing plan that highlights our value proposition—affordability, reliability, and innovation. And Pooja, let's see more design iterations that balance function with forward-looking aesthetics."

The team nodded, each of them already formulating their next steps as they left the room, the initial tension replaced by a focused energy. They all knew that this project wasn't just another product—it was a defining moment for Volt Motors, a chance to revolutionize the market and set a new standard in urban transport.

As the last of his team filed out, Amit stayed behind, staring at the whiteboard where they'd sketched out the project's goals. The words "Affordability, Sustainability, Durability" stood out in bold letters, encapsulating the essence of Volt's vision for the Electric Passenger Auto. These three pillars would be the foundation of their vehicle, the guiding principles that would see them through the challenges ahead. Amit felt the weight of the project settle over him again, a blend of responsibility and excitement for what lay ahead.

This was just the beginning.

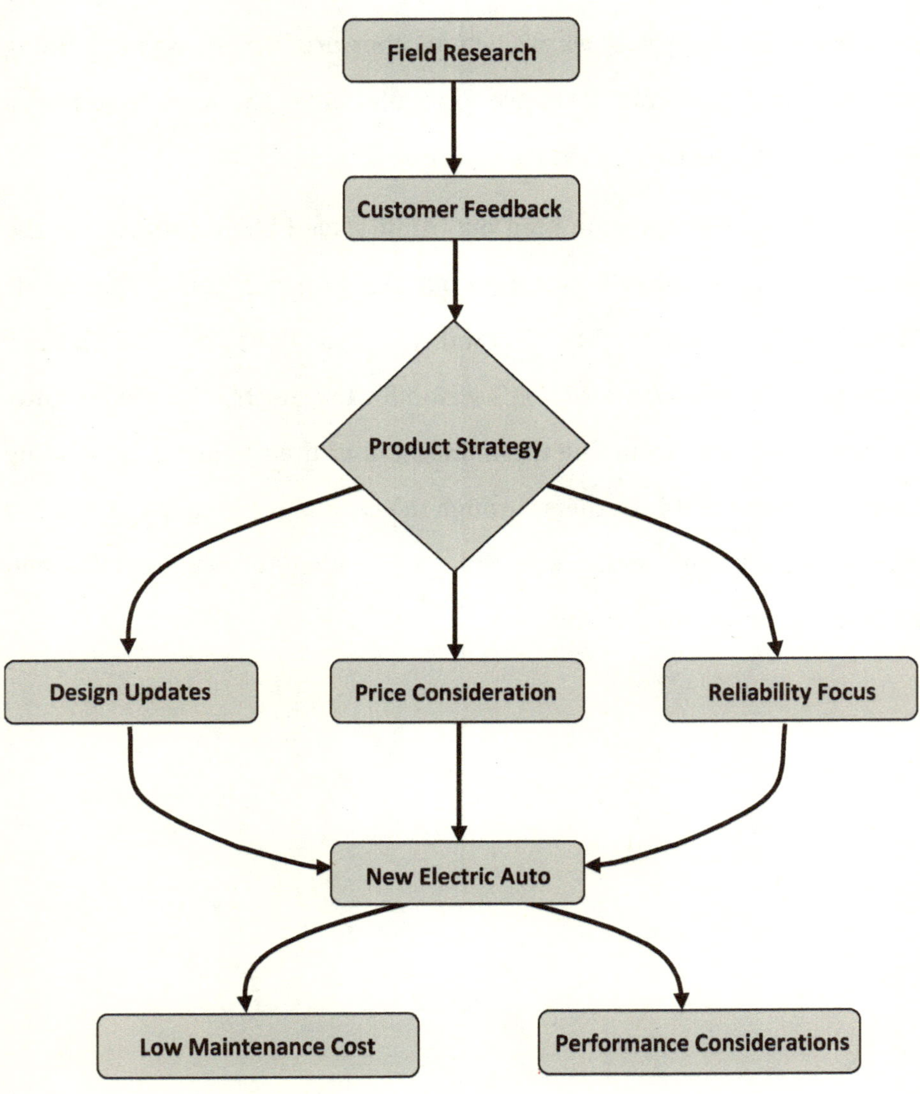

Fig 1.2

Part 3: Internal Resistance

As the meeting progressed, the atmosphere in the Design Lab grew taut, thickening with the tension that comes from unyielding convictions. Amit could feel the pressure mounting around him, a distinct, charged energy that only heightened as each team member fought to uphold their specific priorities. Each department head held tightly to their stance, unwilling to concede an inch. Engineering demanded robustness, finance insisted on stringent cost control, marketing urged customer-centred flexibility, and design pushed for a balance that married practicality with appeal. It was like watching tectonic plates push against each other, each creating fault lines in the conversation that threatened to split the team apart before they had even fully begun.

Amit leaned back slightly, letting his gaze settle on each team member in turn. He knew that the success of this project required more than technical expertise or financial acumen; it demanded an alignment of minds and a willingness to collaborate—a sense that they were in this together, driven by a shared purpose. And that unity was precisely what seemed to be slipping through their fingers as the debate grew more heated.

Deciding it was time to redirect the conversation, Amit cleared his throat and shifted in his chair, exuding calm authority as he addressed the room. "Look," he began, his voice steady and grounded, "I understand where each of you is coming from. The stakes here are incredibly high, and we're all pushing hard because we care deeply about this project. But if we're going to make this work, we must think as a team. We're not just creating another product; we're establishing a product's DNA that's going to define Volt Motors' future—possibly even set new standards for the industry. It's not just a matter of hitting numbers or meeting engineering specs; it's about building something that lasts and creating something that gets it right the first time."

Vivek, who had been silent for a moment, broke in, his tone unwavering and edged with tension. Leaning back with his arms crossed, he gave Amit a serious look. Vivek was known for his methodical, almost stubborn approach to engineering; he wasn't one to accept compromises easily, especially if he felt they could weaken the product. "I get the need to collaborate, Amit," he said, voice tight. "But there's no point in compromising if it undermines the product's integrity from the start. Cheaper materials mean weaker durability. We know what Indian roads are like—the potholes, the heat, the humidity. We can't afford to cut corners on essential components like the battery or the motor. If this auto can't endure daily abuse, it'll be nothing more than a liability, and that's not something I can sign off on."

Suhani, seated directly across from Vivek, barely paused before jumping in, her tone every bit as assertive. She tapped her pen against her tablet rhythmically, as if each tap drove her point further home. "And where do you suggest we find the budget to meet these demands, Vivek? I've run the numbers backward and forward. We're already working with slim margins to keep the product affordable. We can't price ourselves out of the market. Every rupee we add to production costs eats into our profit margin. If we go much higher, we'll alienate the very market we're trying to capture—urban and semi-urban commuters who aren't looking for luxuries; they're looking for something affordable and reliable. You may get the durability you want, but if we're too expensive, there'll be no buyers left. It's simple math."

Amit sensed the friction growing between Vivek's engineering idealism and Suhani's financial pragmatism. Both were experts, equally unwavering, and both unwilling to bend, each holding tight to their perspectives. This stalemate was one Amit knew he'd have to break if they were to get anywhere.

He glanced over at Pooja, who had been sketching furiously in her notebook, her face partially obscured behind her thick-framed glasses. Pooja's creativity and unorthodox ideas often brought a breath of fresh air to these discussions, and Amit could tell by the look on her face that she was deep in thought, likely on the verge of proposing something unexpected. He decided to draw her in, hoping her perspective could shift the conversation.

"Pooja," he said, his tone encouraging, "you've been unusually quiet today. What's going on in that head of yours?"

Pooja looked up, a spark of excitement flashing in her eyes as she set her pencil down. "I'm thinking about how we might approach this from a design perspective. I agree with both Vivek and Suhani, actually. We can't ignore the need for durability, but we also must respect the budget. So, what if we deliver a premium experience that doesn't come with a premium cost? Design has the power to influence perception, to create a sense of value. If we give customers an experience that feels high-quality, they'll believe in it, even if we're using more economical materials."

Vivek raised an eyebrow, his scepticism clear. "Pooja, this isn't about cosmetics. We're talking about performance and durability—design alone can't fix mechanical weaknesses."

Undeterred, Pooja responded with her characteristic conviction, "I'm not suggesting we compromise on essential performance metrics, Vivek. I'm saying that we can use design to bridge gaps where high-end materials aren't an option. For example, we can choose textures and finishes that feel durable but don't cost as much as the actual high-end components. If the auto looks reliable, feels solid, and has an aesthetic that's both modern and practical, customers will believe in the quality and durability, even if we're using cost-effective options for some parts."

She held up her sketchbook, displaying a rough concept of the auto she envisioned. The design was clean and minimalist, with sharp, defined lines that conveyed both strength and style. Her sketch highlighted rugged yet sleek exteriors that could withstand wear and tear without looking clunky, a balance of form and function that hinted at durability without compromising the contemporary appeal.

Kiran, whose eyes had lit up as Pooja spoke, leaned forward, his face animated. "I love where you're going with this, Pooja. There's a real story to be told here—an electric auto that's designed for the future but built for today's reality. If we market it as a reliable, forward-thinking option for urban drivers, something that combines value and vision, we'll capture the attention of a younger, aspirational audience too. They want something that feels progressive, even if they're not paying premium prices."

Suhani, however, remained sceptical, her gaze steady as she addressed the room. "I can see how perception matters, but we must be realistic. Design is important, but it's not going to save us if we can't back it up with actual performance. Vivek's right—we can't ignore things like powertrain quality or battery reliability, especially not if we want this product to last in real-world conditions. If we oversell the look without ensuring durability, the novelty will wear off fast, and we'll be back to square one."

Amit could see the fractures widening once again, each team member's viewpoint steadfast, yet valid. Vivek's scepticism toward anything that could be perceived as superficial, Suhani's wariness of the bottom line, Kiran's enthusiasm for customer connection, and Pooja's bold design concepts—all of it was pushing them further apart rather than closer to a unified direction. He recognized that the moment called for clarity, something that could align everyone on the shared purpose that had initially drawn them to this project.

He decided to shift the conversation. Rising from his seat, he walked to the whiteboard at the front of the room and picked up a marker. "Let's break this down," he said, his voice calm but firm. "We need to identify the core DNA of this vehicle. What are the elements that will make it stand out, that will define it in the market?"

Amit began writing on the board, listing their priorities in large, bold letters, one by one. "First, Affordability. We're not aiming for a premium segment here. Our target is the urban and semi-urban commuter who needs something reliable and cost-effective." He circled the word *Affordability* in thick black lines, underscoring its importance.

"Second," he continued, "Sustainability. We're positioning ourselves as an eco-friendly alternative. This vehicle needs to have a lower carbon footprint. That means efficient battery use, recyclability of materials, and a strong environmental story." He wrote *Sustainability* below *Affordability* and circled it with equal emphasis.

"And third," Amit concluded, "Durability. Vivek, you're absolutely right—we need a product that lasts. Indian roads are no joke, and our vehicle has to withstand daily wear and tear. Without this, the rest won't matter." He added *Durability* to the list, connecting it to the other principles with a line that created a triangle, symbolizing the balance they needed to achieve.

Stepping back, he looked around the room, meeting each of their eyes in turn. "These three principles are non-negotiable. They're the DNA of this project. If we can get these right—if we can find a balance that respects these priorities—we'll have something truly special, something that doesn't just enter the market but redefines it."

Suhani nodded slowly; her expression thoughtful. "I can work with that. But we need to be diligent about managing costs. I'll review the projections and look for places where we can economize without sacrificing key aspects of the product."

Vivek's posture relaxed slightly, though his face remained serious. "I'll go back to the engineering team and look for ways to optimize the materials. May be we can strike a balance with the battery and chassis, but we'll need to source high-quality suppliers. I'll also explore local options in case of supply chain issues. We can't afford disruptions."

Kiran leaned in; his voice infused with new enthusiasm. "This is starting to feel like a real vision. I'll start crafting the narrative—an electric auto that's reliable, future-focused, and accessible. We're creating value, something people can trust without breaking their bank."

Pooja's eyes gleamed with excitement; her creativity sparked. "And I'll refine the design sketches. I'll focus on aesthetics that communicate durability and sustainability while keeping it stylish. We want people to feel like they're stepping into the future, not a compromise."

Amit felt a shift in the room, a subtle yet powerful alignment as each team member committed to their role with renewed clarity. The friction was still there, but it was transformed, channelling the team's energy toward a common goal rather than dispersing it. This was progress, a tentative but significant step toward creating the Electric Passenger Auto they envisioned.

"Good," Amit said, his tone firm yet encouraging. "We have a lot of work ahead, but I think we're on the right path. Let's regroup tomorrow and dive into the specifics. Each of you has your part—let's make sure we're all moving forward together."

As the team began gathering their materials and leaving the room, the atmosphere was different—a shared understanding seemed to settle over them, a sense that they were united in a purpose greater than their individual roles. The journey ahead was long and undoubtedly filled with challenges, but today, at least, they had laid the foundation for a plan.

Alone in the room, Amit took a last look at the whiteboard, where the words *Affordability, Sustainability, Durability* stood out starkly. These three words would define Volt's Electric Passenger Auto. But he knew the real challenge would lie in making those principles tangible, in turning them from ideas on a whiteboard into a vehicle that could roll off the production line and onto the roads of India. The stakes were high, but Amit felt the stirrings of something powerful—a blend of responsibility and ambition that would drive him through whatever challenges lay ahead.

This was just the beginning, and he was ready.

Key Learnings from Chapter 1: What is the DNA You Want to Build to Differentiate in the Market?

1. **Define a Product's Core Identity:** Amit's team at Volt Motors identified the DNA of their Electric Auto—affordability, sustainability, and durability—as the guiding framework for all decisions. This clarity ensured the team stayed focused on creating a product that resonated with the market and differentiated itself from competitors. For professionals and businesses, establishing a core identity early on helps align diverse efforts and fosters consistency.

2. **Balance Aspirations with Practical Market Needs:** The debates between Vivek, who prioritized engineering excellence, and Kiran, who emphasized affordability, showcased the importance of balancing ambitious goals with customer realities. Amit's leadership steered the team toward solutions that addressed practical challenges, proving that aligning aspirations with user-centric needs leads to balanced outcomes in product development.

3. **Leverage Design to Bridge Perception Gaps:** Pooja's innovative approach to using cost-effective materials while emphasizing premium aesthetics demonstrated how design can significantly enhance customer perception. Her vision of creating a sleek and futuristic vehicle appealed to both budget-conscious and quality-driven consumers, underscoring that design is a powerful tool for adding value without inflating costs.

4. **Prioritize Customer-Centric Decision-Making:** Customer feedback revealed that reliability, low maintenance, and affordability were far more critical than high-end features. By keeping these insights at the centre of the project, Amit ensured that the product was aligned with the needs of its target market, proving that customer-focused strategies drive meaningful innovation.

5. **Foster Cross-Functional Collaboration:** The internal conflicts at Volt Motors—between engineering, marketing, finance, and design—highlighted the complexities of aligning departmental priorities. Amit's ability to foster collaboration and unite the team around a shared vision demonstrated that cross-functional teamwork is vital for overcoming resistance and driving progress.

6. **Avoid the Temptation of Shortcuts:** Vivek's proposal to skip critical tests to meet deadlines tested the team's commitment to quality. Amit's insistence on comprehensive testing, even at the cost of delays, emphasized the long-term risks of cutting corners.

This lesson reinforces that maintaining quality is essential for sustaining trust and avoiding costly failures later.

7. **Adapt to Constraints with Innovative Solutions:** The idea of modular design emerged as a solution to balance cost and performance. By offering a basic model with optional upgrades, Volt Motors could cater to both cost-sensitive and performance-driven customers. This adaptability showcases how innovative thinking can address diverse needs within constrained resources.

8. **Define Non-Negotiables to Guide Decisions:** Amit's articulation of the product's core pillars—affordability, sustainability, and durability—served as a litmus test for every decision. This clarity helped the team prioritize and avoid being side-tracked by conflicting interests, illustrating the power of clear, non-negotiable values in decision-making.

9. **Integrate Market Realities into the Development Process:** Volt Motors' approach of incorporating real-world feedback from auto drivers ensured the product was grounded in market realities. This direct engagement provided actionable insights and helped align the team's vision with customer priorities, proving the value of field research in refining strategies.

10. **Deliver a Consistent Value Proposition:** Kiran's marketing strategy of positioning the Electric Auto as "affordable, dependable, and futuristic" aligned perfectly with the product's DNA. Amit's commitment to delivering on this promise through robust engineering and design reinforced the importance of

aligning branding with product reality, ensuring credibility in the marketplace.

These integrated learnings reflect both the challenges and strategies seen at Volt Motors, offering actionable insights for professionals, managers, and academics to navigate product development effectively.

Chapter 2

Put the Customer Right at the Center of Your Decision

Part 1: Customer-Centric Vision

Amit sat alone in the conference room, a tension pulling at his shoulders that hadn't eased since Nisha had called for this meeting on short notice. Today, he would have to present the emerging consensus on the vehicle's DNA—a product philosophy that had taken weeks of intense debate to shape and was still barely holding together under the weight of differing priorities. The Electric Auto project was at a turning point, and Nisha's feedback today could either cement their path forward or send them back to square one. Amit could feel his usual confidence strained, his thoughts racing as he rehearsed his approach. Every choice, every compromise made so far had been an attempt to answer the question at the heart of the project: What did the customer truly need? Today, he would have to show Nisha that they had finally found a focus that resonated with that answer, a direction clear enough to guide them forward.

When Nisha entered, her presence immediately shifted the energy in the room. She moved with her usual precision, a focus that left no room for ambiguity or hesitation. Today, her expression was especially unreadable, her gaze sharper than usual, as though she could see through every detail, every assumption the team had made. She didn't waste time with pleasantries; instead, she placed her tablet on the table, took her seat with purpose, and fixed her eyes directly on Amit. Behind her were Raghav, composed as ever with his calm, assessing demeanour, and Kiran, who was already flipping through a thick stack of customer feedback reports he'd compiled over the past weeks.

"We've got a problem," Nisha began, her voice steady but edged with a directness that left little room for doubt. "I've been reviewing our product development updates, and it feels like we're losing sight of the most crucial factor: the customer. I'm seeing technical specs, internal metrics, and ambitious features, but I'm not seeing how they address what our end-users actually need."

She scanned the room, her gaze settling on each of them, daring anyone to offer a defence. When her eyes returned to Amit, he felt the intensity of her scrutiny. She had zero tolerance for sidestepping the core issue, and he knew she was right. The project had slowly become a tug-of-war between competing priorities. Each department had sought to push their own vision forward, leading to a product that had yet to speak clearly to the people it was meant to serve.

"I've said this before, and I'll say it again—every decision we make should centre around what the customer truly needs, not what looks good on paper," Nisha continued, her tone unyielding. "We're not here to impress with specs; we're here to solve real problems. The only measure of success is whether this vehicle delivers on that."

Amit felt the pressure of her words tighten around him. She had always pushed him to see the bigger picture, but today her insistence carried a new urgency. Somewhere along the way, as engineering, finance, and marketing all clamoured to be heard, they had drifted off course. He knew it, had felt it in the small compromises made with each department, each step drawing them slightly further from the core purpose of the vehicle.

Raghav leaned back, arms folded, and spoke in his usual measured tone, though today even he seemed frustrated. "We have extensive research, Amit. We know exactly what the market is asking for: affordability, durability, low running costs, and ease of maintenance. Yet here we are, debating specs and features that don't speak to any of that."

Kiran, who had been meticulously sifting through customer reports, nodded in agreement. He leaned forward, his expression serious, his voice underscoring the urgency of the situation. "Amit, we're building this for real people. Auto-rickshaw drivers, fleet owners—they've told us clearly what they need. And yet, we're still discussing high-end features that don't align with their priorities. Look at these surveys. The people we're building for are speaking directly to us, and I'm afraid we're not listening."

Amit looked down at the pile of reports Kiran had pushed toward him. Each page was filled with insights from their core market: drivers who navigated the unforgiving roads of cities like Mumbai, Delhi, and Bengaluru, all with high expectations and tight margins. The message was consistent and straightforward—reliability, affordability, and low maintenance costs. These drivers weren't looking for luxury or status; they needed something they could depend on, day in and day out.

He could feel the scrutiny of his team as he flipped through the reports, each of them waiting to hear how he planned to steer them out of the mire they had created. He felt the weight of their concerns settle heavily on him, knowing that he would need to guide the project back to its core purpose.

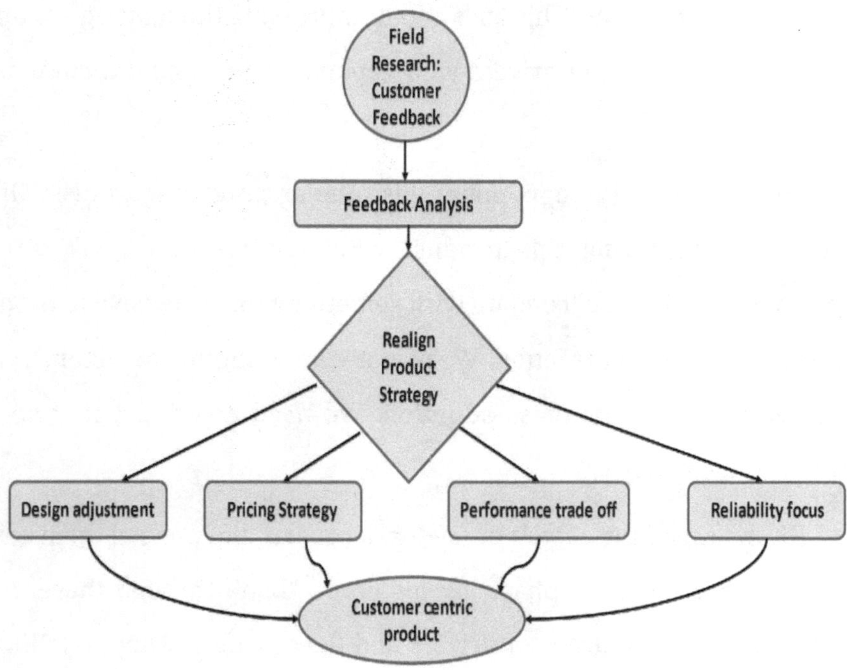

Fig 2.1

"I agree," Amit said finally, meeting each of their eyes with a nod. "I've been thinking about this myself. The more we've debated features and specs, the further we've drifted from the needs of our end-users. These customers don't want a high-end product—they want a dependable tool, something that won't break down and leave them with unaffordable repair bills. We have to get back to basics and design for the reality of their lives."

Nisha leaned forward; her gaze unwavering as she locked eyes with him. "Exactly, Amit. So why are we still talking about premium batteries and top-tier powertrains? The customer doesn't need a vehicle that's optimized for performance beyond what's necessary. They need a vehicle that can survive India's roads, be repaired affordably, and keep running under tough conditions. This isn't about impressing the market; it's about meeting the demands of drivers who depend on us to help them make a living."

Raghav nodded in agreement, his tone as pragmatic as ever. "If we keep overcomplicating this product with features that don't directly address the market, we'll end up with something too expensive to produce and too niche to gain traction. We're not competing in the luxury sector here; we're aiming for mass adoption. We need a product that speaks directly to the majority."

Kiran tapped the customer feedback reports and pushed them across the table once more, emphasizing his point. "Look through these, Amit. We've spoken to hundreds of drivers and fleet owners. They're telling us exactly what they need: a vehicle that's affordable, reliable, and simple to maintain. They don't care about fancy extras or the latest technology. They care about whether they can depend on this vehicle to perform, every day."

Amit took in their words, flipping through the reports, his mind whirling as the reality of their situation became clearer. Each line of feedback reiterated the same sentiment. These drivers were running on tight budgets and needed a vehicle that would support their livelihoods, not one that would turn into a burden. His own assumptions about what would make Volt's Electric Auto stand out had slowly clouded his judgment, leading them away from the true demands of their market.

Nisha's arms crossed, her voice growing even firmer. "Amit, I want us to go back and re-evaluate every single decision we've made so far. If a feature or spec doesn't directly serve the customer, then it's the wrong choice. Period."

Amit felt the weight of her directive settling over him like a challenge and an ultimatum combined. This was a turning point—a moment where he would need to guide his team to reassess every choice they had made so far. To do that, he would need each of them aligned, a united focus on the end-user above all else.

After a pause, he nodded slowly, gathering his resolve. "You're absolutely right, Nisha. We've been caught up in our own debates, losing sight of who we're really building this for. We need to refocus. I'll go back over each component of the design, the performance specs—everything. We'll make sure that every decision we're making truly serves the customer, not just our idea of what might be impressive."

A hint of satisfaction crossed Nisha's face, her posture relaxing slightly as she leaned back in her chair. "Good. That's the direction we need. Go make it happen."

As the team gathered their materials, preparing to leave, Amit remained seated for a moment longer, his mind racing with the shifts they would need to make. This was no longer about competing with other EVs or leading with innovation. It was about listening—truly listening—to the voice of the customer and translating that voice into a product that answered their real-world challenges. The task ahead was demanding, but Amit felt a renewed clarity and commitment.

The Electric Auto was no longer just a product; it was a promise, a response to the genuine needs of their customers. And he was ready to see it through.

Part 2: Conflicting Priorities

After Nisha's directive to put the customer at the heart of every decision, Amit wasted no time gathering his core team—Vivek, Suhani, Kiran, and Pooja—in the Design Lab for a critical brainstorming session. The stakes had never felt higher, and Amit could sense the quiet tension simmering among his team as they settled around the table. They were each experts in their fields, passionate and brilliant, but today's challenge demanded unity in purpose. Yet he knew all too well that achieving that unity would not come without conflict.

Vivek was the first to speak, his expression guarded, his gaze steady. As head of engineering, he wore his perfectionism openly—a dedication that often manifested in his reluctance to cut corners, especially on matters of durability. "I understand what Nisha is saying about affordability and simplicity, but let's be clear about something fundamental. If we don't deliver reliable performance, this product won't survive in the market. These autos are expected to operate under some of the harshest conditions—rough roads, scorching heat, hours of continuous driving. If we compromise too much on the engineering, we'll end up with a vehicle that won't last beyond its first year on the road. We can't just ignore the basic quality standards."

Kiran, leaning forward in his chair, couldn't hold back his response. His experience in marketing had given him an intuitive sense of their customers' financial realities, and he spoke with the passion of someone who had spent hours talking to drivers and fleet owners. "Vivek, I get it—you want something durable. But we're not building this auto for enthusiasts or people with high budgets. Our target customers are urban drivers and fleet operators who are already struggling with tight margins. They want something affordable. If we don't keep our production costs low, we won't even get these people to consider our product."

Vivek's expression hardened, his eyes flashing with frustration. "And what happens when those same customers come back six months later because the vehicle is breaking down? Are they going to thank us for a low upfront cost when they're stuck with costly repairs or stranded on the road? Reliability is not optional. If we lose sight of that, they'll buy once and never come back."

Amit could sense the argument building between Vivek and Kiran, and he stepped in to diffuse the tension before it escalated. "I understand both sides, and you both make valid points. Kiran, you're right that affordability is key for our customers, but Vivek, I also see your point—if the product breaks down, we'll lose their trust, and that's the last thing we want. We need to find a balance. The worst outcome would be delivering a product that's cheap but unreliable. If that happens, it could ruin our reputation before we even have a chance to establish ourselves."

Suhani, who had been sitting quietly with her tablet open, finally spoke, her tone as practical and measured as always. "There's no getting around the fact that we have serious budget constraints. We're already pushing the limits with our current cost estimates. If we keep insisting on premium components, we'll either have to raise the price, which defeats our goal of affordability, or we'll end up absorbing the losses ourselves. Neither option is sustainable."

Amit could see Suhani's point clearly. Her financial prudence was crucial to keeping the project viable, but he knew her stance would only increase Vivek's frustration. If there was any hope of bringing the team together, they'd need a solution that addressed both Vivek's concerns about reliability and Suhani's focus on maintaining a workable budget.

At that moment, Pooja raised her hand slightly, catching their attention with a thoughtful look. "I think we're missing an opportunity here," she said, her voice thoughtful yet infused with a quiet confidence. "What if we consider a modular design approach? We could offer a base model that meets the core needs—affordable and reliable, as Nisha emphasized. But we could also introduce optional upgrades. That way, customers who want a more durable battery or enhanced features can choose those, while those who need a basic model to start out can opt for that. This way, we're not compromising on our core customer needs but are still allowing flexibility for those who want a bit more."

Kiran's face brightened at the suggestion, and he immediately latched onto the potential it offered. "That's actually a great idea. It gives us the ability to hit two different price points—keep the base price low for mass market appeal while still offering premium options for those willing to pay a bit extra."

But Vivek, ever the realist, remained cautious. "Modular designs sound promising, but they're not as straightforward as they seem. You're talking about additional supply chains, managing different inventory levels, and a more complex production setup. Each variation we offer introduces a new layer of logistics and, consequently, additional costs. We can't assume this will automatically bring down production expenses."

Amit could sense Vivek's scepticism, but he also saw a hint of interest—a possibility that he was willing to consider. The team was at a crossroads, but for the first time in the discussion, he felt a sliver of hope, a potential path to a solution that would honour their shared commitment to both customer needs and product integrity.

"Vivek, I hear your concerns," Amit replied, carefully choosing his words to keep Vivek engaged in the idea. "But may be there's a way we can address this without complicating the production too much. What if we identify a few non-negotiable core components—those we can't compromise on for durability—and then allow customization around the peripherals? For example, we can use a standard, reliable battery across all models but offer options for additional performance upgrades or aesthetic customizations."

Suhani nodded, already typing notes into her tablet. "From a financial perspective, this could work, but we'll need to be extremely disciplined about production costs. I'll start running the numbers to see how feasible this modular approach is. If we control which components can be upgraded, we might be able to keep production efficient without inflating costs."

Amit leaned back slightly, feeling a mix of relief and cautious optimism. The modular approach was the first solution that seemed to bridge the gap between their various priorities, allowing the team to address both affordability and durability. He could see the potential to create a product that was adaptable without losing the core values they had outlined in the initial stages of development.

He knew there were still challenges ahead, that Vivek's reservations about modular logistics would require careful planning and Suhani's financial assessments would need thorough analysis. Yet, for the first time, he felt they were on the brink of a breakthrough, an approach that could make the Electric Auto resonate with customers across a spectrum of needs.

"Let's proceed with this direction," Amit said, addressing the team with a renewed sense of purpose. "Vivek, I'd like you to work with the engineering team to determine which components are essential for durability. Suhani, I'll need a clear cost analysis on the modular approach. Kiran, start developing a messaging strategy that speaks to the versatility this offers, and Pooja, I'd love to see some design concepts for a modular model that's functional yet appealing."

Each team member nodded, their focus sharpening as they took on their respective tasks. The initial resistance in the room had softened, replaced by a collective drive to bring the project into alignment with both customer needs and product integrity.

As the team dispersed, Amit felt a renewed sense of determination. The modular approach was a step toward a solution that could balance their competing priorities. It wasn't an immediate answer to every challenge, but it offered the flexibility to cater to their diverse market. Today had shifted the project's direction, and Amit felt that the customer's voice was finally being woven into every step of the journey ahead.

Part 3: Understanding the Market

Amit felt a sense of cautious optimism after the team's breakthrough around the modular approach. By allowing for a customizable vehicle design, they could address both affordability and durability without sacrificing the product's core value. However, Amit knew that the modular concept was still just an idea—a promising one, yes, but one that needed real-world validation before they could proceed. Customer voices had to shape its final form, or the entire approach could end up missing the mark.

With this in mind, Amit resolved to get his team back into the field. The data they had collected over the last several months provided a strong foundation, but now they needed a deeper, segmented understanding. This meant gathering feedback directly from the people they intended to serve—drivers who operated under challenging conditions, fleet owners looking at long-term costs, and urban commuters with tight budgets. It was only by listening to these voices that they could refine the modular approach to meet diverse customer needs.

The next morning, Amit called Kiran, Pooja, and a few other team members into the Design Lab to brief them on his plan. He stood at the head of the table, his expression determined.

"Our conversation yesterday was a turning point," he began, glancing around the table at each team member. "We've come up with a viable direction with this modular concept, but we can't rely on theory alone. This needs validation from actual customers. I want each of you to take this idea into the field, to talk to drivers, fleet operators, and owners. We need to know if they see value in a customizable model. This is going to help us decide what options are essential and which are nice-to-have."

Kiran was the first to respond, his enthusiasm evident. "Absolutely, Amit. I'm glad you're thinking this way. The initial research showed us what customers need, but if we're moving toward a modular approach, we're also talking about customer segments. We're going to get different feedback from a fleet owner managing 50 vehicles than we would from an independent driver."

Amit nodded, his mind already formulating the next steps. "Exactly, Kiran. We need to understand which upgrades each segment values most. For instance, a fleet owner might care about the long-term cost savings of a high-durability battery option, whereas a single driver might just want the lowest possible maintenance cost."

Pooja added eagerly, her creative mind already envisioning designs that could fit different user types. "I love this approach—it means I can start working on design sketches that cater to different profiles. The base model could have a more straightforward look, while an upgraded model could introduce subtle design elements that enhance the user experience. I think these customer conversations could even inspire more ideas for modular features we haven't considered yet."

Amit's expression softened as he heard Pooja's enthusiasm. "Exactly, Pooja. This is a chance for us to learn more than what surveys alone can tell us. Modular design doesn't just mean giving options; it means giving the right options."

Kiran, always eager for fieldwork, began organizing the details, mapping out areas where they could get a range of perspectives. He decided to focus on three major urban centers: Mumbai, with its large base of individual drivers; Delhi, where rideshare companies had started shifting toward electric fleets; and Bengaluru, a tech-savvy city that showed a high interest in eco-friendly transport solutions.

With plans in place, the team split into groups, each group armed with prototypes, detailed drawings, and interactive tablets to showcase the modular features under consideration. Amit watched them depart with a blend of anticipation and nerves. This trip would be critical in validating their direction, a chance to truly hear what the drivers and fleet owners wanted, needed, and valued.

On the Ground: Market Research Begins

Kiran's team began their journey in Mumbai, meeting with a range of drivers in one of the city's busiest districts. The first interview took place under the shade of a large banyan tree, with the din of the crowded street a constant background hum. Kiran and his team spoke with Ashok, a 40-year-old driver who had spent nearly 15 years navigating Mumbai's chaotic traffic. Ashok's diesel auto sat nearby, its age showing in the peeling paint and worn-out seat covers. Kiran could tell this was a man who had seen it all on the road.

"These electric autos—they're supposed to save us money," Ashok said, crossing his arms as he leaned back against his vehicle. "But the ones we've seen so far... they break down too easily. Battery stops holding a charge, the motor fails under long hours. Repairs? Don't even ask; the prices are killing us. If I buy another auto, I need to know it will last."

Kiran nodded, jotting down Ashok's words. "What if you had an option for a stronger battery? It would cost a little more upfront, but it could last longer and save you on repair costs. Would that be something you'd consider?"

Ashok scratched his head thoughtfully, his eyes narrowed in concentration. "May be. But it depends on the price. If I pay more at the beginning, it better come with some kind of guarantee. I can't afford to replace the battery every year. And the price—well, it can't be more than ₹300,000. Even that's a stretch."

The conversation continued, with Kiran gathering feedback from Ashok and several other drivers. The feedback was consistent—reliability and long-term savings mattered more than high-end features. Drivers were willing to consider a slight premium if it promised fewer repair headaches and a lower cost over time.

Meanwhile, in Delhi, Amit and Pooja were engaging with fleet operators. Here, the approach had to be tailored to companies rather than individual drivers. They met Shabnam, a fleet owner managing a network of 30 electric autos for a rideshare company. Shabnam was focused and professional, flipping through pages of maintenance logs as she outlined her needs.

"We're not just looking at the purchase price here," she said, crossing her arms as she reviewed her fleet's maintenance reports. "What matters to us is the total cost of ownership. Repairs, battery replacements, downtime—all of that eats into our margins. If you're saying your auto can save me on repairs and extend the battery life, then we're interested. But I need to see the data, not just promises."

Amit took note of her emphasis on metrics and evidence, sensing an opportunity to showcase their plans. "Shabnam, with the modular approach, you could choose a standard model for most of your fleet and select the upgrades that promise durability and lower maintenance for high-mileage vehicles. We're also considering options for remote diagnostics, so issues can be addressed proactively. Does that align with what you're looking for?"

Shabnam nodded, her interest piqued. "If it brings down our maintenance frequency and reduces downtime, then yes. But again, I'll need evidence. If you can't back it up with performance data, I can't justify the switch. We've had other EV providers make claims that haven't held up, and it's made us cautious."

Amit appreciated her straightforwardness. "We're working on extensive field tests and performance metrics, so we'll get you that data. Our goal is to provide a solution, not just another product."

Pooja observed the exchange, her mind spinning with ideas for fleet-focused design options. This modular approach had opened a new avenue, allowing them to cater to both fleet owners' desire for durable investments and drivers' demand for cost-effective basics.

Returning with Insight: A Clearer Picture

After several days in the field, the team reconvened at Volt Motors, their findings sharper than ever. The customer insights had given Amit a new perspective on the modular approach. While drivers and fleet owners each valued different aspects, they were unified in one priority: the need for a reliable and affordable vehicle that could withstand daily use without extensive repairs or high upfront costs.

Back in the Design Lab, Amit called for an all-hands meeting. The team gathered with a renewed sense of purpose, their notes and observations spread across the table. As Amit looked around, he saw in their faces a shift in understanding—they had gained a more grounded perspective on what the market truly required.

"We've gathered valuable insights," Amit began, nodding as he scanned his team's expressions. "Drivers and fleet owners alike are looking for the same core solution—a durable, low-maintenance vehicle that doesn't stretch their budgets. The modular approach has its potential, but the need for simplicity and reliability has to come first. We need to focus on delivering a dependable base model that meets the most critical customer needs."

Kiran glanced at his notes, nodding in agreement. "Our research is telling us the same story. The demand is clear—a functional, affordable model that gets the job done. If we can nail that, we'll have earned the trust of our customers. Later, if the market shifts or demand grows for upgrades, we can explore modular options to add value."

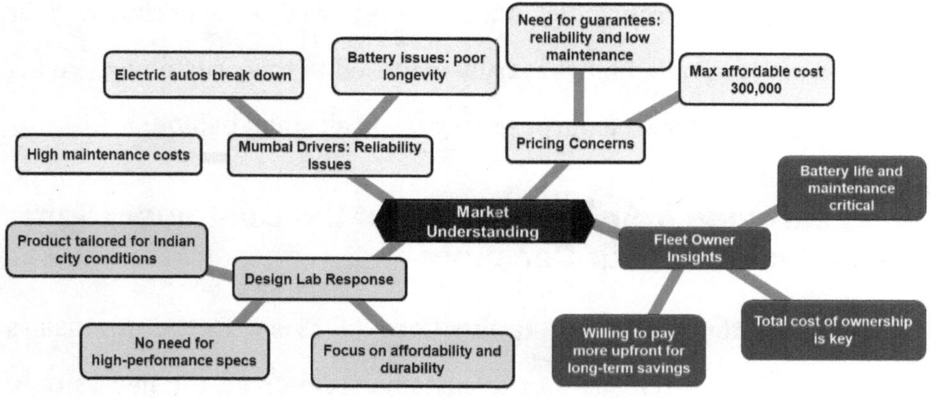

Fig 2.2

Vivek, still holding his notes from the field, added thoughtfully, "Let's keep the essential components as robust as possible without overcomplicating the design. We'll build a foundation of reliability and affordability. If and when customers want more, we'll be prepared to expand the product line with upgradable options."

Amit felt the team's resolve aligning with his own. They didn't need to develop an ambitious modular product right now; they needed to focus on perfecting a vehicle that delivered on the basics—durability, low cost, and simplicity. Only then, after establishing a strong reputation, would they revisit the possibility of an upgrade path.

"Agreed," Amit said, the finality in his voice sealing their collective decision. "Our goal is to earn our place in the market by serving the customer's immediate needs. We'll build a product they can depend on, and in time, we can revisit modular features that add to their experience."

As the meeting concluded, Amit felt a renewed sense of clarity. Their direction was grounded in what truly mattered to their customers, giving the Electric Auto project a purpose they could all stand behind.

Key Learnings from Chapter 2: Put the Customer Right at the Center of Your Decision

1. **Place the Customer at the Core of Every Decision:** Nisha's directive to refocus on the customer reinforced the necessity of aligning the product with real-world needs. The team's earlier drift into internal debates on features was corrected by centring decisions on what urban and semi-urban commuters truly valued—reliability, affordability, and low maintenance. Prioritizing the end-user ensures long-term success in any venture.

2. **Understand and Empathize with Target Audiences:** The team's field visits, such as Kiran's conversation with a seasoned auto driver and Amit's meeting with a fleet owner, revealed invaluable insights. Customers sought vehicles that reduced downtime and maintenance costs rather than cutting-edge features. Direct engagement with the target market helps businesses develop products that solve real pain points.

3. **Balancing Conflicting Priorities:** There was a significant focus on managing the ongoing tension between engineering's demand for quality, marketing's push for cost-effectiveness, and finance's insistence on controlling the budget. Success requires compromise, with both sides acknowledging each other's concerns while keeping the customer in mind.

4. **Design Solutions for Total Cost of Ownership:** The feedback from fleet owners, emphasizing long-term savings over upfront costs, led the team to focus on durability and maintenance-friendly designs. Customers care about value throughout a product's lifecycle, not just its initial price—a crucial insight for developing sustainable offerings.

5. **Reassess Decisions Against Customer Feedback:** When Amit and his team revisited their earlier decisions, they identified areas where they had prioritized internal goals over customer needs. This recalibration ensured that the Electric Auto's features, like robust batteries and reliable powertrains, were designed to address market demands. Regularly evaluating decisions against customer insights prevents costly misalignment.

6. **Use Field Research to Inform Strategy:** The team's first-hand interactions with auto drivers and fleet owners validated their design and feature choices. Field research allowed them to identify critical priorities such as low repair costs, durability, and ease of maintenance, reinforcing the importance of grounding strategies in real-world data.

7. **Simplify the Product to Meet Core Needs:** Raghav's insistence on simplifying the design to address basic requirements like affordability and reliability helped the team avoid overengineering. Focusing on essential features that customers value is more impactful than adding unnecessary complexity or luxury elements.

8. **Craft a Modular Design for Diverse Needs:** Pooja's proposal to offer a modular design—with a base model and optional upgrades—emerged as a practical way to serve both cost-conscious customers and those willing to pay for performance enhancements. This approach showcases the value of adaptability in product offerings to cater to a broad audience.

9. **Communicate a Clear and Realistic Value Proposition:** The team's customer-first mindset drove their marketing strategy to emphasize reliability, affordability, and ease of maintenance over luxury or cutting-edge technology. This clear, relatable messaging builds trust and attracts the right audience, illustrating the power of authentic communication.

10. **Align the Team Around Shared Goals:** Amit's leadership brought together the diverse priorities of engineering, marketing, and finance, aligning them with the goal of creating a product that met customer needs. Unified vision and teamwork are essential for overcoming internal conflicts and delivering successful outcomes.

These key learnings, drawn from Volt Motors' journey in Chapter 2, highlight the importance of customer-centricity, collaboration, and adaptability in navigating complex product development challenges.

Chapter 3

Shortcuts of Today are Problems of Tomorrow

As the first few weeks of development rolled forward, Amit could feel the initial sense of direction from their field research solidifying into a concrete plan. With customer insights shaping their core priorities, the team had rallied around the product's essential DNA: an Electric Auto that was affordable, reliable, and built to handle the demands of India's urban landscape. The modular approach, while promising, had been wisely set aside as a future possibility, leaving them to focus on delivering a durable, cost-effective base model.

But translating those ideals into reality was proving to be more complicated than anyone had anticipated. One by one, the challenges emerged: supply chain bottlenecks, software glitches in the Battery Management System, and delays from key vendors in their supply chain. The difficulties came in waves, each one more complex than the last, testing the team's resolve and pushing their deadlines into dangerous territory. Every small setback forced them to re-evaluate their timelines and balance urgency against quality—a precarious dance that felt as though one wrong move could throw the entire project off course.

Amit could sense the weight of it all bearing down on his team. Vivek, their head of engineering, was visibly fraying under the pressure. Every day brought a new engineering compromise or a fresh concern about the reliability of their suppliers. He had been tracking the smallest of issues with a meticulousness that bordered on obsession, driven by an urgency that Amit understood but couldn't entirely support. Amit, too, felt the pressure, but he knew that compromising too soon would only create larger problems down the road.

Now, with delays mounting and tensions simmering, the team's hard-won consensus on product priorities was being challenged by the reality of deadlines and the limits of their resources. The strain was becoming visible in every corner of Volt Motors, and Amit knew the team was close to a breaking point. Each meeting, each decision, felt like navigating a high-stakes maze where shortcuts tempted at every turn, promising relief but risking future disaster.

In this atmosphere of mounting pressure, Amit felt the first tremors of conflict within his team. What had begun as a shared vision was now fragmenting under the demands of execution, leaving each of them grappling with the question that haunted every step of development: How far were they willing to compromise to get the product to market on time?

Part 1: Engineering Proposals

Amit sat at his desk, the hum of Volt Motors' open office barely registering as he reviewed the engineering reports scattered in front of him. Despite the team's consensus on the product's core design, the project had become anything but straightforward. Delays were cropping up in every direction—testing schedules slipping, parts suppliers struggling to meet quality standards, and software glitches surfacing at the worst possible times. Each setback brought a new cascade of decisions, each one forcing Amit to weigh their commitment to quality against the relentless ticking of the clock. They had promised a product that was affordable and reliable, but every corner of the project now seemed strained to keep that promise.

His thoughts were interrupted by a brisk knock, followed by Vivek entering with his characteristic intensity. Amit could see the strain in Vivek's expression—the way his eyes narrowed as though he were trying to hold back his frustration. In his hands was a thick folder of technical documents, his latest engineering proposals.

"We need to talk," Vivek said without preamble, dropping the folder onto Amit's desk. His voice carried a sharp edge, weighed down by weeks of delays and mounting pressure.

Amit looked up, bracing himself. He knew what was coming. "What's the issue now?" he asked, though he already had an idea from the look in Vivek's eyes.

Vivek didn't waste a moment. "We're up against it, Amit. Testing timelines for the BIW (Body In White) rigidity, the powertrain, and especially the battery systems have blown out. The vendor quality for the body electronics is barely meeting baseline, and honestly, if we don't make some cuts or start taking serious concessions, we're staring at a significant delay." He paused, leaning over the desk. "We can't keep this up without changing our approach."

Amit frowned, his fingers tapping the edge of his desk. "What kind of concessions are you suggesting?"

Vivek crossed his arms, his tone betraying his irritation. "We need to cut down on non-critical testing phases. We're over-engineering the BIW for a three-wheeler auto, Amit. Do we really need steel cross-members when an alloy could do the job? We could switch to a lighter material, cut down costs, and save weeks on production. That alone would help us gain back precious time."

Amit felt his stomach tighten. "You're proposing we reduce BIW testing and switch to lighter materials?"

Vivek nodded, his voice sharper now. "Yes. We're building an auto-rickshaw, not a tank. The current BIW setup is more than enough for a product at this price point. Reducing the weight will even help with battery range. It's a practical compromise."

Amit glanced down at the folder, flipping through Vivek's highlighted sections. "And what about the powertrain integration? We set specific torque requirements for urban driving, and a lighter frame might affect that load-bearing capacity. What happens when drivers push the vehicle hard during peak hours?"

Vivek shook his head, his frustration evident. "The powertrain can handle it. We've run simulations to verify the load-bearing capacity under traffic conditions, and the BMS is already compensating for torque spikes. We don't need to over-engineer every part of this vehicle, Amit. Right now, the problem isn't performance; it's time."

Amit leaned back, feeling the tension mount. The thought of cutting back on testing cycles, especially structural testing for the BIW, felt like a gamble. "Vivek, you know this isn't just about trimming a few testing phases. If we skip durability testing on the BIW and start using unproven alloys, we're putting long-term reliability at risk. The BIW isn't just holding up the frame; it's supporting the suspension and the motor mounts. What happens when the auto hits a pothole at speed?"

Vivek's jaw tightened, his impatience seeping through. "We've done finite element analysis, Amit. The stress points hold under the conditions we've simulated. But if we sit around waiting for every last test to complete, we'll miss the deadline."

Amit crossed his arms, feeling a familiar tug between urgency and integrity. "And the battery system? We've had thermal management issues, with charger failures reported from our suppliers. If we start cutting back testing for thermal stability, we risk thermal runaway. Are you prepared to deal with the fallout if these systems fail in the field?"

Vivek's response was swift, his tone clipped. "The BMS team is confident that our current passive cooling setup can handle the load. Yes, we had issues with some chargers, but switching to a new MOSFET (Metal-Oxide-Semiconductor Field-Effect Transistor) configuration has resolved it. The BMS is stable. I've checked with the team myself."

"Stable?" Amit echoed, his skepticism unmistakable. "A 'stable' system from a vendor who's already failed us on two separate batches? We had unacceptable failure rates in the charge controllers. Simply switching components isn't a solution. Without a complete integration test, we don't know if the system will withstand real conditions."

Vivek threw his hands up, his frustration uncontained. "You're complicating this, Amit! We've tested BMS stability. If there was a failure in the core system, it would've surfaced by now. This isn't a quality issue—it's a time issue. We're running out of it."

Amit leaned forward, his voice calm but resolute. "Vivek, I understand the urgency, but we're talking about critical systems here. If we skip testing now, we'll be gambling on durability. The SOC (state-of-charge) misreads we've seen during discharges are already an indicator that we need more tests. If we launch a product that misreports battery charge or worse, shuts down unexpectedly under high loads, we're looking at disaster."

Vivek exhaled sharply, his patience thinning. "Then tell me how we get back the time, Amit. Between vendor delays, glitches in the ECU, and sensor shipments stuck overseas, we're buried under delays. If we don't take some action, we're going to blow this timeline, and Raghav and Nisha are already at the edge of their patience."

Amit's hands clenched as he considered Vivek's words. He knew the pressure was real, and that every day of delay increased the strain. "Vivek, I understand the need for urgency, but cutting corners here isn't just a risk—it's a certainty that we'll be dealing with recalls, warranty claims, and customer dissatisfaction. Every shortcut we take today becomes tomorrow's problem, and we can't afford to gamble on this product's integrity."

Vivek's shoulders sagged slightly, and he leaned back, his frustration tempered but not gone. "Then we need another plan, Amit, because we're heading toward a delay that we can't afford. And when that happens, we're all going to be facing the consequences."

Amit looked down at the engineering documents, feeling the weight of their conversation settle on him. They were nearing a tipping point, where every decision felt fraught with compromise. But despite the time constraints, he knew he couldn't afford to take shortcuts on the very values they had built their product around.

Part 2: Rushed Decisions

The meeting room felt tense as Amit sat down with his core team—Vivek, Suhani, Kiran, and Pooja. Each member's face mirrored the strain of looming deadlines and the growing realization of how far they were being stretched. Vivek, visibly worn down from his earlier discussion with Amit, sat at the end of the table, flipping through his notes with restless energy. Amit knew today's conversation needed to produce a clear path forward, one that would address their timelines without compromising the product's core values. But he could see the toll the delivery pressure was taking on Vivek, who'd always championed rigorous testing yet now seemed to be buckling under the relentless push to launch on time.

Amit took a breath, glancing around the table. "We're behind on testing for the chassis, battery, and powertrain integration. Our BMS stability is still inconsistent, and supply chain delays on critical body electronics aren't helping. I know everyone feels the weight of this project, but we need to find a solution that doesn't sacrifice quality."

Vivek, his patience clearly wearing thin, spoke up first. "I've said it before, Amit—we can't keep testing every single component as if we're developing a luxury sedan. The BIW is over-engineered for what we're trying to accomplish here. We're building a three-wheeler, not a high-performance vehicle, and reducing testing on non-critical aspects of the chassis is a straightforward way to keep this project moving."

It wasn't lost on Amit that Vivek, usually a staunch advocate for thorough testing, was now arguing to cut it back. He could see the delivery pressure weighing heavily on Vivek, affecting his priorities and pushing him toward concessions he wouldn't normally consider.

Suhani, who had been quiet until now, adjusted her glasses and leaned forward, her voice resolute. "And what about the financial impact, Vivek? If we cut testing and end up facing warranty claims and repairs down the line, the costs will outweigh any time saved. These aren't minor adjustments—if we get this wrong, it could lead to recalls and customer dissatisfaction. Is that something we're prepared to risk?"

Vivek rolled his eyes, his tone edged with exasperation. "Suhani, I've run the numbers. We're talking about marginal adjustments—a lighter alloy for the BIW and shorter testing for battery discharge cycles. None of these changes will significantly impact performance. It's not like switching materials will make the entire product fail."

Suhani's gaze didn't waver. "It's not just about marginal changes, Vivek. It's about managing risk. We're already facing vendor issues, and the quality of components isn't guaranteed. Rushing through this process only increases the chance of something going wrong."

Vivek clenched his hands, his frustration more evident. "We're not gambling, Suhani. We've done simulations. The lighter alloy holds up, and the design is optimized for the power-to-weight ratio. We're within acceptable limits, and these changes would even benefit battery range." He paused, then added, his tone more reflective, "But the longer we delay, the more pressure we face—from the board, from Raghav, from the market. This delay is starting to feel like a noose tightening around our necks."

Amit, observing the strain in Vivek's expression, leaned forward to address him directly. "I understand the time pressure, Vivek, and I know the deadlines aren't getting any friendlier. But simulations don't account for real roads. Our customers are navigating streets full of potholes and abrupt stops. If we compromise on BIW strength, it's not just about weight—it's about long-term durability."

Kiran, who had been watching the exchange in silence, added, "We've been positioning ourselves as a brand built on reliability. Cutting corners now would undo everything we've been working toward. Customers need to trust that we're delivering a vehicle that lasts beyond a few months."

Vivek threw up his hands, frustration overtaking him. "And what happens if we don't launch at all, Kiran? We're already trailing Zephyr EV, and they're set to launch next quarter. If we don't get this product to market, the customers we're so concerned about won't have anything to buy from us. Every delay is costing us momentum."

Amit listened, feeling the weight of Vivek's words but unable to ignore the consequences of taking shortcuts. "I hear you, Vivek. But if we rush a product to market with weaknesses, we risk destroying the trust we're trying to build. One battery failure, one structural flaw, and we lose customer loyalty faster than we built it."

Vivek's voice grew sharp. "You're betting on a flawless launch, Amit. But we need to be realistic. Progress is made by taking calculated risks, not by waiting for every test to go perfectly."

Amit's tone matched Vivek's intensity. "This isn't about perfection; it's about safety and dependability. If we sacrifice core values now, we'll be paying for it later through warranty claims, recalls, and reputational damage. Shortcuts today become tomorrow's liabilities."

The room fell silent, with Suhani and Kiran exchanging glances that reflected the uncertainty of their position. Everyone knew the project had reached a critical juncture and that finding a middle ground was essential. The timelines were volatile, but compromising quality could bring irreversible damage.

Pooja, who had been quietly listening, finally spoke, her voice calm but confident. "What if we prioritize the most critical testing phases? Focus on the essentials—powertrain durability, BMS integration, and charger reliability. We could cut back on non-essential tests, like aesthetic durability, for now. It's a compromise, but one that allows us to protect the critical systems while finding some time savings where we can afford it."

Amit considered her suggestion, nodding slowly. "It's a start. Vivek, go back to the engineering team and adjust the testing schedule to prioritize the necessary tests. Focus on battery thermal management, structural integrity for the BIW, and charger performance. If we're going to cut anything, it'll be non-critical, and it will be a temporary concession."

Vivek sighed, his reluctance clear, but he nodded. "Fine. I'll revise the testing phases and bring it back for review. But let's be clear—these changes might still not be enough to keep us on track without further adjustments."

Amit leaned back, sensing the underlying tension but feeling a small sense of victory in securing the team's tentative agreement. They were walking a fine line, and while compromises were necessary, he knew they needed to balance the integrity of the product with the realities of delivery.

Part 3: First Major Setback

The two-month delay had officially been announced, and Amit could feel the tension as thick as the humid air outside Volt Motors' sleek office. The weight of the decision to extend the testing phase and avoid shortcuts had started to crush the team's morale. The board was demanding answers, and Amit's phone hadn't stopped ringing with calls from Nisha and Raghav, each more frustrated than the last.

The biggest problem, however, lay in the meeting he was about to step into. Raghav had called an emergency strategy session, and Amit knew the conversations would get heated.

As he walked into the strategy room, he saw the key figures waiting for him: Raghav sat at the head of the table, his face unreadable but his impatience clear in the way he tapped his fingers on the desk. Nisha was seated beside him, her expression a mixture of frustration and concern. Vivek was already in his seat, flipping through notes, clearly still irritated from their last conversation. Suhani and Kiran exchanged anxious looks, and even Pooja seemed unusually tense, twirling her pen nervously.

Amit knew this wasn't going to be a pleasant discussion. The project had officially hit its first major setback, and the leadership team was about to dive headfirst into it.

Raghav started the meeting without any pleasantries. "We're looking at a two-month delay," he said flatly, setting the tone. "That's a reality we can't ignore. The board is furious, the investors are on edge, and Zephyr EV is already gearing up for their launch next quarter. Amit, we need to understand what the hell is going on."

Amit glanced around the room before speaking, feeling the pressure from every direction. "We ran into issues with the BMS during the integration with the charger units. We've had charger failures during stress testing, specifically during the fast-charge cycles, which led to overheating. The new MOSFET configurations weren't handling the voltage spikes well enough."

Vivek interjected, his voice tight with frustration. "We had this conversation already, Amit. We could have cut the testing time and pushed forward. Yes, there were issues with the charger, but we solved them by switching to a new supplier for the gate drivers. You didn't need to extend testing by another month just to double-check the thermal performance of the BMS."

Amit turned to Vivek, his voice calm but firm. "I'm not going to sign off on a product that hasn't been thoroughly tested. You saw the same reports I did—the thermal runaway risk was still higher than we anticipated during the fast-charging cycles. If we had ignored that and gone ahead with production, we could have had battery fires on our hands."

Raghav, who had been listening quietly, leaned forward, his voice sharp. "You're talking about thermal runaway as if it's an everyday problem. Is this something that would have been fixed in the field, or are we talking about catastrophic failures here?"

Amit didn't flinch. "If we had skipped those tests, we would have had major issues within the first six months. The BMS was misreading the SOC during fast charges, causing the system to overestimate the battery's available capacity. That led to overcharging, which, under certain conditions, could have caused the batteries to overheat. In the worst-case scenario, it could've led to fires."

Raghav's face hardened. "So you're telling me we delayed the entire project because of a problem that might not even show up under normal driving conditions?"

Amit met Raghav's stare without backing down. "It's not about what might show up—it's about what could show up under extreme conditions. We're talking about a product that will be used in cities where autos are on the road for 12-16 hours a day, in extreme heat. The risks of overheating and thermal failures are real, especially if we don't fully address the charge-discharge cycling issues."

Vivek slammed his notebook shut, clearly frustrated. "Fine. I get the safety concerns, but we're bleeding time here. And this isn't just about the battery. The powertrain integration has been slowed down by the extended testing on the BIW structure. We could've switched to a simpler material composition weeks ago and shaved off some of the testing. Instead, we're still hung up on load-bearing stress tests that haven't produced any failures so far."

Amit turned to Vivek, his patience wearing thin. "The BIW testing is necessary because we're relying on lower-grade materials for the chassis. We've already seen micro-cracks forming at the suspension mounts during high-stress scenarios in the finite element analysis. You really want to risk that on a production model? One bad pothole at high speed and we could have structural failure on our hands."

Nisha, who had been silent until now, finally spoke. "Amit, I understand the safety concerns, but Vivek has a point. We're running out of time. Is there a way to prioritize critical testing without delaying everything? We can't afford to fall too far behind Zephyr EV."

Amit took a deep breath, feeling the weight of her question. "We've already cut non-essential tests. What's left is powertrain durability, thermal management, and charger reliability. I'm not willing to compromise on those. We've had three charger failures in the last testing cycle alone, and we're still seeing inconsistencies with the BMS communicating with the CAN bus. If that issue isn't resolved, we're going to have inconsistent charging across the fleet. That's a huge red flag for fleet operators, especially when they're trying to minimize downtime."

Suhani leaned in, her voice calm but laced with urgency. "What's the real cost of this delay, Amit? I've been running the numbers, and we're losing cash flow every week this project is pushed. The vendors are pressuring us to finalize orders, but if we don't have the product ready, we're risking penalties from long-lead suppliers."

Amit exhaled slowly. "I get it, Suhani. But the costs of launching with an unreliable product will be far higher. We'll be dealing with warranty claims, recalls, and damage to our reputation that we can't afford to lose, especially on our first major product."

Kiran, the marketing head, jumped in next, his frustration evident. "We've built this entire campaign around reliability and innovation. If we launch and the autos start breaking down, or worse, catch fire because of a BMS failure, we're done. Customers won't care that we were first to market—they'll remember that we sold them a product that couldn't deliver on its promises."

Vivek, still visibly frustrated, couldn't hold back. "We've been stuck in analysis paralysis for weeks! Every test brings up more issues, and every issue pushes the timeline further. If we don't take some calculated risks, we'll never launch."

Amit turned to face Vivek, his voice measured but firm. "This isn't paralysis. This is due diligence. The powertrain is under more stress than we originally anticipated during extended use, especially when drivers push it at full torque. If the battery discharge rate isn't properly managed, we'll see range issues, and if the BMS fails to regulate heat during fast charging, we risk thermal failures. We've already seen the SOC inaccuracies during rapid discharge. Ignoring these now means launching a product that could start failing within months."

Raghav leaned back in his chair, pinching the bridge of his nose in frustration. "So what are we supposed to tell the board, Amit? That we're two months behind because we're worried about worst-case scenarios?"

Amit didn't flinch. "You tell them we're two months behind because we're building a product that's safe and reliable. The moment we start compromising on the core systems—the battery, powertrain, and BMS—we're compromising the entire product's future. If we launch a product with charger failures or BIW weaknesses, we'll be looking at recalls and long-term damage to the brand."

Nisha sighed heavily, clearly torn. "I get that, Amit. But the investors are expecting results. We've made commitments, and every day we delay, we're losing credibility. If this doesn't pay off, it's not just the product that's at stake—it's the entire company's future." Amit nodded slowly, feeling the weight of her words. "I understand the risks of a delay, Nisha. But the risks of launching prematurely are worse. We've seen this play out with other companies. Rushing a product to market, only to deal with massive recalls and customer backlash. If we do this right, we'll build something that lasts. But if we cut corners, we're just setting ourselves up for disaster."

Raghav rubbed his temples, clearly exhausted by the debate. "Alright, Amit. You've made your point. But you'd better be ready to defend this decision to the board. They're going to want answers, and I'm not sure they'll be as patient as we've been."

Amit felt the tension ease slightly, but the weight of the situation hadn't lifted. He had won the battle to maintain the integrity of the product, but the delay was a reality they couldn't ignore. The next few months would be critical, and there was no guarantee the board—or the market—would be as forgiving as he hoped.

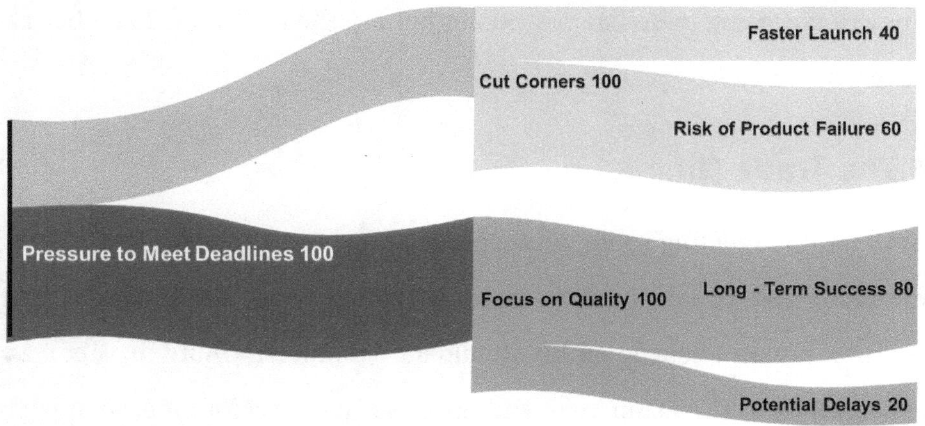

Fig 3.1

As the meeting adjourned, Amit stood by the door for a moment, watching the team file out, each of them carrying their own frustrations and concerns. He knew they were walking a fine line, and the decisions they were making now would define the company's future—for better or worse.

Nisha and Raghav waited till Amit returned to his seat. Raghav pressed in once again, "We are playing with time, money, and trust of our investors. If this doesn't pay off, the repercussions are going to be massive."

Amit nodded. "I know. But I'm willing to take the heat for it. I'm not willing to gamble on a product that isn't fully ready. If we compromise now, we'll be dealing with recalls, warranty claims, and worse—customers losing faith in Volt Motors."

Raghav studied him for a long moment before sighing. "Fine. But you're going to need to justify this to the board when the time comes.

They're not going to be happy, and neither are the investors. You'd better have a damn good explanation."

4.The Trade-Off

Amit left the meeting room with a sense of unease. The delay had been a necessary step to safeguard the product's integrity, but the weight of that decision pressed heavily on his shoulders. The Electric Auto project was approaching a critical juncture, and there was no room for indecision.

Gathering the leadership team later that day, Amit addressed them with quiet determination. "We've reached a crossroads," he began, his voice steady but carrying the strain of weeks of unresolved tension. "We need to make trade-offs that prioritize our core pillars—affordability, durability, and sustainability. The truth is, we've been chasing perfection, but that's not what our customers need. They want something reliable, affordable, and low-maintenance. We can't keep trying to achieve everything at once."

The room fell into an uncomfortable silence, the weight of his words settling over the team like a heavy fog. Vivek, as expected, was the first to break it.

"So, we're compromising the powertrain?" he asked, his tone sharp and incredulous. "The torque requirements we've set are already pushing limits. If we cut those, the auto won't perform under heavy loads. Drivers will overload these vehicles; you know that, Amit. If the motor can't handle the strain, the battery system will suffer too."

Amit met Vivek's gaze, his response calm but firm. "We're not compromising—we're optimizing. The torque-to-weight ratio will be adjusted to match real-world use cases. This isn't about luxury performance; it's about meeting customer needs. We'll reduce BIW reinforcements where they're redundant and shift our focus to battery thermal management. These changes ensure the vehicle lasts and fits within customers' budgets."

Suhani leaned forward, tapping her tablet for emphasis. "We've modeled the cost impacts of these adjustments," she said. "If we implement them, we'll bring costs back within 12-15% of our target price, which is manageable. But if we stay the current course, we'll overshoot by a margin we simply can't sustain."

Kiran, who typically infused the room with energy, tempered his usual enthusiasm. "We'll need to reframe the narrative in our marketing," he said thoughtfully. "The message has to focus on reliability and affordability instead of high-end performance. Customers aren't asking for torque metrics—they want fewer breakdowns and lower maintenance costs."

The discussion grew tense as Vivek pushed back, his perfectionism clashing with the practicalities being laid out. "We've been developing a powertrain that outperforms anything in its class," he argued. "If we water that down now, we're undermining our engineering principles. The payload requirements alone demand high torque output. Reducing specs risks failure under stress, especially in overloaded conditions."

Amit let Vivek's words linger in the air before responding. "And what happens if we price ourselves out of the market? A flawless product that no one can afford doesn't serve our customers. By optimizing the powertrain and focusing on battery thermal management, we reduce strain on the motor while improving longevity. This isn't compromise—it's adaptation."

Pooja added, "The changes to the chassis will help too. We'll adjust BIW reinforcements to critical areas only. That'll reduce weight, improve range, and still maintain structural integrity under stress."

Vivek hesitated, his resistance softening as the logic began to take hold. "Fine," he said reluctantly. "But if we're cutting torque output, the battery system needs to be rock-solid. SOC mis readings during high-load cycles have already caused issues in testing. If we're pushing the battery harder to compensate, thermal management has to be bulletproof."

Amit nodded. "Agreed. Battery performance and thermal stability remain top priorities. Vivek, I want your team to focus on refining the BMS algorithms and ensuring seamless integration with the CAN bus. We'll also continue rigorous testing on the new MOSFET configurations. Suhani, keep an eye on supply chain costs for these changes, and Kiran, start updating the marketing framework to reflect this shift."

By the end of the meeting, a reluctant but clear consensus had been reached. The team would adjust powertrain specifications to balance cost and performance. BIW reinforcements would be localized, reducing excess material use, and thermal management for the battery would take precedence over marginal performance gains.

As the group dispersed, Amit lingered in the room, staring at the whiteboard where the words Reliability, Affordability, Durability were written in bold. These weren't just marketing phrases—they were the lifeblood of their vision. The trade-offs had been painful, but they were necessary. Amit only hoped the road ahead would vindicate the choices they had made.

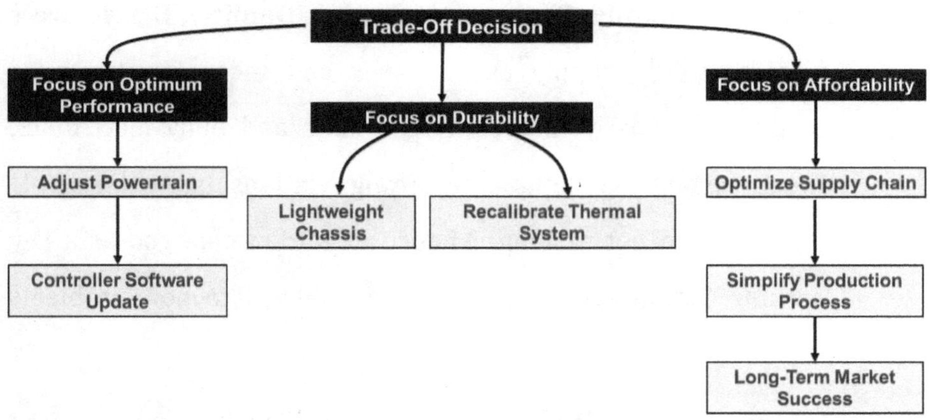

Fig 3.2

Key Learnings from Chapter 3: Shortcuts of Today Are Problems of Tomorrow

1. **The Dangers of Cutting Corners:** The core lesson of this chapter is the long-term risk of taking shortcuts in product development. While the pressure to meet deadlines is immense, compromising on quality and safety—particularly in key areas like the BIW (Body-in-White), powertrain, and BMS (Battery Management System)—can lead to catastrophic outcomes, such as product failures, recalls, or worse, safety incidents like battery fires.

2. **Real-World Testing is Crucial:** Simulation and theory can only take a project so far. Real-world conditions—especially in markets like India, where roads are harsh and vehicles face constant wear and tear—must be accounted for. The importance of real-world testing was highlighted, particularly with the BIW strength, charger failures, and thermal management of the battery during fast charging.

3. **Managing Supply Chain and Vendor Quality:** Delays were exacerbated by supply chain issues and inconsistent vendor quality, particularly in the charger units and body electronics. The importance of maintaining strong relationships with reliable suppliers and not rushing vendor integration emerged as a key learning. Cutting corners in this area would lead to more problems down the line.

4. **Taking Calculated Risks vs. Over-Testing:** The chapter showcased the tension between speeding up the development process and the risk of over-testing. While Vivek argued for reducing testing to save time, Amit defended the need for thorough testing to avoid long-term damage. The right balance between testing efficiency and due diligence is critical in ensuring both time-to-market and product reliability.

5. **Communication with Stakeholders:** The delay in the project underscored the importance of communicating effectively with key stakeholders, including the board and investors. Even though the delay was necessary to ensure the product's safety and reliability, the team realized the importance of preparing solid justifications and being ready to defend decisions with clear, data-backed arguments.

6. **Customer Expectations and Brand Trust:** Kiran's concerns around marketing and brand positioning highlighted that the product's success depends on meeting customer expectations of reliability and quality. The potential damage from launching

a product that failed to meet these expectations would be far worse than any delays, as it would harm the company's long- term reputation.

7. **The Cost of a Delay vs. The Cost of a Recall:** Suhani's insights into the financial implications of delays vs. recalls reinforced a key lesson: while delays can hurt cash flow and credibility in the short term, the cost of launching a defective product—dealing with recalls, warranty claims, and customer dissatisfaction — is far greater. Careful risk assessment and financial foresight are necessary when making such decisions.

8. **Internal Conflict and Team Alignment:** The chapter also demonstrated the internal tensions between departments—engineering, finance, marketing, and operations—and the need for strong leadership to align them toward a common goal. The debates highlighted that every department had valid concerns, but ultimately, the team had to work together to prioritize long-term success over immediate gratification.

9. **Making Strategic Trade-Offs:** One of the important takeaway from this chapter is the need to make early trade-offs in a project to avoid bigger issues later. Amit's decision to shift the focus from high-end performance to durability and affordability demonstrates that success in product development often comes from strategic compromises. This avoids a scenario where chasing perfection leads to delays and over-engineered products that may miss the target market.

10. **Balancing Performance and Cost:** The debates highlighted the technical challenge of balancing performance with cost efficiency. Reducing the powertrain's torque output to lower strain on the battery system and optimizing the chassis design for weight and cost savings were key examples of this. The decision to prioritize long-term reliability over peak performance aligned with both customer expectations and financial constraints.

These learnings illustrate the complexity of launching a new product in a highly competitive market and the importance of making long-term decisions that prioritize quality and customer satisfaction over short-term gains.

Chapter 4

Have Self-Belief and Be Authentic

Part 1: A Crisis of Confidence

The two-month delay was looming over Amit like a storm cloud. The weight of the Electric Auto project—its technical challenges, financial constraints, and now the constant doubts from his team— was beginning to chip away at his confidence. For the first time since joining Volt Motors, Amit felt the crushing pressure of not just leading a project but owning every decision. And some of those decisions were not sitting well with key members of his team.

In recent meetings, the tension had been palpable. Vivek's ongoing resistance to the trade-offs they'd made in the powertrain design hadn't eased, and while the BMS issues had been mitigated, the complexity of integrating the new MOSFET configurations without delaying production was proving more difficult than anticipated. Even Suhani, who had always been a voice of reason, was starting to show signs of stress as the financial strain on the project worsened.

Amit sat in his office, his fingers massaging his temples as he stared blankly at his desk. His phone buzzed, snapping him back to reality. It was a text message from his wife, Rina.

"Amit, I'm at the hospital. Dad's not well. I think it's serious."

His heart skipped a beat. Amit stood up abruptly, his head spinning. His father-in-law, who had been dealing with a heart condition for months, had just been admitted to the hospital. Amit's world began to tilt. He needed to be there for his family, but the pressure of the project weighed equally heavy on him.

In the hours that followed, Amit rushed to the hospital, his mind torn between his personal crisis and the looming project decisions. At the hospital, he was met by his wife, pale and shaken.

"Amit," Rina began, her voice trembling. "They're saying it's a blockage. He needs surgery."

Amit hugged her tightly, his heart pounding. "I'm here. We'll get through this."

The next few hours were a blur of medical updates, hurried phone calls, and a mind divided between his family and his team. Amit tried to stay present, but the constant ping of emails and messages from Volt Motors reminded him that the project wasn't going to wait for his personal crisis to resolve.

Amit sat outside the hospital's waiting room, staring blankly at the rows of chairs in front of him. His father-in-law had just been rushed into surgery for a heart blockage, and while the doctors were hopeful, there were no guarantees. The family was shaken—his wife, Rina, had barely left her father's side, and Amit felt the immense weight of both his personal crisis and the professional one back at Volt Motors. The Electric Auto project, which had consumed his life for months, was struggling under delays, technical challenges, and growing doubts within the team.

Amit's phone buzzed again. A message from Vivek asking for updates on the latest motor-controller calibration tests. Amit didn't even have the energy to open it. He was exhausted—physically, emotionally, and mentally. He felt like he was failing both at home and at work, unable to be there for his family and his team in the way they needed.

His confidence, something that had carried him through many difficult moments in his career, was now at its lowest. In this moment of uncertainty, Amit knew he needed guidance—someone who could help him regain his footing. He scrolled through his phone and dialed the number of his long-time mentor, Manav.

Manav answered on the second ring, his voice calm and steady. "Amit, how are you holding up?"

Amit exhaled slowly, feeling the tension in his chest. "Manav, I... I'm struggling. I'm at the hospital—Rina's dad is in surgery, and it's serious. But I can't stop thinking about the project. The team is falling apart, the technical issues are piling up, and I don't know if I'm making the right decisions anymore. I'm... I'm doubting myself."

Manav was silent for a moment, allowing Amit's words to hang in the air. "It sounds like you've got a lot on your plate, Amit. But let's start with this—what's making you doubt yourself?"

Amit rubbed his eyes, feeling the exhaustion creep in. "I'm torn. I need to be here for my family, but the project is critical. We're behind on deadlines, and the team—Vivek, Suhani—they're questioning my decisions. The trade-offs we made? I thought they were right, but now I'm not so sure. I don't know if I can keep balancing everything. What if I'm making all the wrong choices?"

Manav's voice remained steady. "Amit, first of all, it's okay to feel overwhelmed. What you're going through—both personally and professionally—is incredibly tough. But let me ask you something: Do you still believe in the vision of the project?"

Amit paused, considering the question. "I do. I know the product can work. It's not about the vision. It's about... everything else. The technical setbacks, the delays, the team losing faith in me. And on top of that, I feel like I'm not being there for my family. How can I focus on work when I know my father-in-law is in surgery right now? How do I balance these two worlds without failing at both?"

Manav's tone shifted slightly, more empathetic now. "Amit, what you're feeling is normal. Balancing personal and professional priorities is one of the hardest challenges anyone can face, especially in moments of crisis. But let's break it down. First, about the project. You said you still believe in the vision. That's important. But what's making you doubt your decisions on the technical front?"

Amit leaned back against the cold hospital wall, thinking carefully. "The team—Vivek especially—keeps pushing back on the decisions we made to sacrifice performance for durability. The powertrain, the torque output—he thinks we're going to lose our edge in the market if we don't deliver high performance. And Suhani is worried about the financial strain with the suppliers. I thought making those trade-offs would keep us on track, but now I'm not so sure. The feedback I'm getting is making me second-guess everything."

Manav listened intently, then responded with his characteristic calm. "Amit, leadership often means making decisions that not everyone will agree with. And yes, sometimes you will face pushback. But that doesn't mean your decisions are wrong. When you made those trade-offs, what was your guiding principle? What was the goal you were trying to achieve?"

Amit thought for a moment, recalling the discussions they'd had in the design lab. "The goal was to deliver a product that was reliable and affordable for our target market—urban and semi-urban commuters. We knew we couldn't push performance at the expense of cost or durability. We needed to focus on what mattered most to the customer."

Manav nodded. "Exactly. And has that goal changed?"

"No," Amit admitted. "But it's just... everything feels like it's falling apart. The team is questioning my leadership, and I don't know how to keep pushing them forward when I'm barely keeping it together myself."

Manav's voice softened. "Amit, it's okay to feel like you're not in control right now. But here's what you need to understand— leadership isn't about having all the answers or never feeling doubt. It's about staying grounded in what you believe, even when things get tough. It's about being authentic. Your team is questioning things because they're stressed, too. They're looking to you for clarity, and if they sense that you're losing faith in yourself, they'll start doubting the entire project."

Amit swallowed, the weight of Manav's words sinking in. "So what do I do? How do I regain their trust when I'm not even sure of myself right now?"

Manav's response was gentle but firm. "Amit, the first step is accepting that it's okay to feel unsure. But you need to separate doubt from fact. The facts are that you made those decisions with a clear purpose in mind. You had a strategy—reliability over performance— and it was the right strategy given the circumstances. Your doubt is just the noise that comes when the pressure mounts. Don't confuse the two."

Amit was quiet for a moment, thinking it over. "But how do I communicate that to the team? They're expecting answers. They're looking to me to guide them, and I don't want to pretend like I have everything under control when I don't."

Manav smiled on the other end of the line, sensing Amit's conflict. "Amit, leadership isn't about pretending. In fact, the more you try to fake confidence, the more disconnected you'll feel from the team. What they need right now isn't a leader who has all the answers— they need a leader who's willing to be real with them. Be transparent. Tell them what the challenges are, but also remind them of why you made the decisions you did. Reaffirm the vision. Be authentic, and they'll follow you."

Amit felt a shift inside him, a flicker of clarity breaking through the fog. "You're saying I need to stop trying to fix everything myself and start leading with... vulnerability?"

Manav chuckled softly. "Exactly. Vulnerability isn't weakness— it's strength. It takes courage to admit that things are tough, but it also shows your team that you're still committed to finding a way through. When they see that you believe in the vision, even if there are bumps along the way, they'll regain their confidence in the project. They'll rally."

Amit thought back to his recent meetings, how he had felt the need to project an air of control even when he was crumbling inside. May be that's where he had gone wrong.

"And what about my family?" Amit asked, his voice softer now. "How do I focus on work when I feel like I should be here, with Rina and my father-in-law? How do I balance it all without letting one side down?"

Manav took a deep breath before answering. "Amit, balance doesn't mean giving equal weight to everything at all times. It means being present where you're needed most in that moment. Right now, you're with your family—and that's where you should be. But that doesn't mean you've abandoned your work. When you return to the project, be present there. Communicate with your team. Delegate where necessary. You can't be everywhere at once, and that's okay. The key is to give your full attention to the priority in front of you."

Amit felt a sense of relief wash over him. "So, you're saying I don't need to feel guilty about being here, with my family."

"Exactly," Manav said. "You're doing what needs to be done. When you're back at work, focus on what needs to be done there. Trust your team to handle things in your absence, and when you return, lead them with the clarity and authenticity that you've always had. It's not about perfection—it's about being genuine and present."

Amit nodded, feeling the tension in his chest ease. "Thank you, Manav. I've been feeling like I'm failing at both, but what you're saying makes sense. I need to be present—whether that's here or at work. And I need to trust that I've made the right decisions, even when things get tough."

Manav's voice was warm. "Exactly, Amit. You're stronger than you think, and you're not alone in this. You have a team at work, and you have a family that supports you. Believe in yourself, trust in the process, and remember—leadership isn't about being perfect. It's about being real."

Amit smiled, the clarity he had been searching for finally beginning to take root. "You're right, Manav. Thank you. I needed this."

"Anytime, Amit. Take care of your family, and when you're back at Volt Motors, take care of your team."

As the call ended, Amit sat in the quiet of the hospital, feeling a new sense of balance. The crisis of confidence was still there, but it no longer felt insurmountable. He knew he could handle both his personal and professional challenges by being present, being real, and trusting in himself—and his team.

Part 2: Authentic Leadership

Two days after his father-in-law's surgery, Amit returned to Volt Motors, feeling the weight of both his family crisis and the project's growing challenges. He had spent the night at the hospital, his thoughts torn between the Electric Auto and his personal responsibilities. His confidence was wavering, and even though Manav's advice had been reassuring, Amit knew he needed more than just words to regain his footing. He needed to understand how to lead authentically under intense pressure.

The tension in the office was obvious as soon as he walked in. The project was moving forward, but without the energy or momentum it needed. The team was fragmented, and although Amit had kept the project from derailing entirely, it felt like they were heading toward a crisis. The technical issues were piling up—powertrain calibration, BMS integration, and financial constraints were all snowballing, adding layers of complexity to an already strained situation.

Amit had scheduled a team meeting to address these concerns, but before it could begin, Nisha Mehta, the CEO, called him to her office.

Nisha's office was minimalist, the walls adorned with sustainability awards and photos from Volt Motors' early days—a company she had built from the ground up. As Amit entered, Nisha motioned for him to sit across from her at the sleek, glass-topped desk.

"You wanted to see me, Nisha?" Amit asked, trying to keep his voice steady.

Nisha nodded, her expression calm but focused. "Yes, Amit. I've been following the progress of the Electric Auto closely, and I wanted to talk to you before we head into this next phase. There's something I need you to understand about leadership, especially now."

Amit leaned forward slightly, intrigued. "I'm listening."

Nisha paused, choosing her words carefully. "Leadership, especially in a time of crisis, isn't about having all the answers. It's about having the confidence to be authentic. You can't lead effectively if you're constantly doubting your own decisions or trying to meet everyone's expectations. I've seen you struggle with this recently, and I understand why—there's a lot riding on this project. But the team is looking to you for clarity, and you need to provide that by being true to who you are as a leader."

Amit frowned slightly, still processing. "But what does that really mean, Nisha? 'Being authentic' sounds straightforward, but when everything's on the line—when the team is questioning my decisions, when we're behind on deadlines—it feels like I need to be someone else. Someone who has all the answers."

Nisha smiled faintly. "I know it feels that way. But let me give you an example. When I was starting Volt Motors, we were building our first electric bus, and everything was going wrong. Our battery supplier had backed out last minute, the chassis design was flawed, and we were running out of cash. The board wanted me to cut corners, use cheaper materials, and just get the product out to market. But deep down, I knew that if we did that, we'd be sacrificing the very vision that Volt Motors was built on—sustainability and quality. So I made a tough call. I delayed the launch, much to the board's frustration. It was a hard decision, but I communicated it to the team, honestly and transparently. I told them why I believed in what we were doing and why we had to stick to our principles."

Amit leaned in, interested. "But how did you handle the pressure? The board, the team, the financial strain—how did you not compromise when everything seemed to be pushing you in that direction?"

Nisha nodded, acknowledging the difficulty. "It wasn't easy. There were sleepless nights. I was worried about whether I had made the right call. But here's the thing, Amit—when you lead with authenticity, you're not pretending to have all the answers. You're acknowledging the reality of the situation, and you're bringing the team into that reality with you. I didn't stand in front of my team and tell them everything was fine when it wasn't. I told them the truth: that we were in trouble, but that I believed in our product and our values. And because I was honest and transparent, the team rallied. They worked harder than ever because they knew I wasn't hiding anything from them."

Amit considered this, frowning. "But don't you think being too transparent might make the team panic? If they know things are bad, won't that just add to their stress?"

Nisha smiled, shaking her head slightly. "It's not about giving them a doomsday scenario. It's about giving them the truth along with a plan. When you're authentic, you acknowledge the challenges, but you also communicate your belief in the team's ability to overcome them. That's what rallies people. They don't follow you because you promise them perfection. They follow you because they trust that you're not going to sugarcoat the situation, but that you'll also guide them through it with integrity."

Amit felt a flicker of understanding. "So, it's about owning the situation and being honest about the difficulties, but also showing the team that you believe in the path forward."

"Exactly," Nisha said, her eyes brightening. "When you're authentic, people don't expect you to be perfect—they expect you to be real. Right now, the team senses your doubts, and it's making them uncertain. But if you stop trying to be the leader with all the answers and start being the leader who's honest about the challenges and confident in the team's ability to solve them, you'll earn their trust. It's about self-belief—and when you believe in yourself and your decisions, the team will follow."

Amit sat back, absorbing her words. "I've been trying to hold everything together on my own. I've been so focused on fixing every problem that I've stopped trusting the team to help me."

Nisha smiled softly. "Leadership isn't about doing everything yourself. It's about empowering your team, trusting their expertise, and being confident enough in your own decisions to let them take ownership. You've made some tough calls already—the trade-offs we discussed, the focus on reliability over performance. Stand by those decisions. Be clear and transparent about them, and the team will trust you. But you have to trust yourself first."

Amit nodded slowly, feeling the clarity return. "I get it now. I need to stop doubting my decisions and start leading with the conviction that we made the right choices. I need to communicate that to the team."

Nisha leaned forward, her tone gentle but firm. "Exactly. Authentic leadership is about self-belief, but also about being vulnerable enough to admit when you don't have all the answers. It's okay to tell your team that there are challenges we're still solving— but let them know you believe they're the ones who can solve them. That's where leadership truly shines."

Amit smiled, feeling a renewed sense of purpose. "Thank you, Nisha. I needed this. I've been so wrapped up in trying to fix everything that I forgot the most important part—trusting the team and staying true to why we're here in the first place."

Nisha smiled back, her confidence in him clear. "You've got this, Amit. Just be yourself. The team will follow if you lead with authenticity and belief in your vision. Now, go remind them why we're building this Electric Auto in the first place."

Authentic Leadership
Core Principles
Self-Belief
Confidence under pressure
Vision and values
Transparency
Balance realism with optimism
Openly share challenges
Key Actions
Acknowledge Reality
Admit challenges
Honesty about difficulties
Empower the Team
Trust and delegate
Involve in problem-solving
Inspire Vision
Align with values
Remind team of purpose
Core Idea
Empowering others collaboratively
Honesty, self-bell and trust
Outcomes
Sustainable Success
Values-based decisions
Resilience
Overcome obstacles together
Build Trust
Secure and motivated team
Emotional Intelligence
Supportive Communication
Encourage and reassure
Vulnerability
Leaders don't need all answers
Show humanity

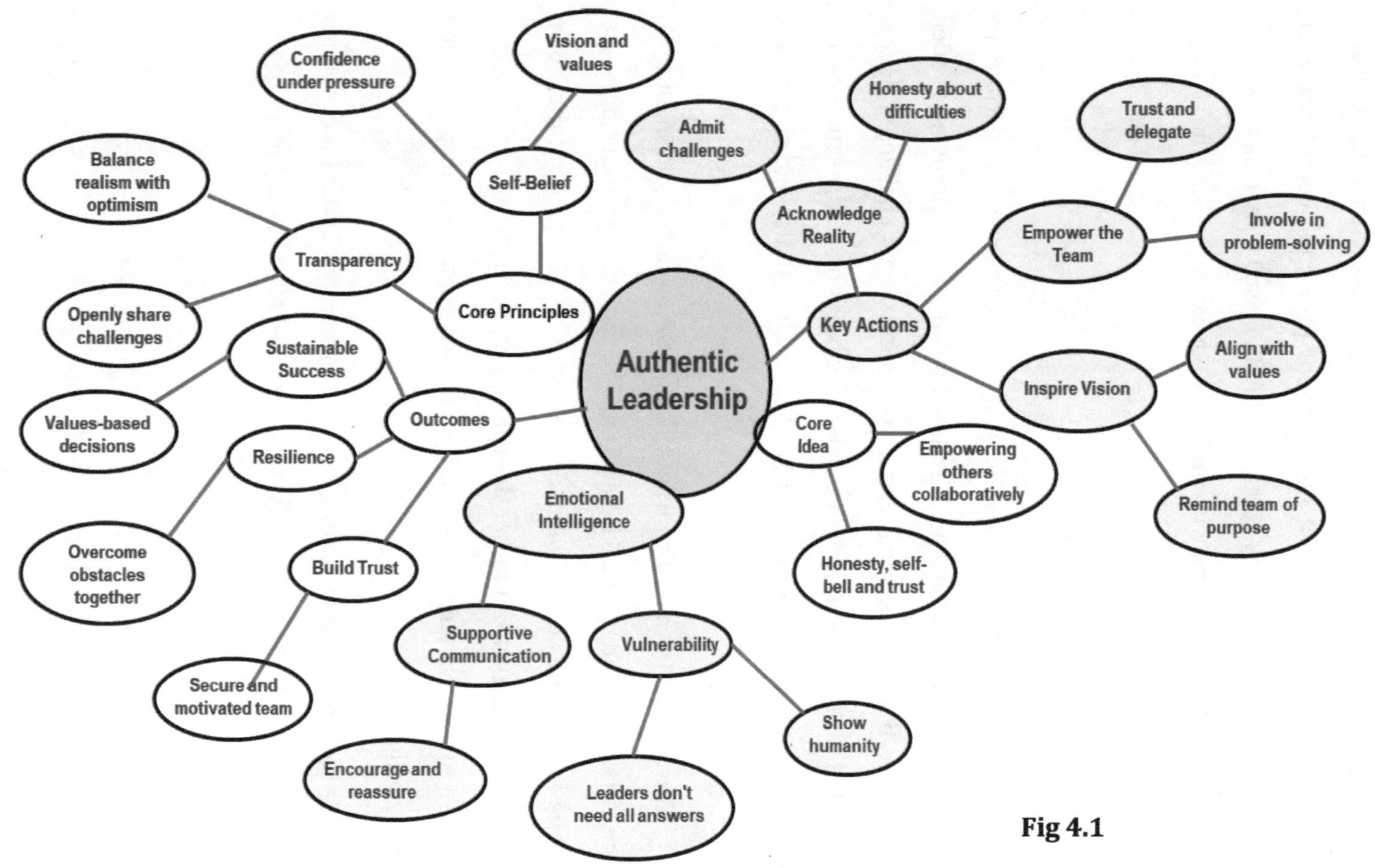

Fig 4.1

This conversation left Amit with a deeper understanding of what it meant to lead authentically. It wasn't about projecting confidence even when he didn't feel it; it was about owning the reality, sharing it with his team, and empowering them with the knowledge that they had the strength to face the challenges together.

Part 3: Team Rally

Amit returned to Volt Motors with a renewed sense of clarity. His conversations with Manav and Nisha had given him the tools he needed to navigate both his personal crisis and the project's challenges. He no longer felt the need to project an air of invincibility. Instead, he understood that true leadership came from authenticity, vulnerability, and trusting his team.

The tension in the office was still thick when he walked in, but this time, Amit was ready to face it head-on. The project was under pressure, and he knew the team had been dealing with his absence and their own growing frustrations. But rather than pretending everything was fine, Amit planned to address the issues directly, in a way that was transparent and empowering.

He decided to start with one-on-one conversations with his core team members—Vivek, Suhani, Pooja, and Kiran—before bringing everyone together.

Conversation with Vivek

Amit found Vivek in the engineering lab, hunched over a stack of reports. Vivek's face was lined with fatigue, and the frustration Amit had sensed in their recent meetings still lingered. He took a deep breath and approached.

"Vivek, can we talk?" Amit asked, keeping his tone open.

Vivek glanced up, clearly surprised but nodded. "Sure, Amit.

What's on your mind?"

Amit pulled up a chair, sitting across from him. "I know things have been tense between us lately. The decisions we've made on the powertrain, the trade-offs—there's been a lot of disagreement. I've

been thinking about it, and I want to acknowledge that I haven't been as open as I should have been. I've been trying to hold everything together, but I realize now that I need to be more transparent with you—and with the team."

Vivek leaned back slightly, the edge in his expression softening. "I appreciate you saying that. I've been frustrated, yes. But I also understand that the pressure is immense. We're trying to do something ambitious here, and when the deadlines start slipping and the technical issues keep piling up, it's easy to feel like we're losing control."

Amit nodded, relieved that Vivek was being honest. "I know. And I've been feeling the same way. But here's the thing—I believe in the decisions we made, even if they were difficult. The trade-offs were necessary to keep the product on track. But that doesn't mean we can't keep improving. If the motor-controller synchronization still isn't where it needs to be, let's tackle it together. I want your input—your honest input—on how we can fix it."

Vivek's expression shifted, and Amit could see the tension easing. "Honestly, Amit, I've been thinking about that a lot. I've run more tests on the recalibration, and while we've fixed the high-end issues, the low-speed performance is still lagging. If we can tweak the torque distribution algorithm and adjust the motor response curves for lower speeds, I think we can improve the overall responsiveness. But it's going to take time, and I need the team to be aligned on that."

Amit smiled, feeling a genuine sense of collaboration. "Then let's make that the focus. We'll prioritize the low-speed performance, but I want to make sure we're all on the same page. I'm not going to pretend that I have all the answers, Vivek. What I do have is trust in this team—and I'm counting on you to help us get there."

Vivek nodded, his respect for Amit clear. "Alright. Let's do this.

I appreciate the openness, Amit. It makes a difference."

Conversation with Suhani

Next, Amit sought out Suhani in her office, where she was poring over financial spreadsheets, her brow furrowed in concentration. She looked up as Amit knocked on the doorframe, motioning for him to come in.

"Amit, good timing. I was just about to send you an update on the supplier negotiations. The costs are still fluctuating, and we're not where we need to be yet."

Amit took a seat, exhaling slowly. "Suhani, I know you've been carrying a lot of weight on the financial side, and I haven't made it easier by pushing the team so hard. I want to apologize for not being more upfront with you about the pressures I've been under."

Suhani's expression eased. "Amit, I understand. We're all under pressure. But it's been tough managing the finances with so many uncertainties. The supply chain issues, the MOSFET supplier delays—it's all adding up. We need to make sure we don't blow the budget, but we also can't compromise the core components."

Amit leaned forward, appreciating her candor. "I completely agree. I'm not here to pretend we're not facing a crisis. But I believe we can get through it. I had a conversation with Manav recently, and it helped me realize something—our success doesn't come from avoiding problems. It comes from facing them together, with clarity and transparency."

Suhani smiled slightly. "That's good to hear. I've been worried that we've been pushing too hard without thinking through the long- term financial impact. But if we're all on the same page, we can start finding solutions. I've been looking into alternative suppliers for some of the components, especially for the BMS electronics, and I think we can make up for some of the cost overruns there."

Amit's face brightened. "That's exactly what we need. I want you to keep pushing on that, but I also want you to know that you have my full support. We're going to make this work, Suhani. Let's stay aligned and keep the communication open."

Suhani nodded. "We will. And Amit, I appreciate you being more transparent with the team. It's what we needed."

Conversation with Pooja

Amit found Pooja in the design lab, where she was reviewing the latest simulations on the airflow system around the powertrain. She looked up as Amit approached, offering a small smile.

"Amit, I've been running the models you asked for. The cooling system is holding up well under the revised load, but I'm still worried about heat dissipation during prolonged low-speed operation. We might need to adjust the venting system to avoid hotspots."

Amit nodded, impressed by her dedication. "Pooja, that's great work. And I want to say something before we dive into the details. I know I haven't been as communicative as I should have been with the team. I've been caught up in the pressure of the project, but that's no excuse. I want you to know that I trust your expertise, and I want us to be more open moving forward."

Pooja's face relaxed. "I appreciate that, Amit. I've been worried about the direction of the project, especially with all the technical trade-offs we've made. But I've also seen how hard you've been working to keep everything on track. We just need to make sure we're balancing the technical needs with the timeline."

Amit leaned in, his voice steady. "Exactly. And I want you to know that I'm listening. If the cooling system needs adjustments, let's make those adjustments. We can't afford to cut corners, but we also need to keep pushing forward. I'm counting on you to help us find that balance."

Pooja **smiled**. "You've got it, Amit. Let's make this work."

Conversation with Kiran

Amit's final one-on-one was with Kiran, the head of marketing. Kiran had been busy preparing the initial customer feedback reports and was clearly eager to discuss the next steps.

"Amit, I've been going over the latest feedback from our test drivers. The consensus is clear—customers are prioritizing reliability over performance, just like we anticipated. But we need to be careful. If the low-speed torque lag isn't fixed, we might have issues with customer satisfaction."

Amit nodded, grateful for Kiran's insight. "Kiran, thank you for flagging that. And I also want to acknowledge something—I haven't been as transparent with you and the rest of the team as I should have been. I've been carrying a lot of stress, but that's not an excuse. From now on, I want to make sure we're fully aligned on both the technical side and the customer-facing side."

Kiran smiled, leaning back in his chair. "I appreciate that, Amit. And honestly, I think the team's felt the pressure, but we've also seen how committed you are. If we can work together to align the product with the customer's expectations—and fix the technical issues—we'll be in a strong position. I've been refining the messaging to focus more on total cost of ownership and long-term savings for the fleet operators. If we get that right, the performance trade-offs won't matter as much."

Amit smiled, feeling the pieces starting to come together. "That's exactly what we need. Let's keep the communication flowing. We're all in this together."

Team Meeting: Collective Rally

Later that day, Amit gathered the entire core team—Vivek, Suhani, Pooja, Kiran, and Raghav—in the main conference room. The atmosphere was still tense, but Amit felt a shift. He had had the difficult conversations with each of them individually, and now it was time to bring everyone together.

"Alright, everyone," Amit began, standing at the head of the table. "I know the past few weeks have been challenging. We've faced setbacks, disagreements, and a lot of uncertainty. But I want to start by saying this—I believe in every decision we've made so far. I also believe in this team."

He paused, letting his words settle. "I haven't always been as open with you as I should have been. I've been trying to shoulder the responsibility of this project on my own, but I realize now that leadership isn't about doing everything alone. It's about trusting your team. And I trust each and every one of you."

Vivek, sitting across the table, leaned forward slightly. "Amit, I appreciate that. And I think I speak for the team when I say we've all felt the pressure. But if we're aligned, if we know what the next steps are, we can make this work."

Suhani concurred. "Agreed. If we keep the communication open and tackle the issues head-on, we can stay on course. The financials are tight, but I'm confident we can find a way to stabilize the costs."

Pooja nodded. "The technical issues with the cooling system and the torque lag are manageable. We just need to stay focused and push through the next round of tests."

Kiran smiled. "And on the customer side, we're ready. We've got the messaging aligned with the product's strengths, and if we stay on track, I'm confident we can hit the market with a strong offering."

Amit felt a surge of pride as he looked around the table. The team was rallying, not because everything was perfect, but because they believed in the shared vision.

"Thank you, everyone," Amit said, his voice steady and filled with conviction. "Let's move forward with clarity, transparency, and confidence. We're going to make this work—together."

The team nodded in agreement, and for the first time in weeks, the tension in the room felt lighter. They had a long road ahead, but with renewed trust and alignment, they were ready to face the challenges together.

Key Learnings from Chapter 4: Have Self-Belief and Be Authentic

1. **The Importance of Self-Belief:** One of the core takeaways from this chapter is that self-confidence in leadership is crucial.

Amit realized that in order to lead his team effectively, he had to first believe in himself and in the decisions he had made for the project. His ability to regain this belief after conversations with his mentor Manav and Nisha helped him become a stronger and more grounded leader.

2. **Authentic Leadership Builds Trust:** Amit learned that being transparent and vulnerable with his team was essential to building trust. By admitting his doubts and openly discussing the project's challenges, he fostered a more open and collaborative environment. His team responded positively to his authenticity, which helped to restore alignment and trust in his leadership.

3. **Balancing Personal and Professional Priorities:** Amit struggled with balancing the personal crisis of his father-in-law's health with the demands of his job. Through his conversation with Manav, he learned that leadership is about being present in the moment and prioritizing what needs attention at different times. This insight helped him handle both his family and work crises without feeling overwhelmed or guilty.

4. **Team Empowerment:** Amit realized that leadership is not about carrying the entire burden alone, but about empowering the team to contribute and solve problems together. By seeking input from team members like Vivek, Suhani, Pooja and Kiran, Amit recognized the importance of trusting his team's expertise and allowing them to take ownership of the technical and financial challenges they were facing.

5. **Clear and Transparent Communication:** Amit understood that effective communication is about being honest with the team about the difficulties they are facing while reaffirming the vision and the path forward. His transparency helped the team rally behind the project, and they were more willing to engage with the challenges once they felt included in the decision-making process.

6. **Resolving Differences through Collaboration:** The chapter emphasized that team members may have different perspectives and opinions, but these differences can be resolved through collaborative discussion. By speaking to Vivek, Suhani, Pooja, and Kiran individually, Amit addressed their concerns and found common ground, allowing the team to move forward with collective understanding.

7. **Empathy in Leadership:** Amit also learned that showing empathy toward his team's concerns, while remaining firm in his vision, is a key element of authentic leadership. The team respected Amit more when he acknowledged their frustrations and worked with them to solve the problems rather than imposing decisions from above.

8. **Taking Ownership and Accountability:** The chapter highlighted the importance of a leader taking ownership of their decisions and being accountable for the project's outcomes. Amit acknowledged the difficulties and took responsibility for the direction the project was heading, which strengthened his relationship with his team and reinforced their collective commitment to success.

9. **Aligning the Team Toward a Shared Vision:** A major learning was that leadership involves aligning the team around a shared goal. Despite their initial disagreements, Amit's open communication helped the team rally behind the core vision of delivering a reliable, affordable product that meets customer needs. This alignment increased the team's sense of purpose and momentum.

10. **Balancing Technical Challenges and Strategic Priorities:** The technical debates around motor-controller synchronization, BMS integration, and cooling system adjustments highlighted that even in a high-stakes project, it's essential to balance technical challenges with the overall strategic priorities of the project. By focusing on what truly mattered—reliability and customer satisfaction—Amit led the team to make the necessary adjustments without losing sight of the end goal.

These key learnings from Chapter 4 underscore the importance of self-belief, authenticity and open communication in effective leadership, especially in moments of crisis. They also highlight the value of trusting the team, collaborative problem-solving, and staying grounded in the project's core mission.

Chapter 5

Learn to Deal with Reality, Not Perceptions

Part 1: Internal Perception vs Reality

The tension at Volt Motors had taken on a new form. Despite the progress Amit and his team had made in the Electric Auto project, a dangerous narrative was beginning to take hold within the company's corridors: Volt Motors was falling behind. Amit could sense it in the way his colleagues spoke in hushed tones, the uneasy glances exchanged during meetings, and the not-so-subtle questions about how far along the competitors, especially Zephyr EV, had come with their own auto-rickshaw.

Amit was sitting at his desk when Kiran knocked on the doorframe and stepped into his office. There was a serious look on Kiran's face that immediately caught Amit's attention.

"Amit, we need to talk," Kiran began, closing the door behind him. "I don't know how to say this, but there's been a lot of... gossip going around."

Amit raised an eyebrow, motioning for him to continue. "Gossip?

About what?"

Kiran hesitated for a moment. "About the Electric Auto project. People are saying we're falling behind, that Zephyr EV is already ahead of us. Internally, some teams are starting to believe that the project's in trouble, that we're not going to make the launch date."

Amit sighed, leaning back in his chair. He had felt this creeping in—the perception that Volt Motors wasn't keeping up. "Let me guess, they think Zephyr's going to beat us to market?"

Kiran nodded. "It's more than just that. Some of the senior managers are worried we've lost momentum. They think the setbacks with the powertrain calibration, the supply chain issues with the

MOSFETs, and the delays in the prototype testing mean the project is on the verge of failure. It's starting to create a sense of panic."

Amit's jaw tightened. He had worked hard to regain control of the project after the initial delays, and while he knew they had faced significant obstacles, he was confident they were still on track for a successful launch. But perceptions, especially within a company, could be as damaging as the reality.

"Kiran, I need to know something," Amit said, his voice calm but direct. "What's your perception? Do you think we're falling behind?"

Kiran paused, weighing his response carefully. "Honestly? No, I don't. I know we've had setbacks, but I also know the work that's gone into correcting them. The testing results have been improving, the financials are stabilizing, and the customer feedback has been overwhelmingly positive. But the problem is that not everyone knows what we know. They only see the delays, the missed deadlines, and they assume the worst."

Amit nodded. "Perception is a powerful thing. But we can't let it dictate how we move forward. The reality is that we've made progress—real progress. But I also understand why people are starting to doubt us.

We haven't been as transparent with the broader teams as we've been internally."

Kiran leaned forward. "So how do we deal with this? We can't let the team start doubting the project when we're this close to the finish line."

Amit thought for a moment, his mind racing through possible solutions. "We need to confront the perception head-on. I'll have to talk to the broader team, address the rumors, and give them a clear picture of where we really are. But first, I want to meet with Nisha. I need her backing on this. If we're going to fight perceptions, we need to do it from the top down."

Kiran nodded. "I agree. If we let these rumors fester, it'll affect morale, and that's the last thing we need right now."

Amit stood up, feeling a surge of determination. "Let's get ahead of this before it spirals."

Part 2: The Market's Perception

Later that afternoon, Amit was called into a boardroom meeting with Nisha and several senior executives. As he entered the room, he immediately sensed the tension. Nisha was seated at the head of the table, flipping through a stack of documents, her expression unreadable. Across from her sat Raghav, head of operations, and a few other department heads. The atmosphere was charged with a sense of urgency.

"Amit, take a seat," Nisha said, gesturing to the chair beside her. Her tone was calm, but Amit could sense the underlying intensity.

As soon as Amit sat down, Raghav launched into the conversation. "Amit, we've been monitoring the market trends, and there's growing concern. Zephyr EV has started heavily marketing their auto-rickshaw, and it's creating a buzz. They're presenting it as the next big thing, and the perception in the market is that they're about to leap ahead of us."

Amit nodded, having anticipated this moment. Zephyr EV, Volt Motors' biggest competitor, had always been aggressive with their marketing strategies, but lately, their efforts were amplified. The perception they were building—that Volt Motors was lagging behind— was gaining traction not just in the market but also within the walls of Volt Motors itself.

"I've heard the same from Kiran and some of the team," Amit replied. "Internally, there's talk that we're falling behind. It's starting to affect morale."

Nisha leaned forward, her fingers tapping lightly on the desk. "The board is getting anxious, Amit. They're seeing Zephyr's marketing push, and they're asking why we haven't been more aggressive. They've even started questioning if we'll make the launch date. We need to address this head-on."

Amit took a deep breath, knowing this was a crucial moment. "Here's the truth—we're not behind. We've faced challenges, yes, but we're not losing to Zephyr. What we're seeing right now is perception— the noise they're generating in the market. But if you look deeper, their product is full of compromises. They're cutting corners in critical areas, like battery thermal management and range stability. They're focusing on quick wins in their marketing, but the reality is their product isn't built to last."

Raghav, who had been scanning a report in front of him, looked up. "But how do we counter that perception? Zephyr's getting ahead of the narrative, and that's what the board is worried about. We can't afford to let them dominate the conversation."

Amit nodded, understanding the gravity of the situation. "We need to communicate the real strengths of our product, and we need to do it confidently. Yes, Zephyr's marketing has been slick, but we're offering something they aren't—durability, comfort, and a completely redesigned driver and passenger experience."

Nisha's interest piqued. "Tell us more."

Amit stood up and moved to the whiteboard, sketching a rough outline of the Electric Auto. "We've made significant improvements to the design and styling of our auto. It's not just about what's under the hood anymore—it's about creating a more comfortable and spacious experience for both drivers and passengers. This isn't just another auto-rickshaw; we've reimagined the whole interior to provide more legroom, better ergonomics for the driver, and additional storage space for luggage, which is something drivers and passengers have been demanding for years."

He pointed to the driver's section. "We've focused on improving driver comfort, especially for long shifts. The seat now offers better lumbar support, and we've optimized the dashboard layout so that drivers have easy access to controls without having to stretch or twist awkwardly. This might seem like a small detail, but it's a big deal for drivers who are spending 12-14 hours a day behind the wheel."

Nisha nodded, clearly impressed. "This is the kind of differentiation we need to emphasize."

Amit continued, moving to the passenger section. "For the passengers, we've increased legroom and added cushioned seating that's more comfortable for longer rides. The cabin is wider, providing a more open feel. This design also adds more luggage space behind the seats, which addresses one of the biggest complaints from commuters—there's never enough room for their bags. Zephyr's design is flashy, but they haven't prioritized these practical features."

Raghav leaned in, his interest piqued. "So, you're saying our product isn't just about the powertrain—it's about the overall experience?"

"Exactly," Amit replied. "We've kept the engineering fundamentals strong—reliable powertrain, robust battery system, and durable chassis design—but we've also improved the user experience. Zephyr is relying on sleek marketing and flashy features, but they're missing the practical needs of drivers and passengers. Our product will deliver on both fronts—performance and comfort."

Nisha looked thoughtful for a moment. "What about the space optimization? How does it compare to Zephyr's model?"

Amit smiled, prepared for the question. "Zephyr's model has focused heavily on appearance, but they've sacrificed interior space. Their cabin is narrower, and while it looks futuristic, it's not as practical. Our Electric Auto offers 10% more cabin space than Zephyr's, which directly translates into a more comfortable ride for passengers, especially in crowded urban areas. And the additional luggage space will be a game-changer for drivers who often have to turn away customers with heavy bags."

Nisha's face lit up. "This is exactly what we need to push in our marketing. The reality is that our product is built for the real-world conditions our drivers face. It's not just about aesthetics—it's about functionality and comfort."

Raghav, who had been one of the skeptics earlier, seemed to be coming around. "This sounds promising, Amit. But the market perception right now is that Zephyr is ahead. How do we communicate these advantages without seeming like we're playing catch-up?"

Amit met Raghav's gaze with confidence. "We don't need to react to Zephyr's marketing directly. Instead, we double down on what we know our customers value. We position the Electric Auto as the more thoughtful, reliable choice. We show the market that we've built something that's designed for the long haul, both in terms of performance and comfort. Our product is built to last, not just to impress."

Nisha nodded, clearly impressed by Amit's focus. "And the new design elements—the additional space, the driver and passenger comfort—that's going to resonate with our audience?"

"Absolutely," Amit replied. "When drivers see the improved ergonomics and the fact that they won't be as fatigued after long shifts, and when passengers experience the extra space and comfort, that's what will set us apart. Zephyr is chasing the flash, but we're focused on substance."

Raghav still had a thoughtful look on his face. "The board is going to ask tough questions. They'll want to know how we plan to position this in the market without looking like we're responding to Zephyr's moves."

Amit met his gaze steadily. "I'll take those questions head-on. We're not responding to Zephyr—we're staying true to our vision. I'll explain to the board that the reason we've had delays is because we refused to compromise on what matters. The Electric Auto will speak for itself once it's launched. The market will see the difference between a product built for reliability and comfort versus one built for hype."

Nisha smiled, clearly satisfied with Amit's approach. "Alright, let's go with that. We'll prepare for the board meeting, and I want you to take the lead, Amit. We're not here to chase after perceptions—we're here to deliver a product that's grounded in reality. Make sure the board knows that."

Amit nodded, feeling a renewed sense of confidence. "Understood.

We'll show them the reality behind our progress."

Part 3: Grounding in Reality

The days following the board meeting were filled with a sense of urgency, but also a growing sense of purpose. Amit knew that the biggest challenge he faced wasn't the technical complexities of the Electric Auto—it was getting his team fully aligned and grounded in reality. The perception that Zephyr EV was leading the market had caused anxiety, but Amit was determined to refocus the team on what truly mattered: the substance of their product, not the noise from competitors.

He gathered his core team—Vivek, Pooja, and Kiran—for a detailed strategy session. He wanted to break down each critical aspect of the vehicle, from technical performance to design features and marketing strategy, and ensure they all moved forward with clarity and confidence.

Vivek's Technical Insight: Powertrain and Battery System

Amit started with Vivek, who had been overseeing the technical aspects of the powertrain and BMS. The Electric Auto's motor-controller synchronization had been a major hurdle, and Amit knew they couldn't afford any more delays on this front.

"Vivek let's start with the powertrain," Amit said, leaning forward. "Where do we stand with the latest test results on the torque distribution? I know the low-speed performance was still an issue."

Vivek nodded, adjusting his glasses as he pulled up the latest data on his tablet. "We've made significant progress there. The torque distribution algorithm has been optimized for better low-speed acceleration. We focused on recalibrating the power curve to ensure smoother transitions when the vehicle is fully loaded, particularly in stop-and-go traffic. The drivers will notice a much more responsive throttle at low speeds now."

Amit looked at the data on the screen, impressed by the improvements. "That's great to hear. How's the battery discharge rate holding up under the revised torque settings?"

Vivek tapped on the tablet, showing the battery performance graphs. "With the new configuration, the strain on the battery during rapid acceleration has been reduced by about 12%. The thermal management system has been working as expected, and we've seen a decrease in heat spikes during long-duration drives. The BMS is now better aligned with the powertrain output, so we're seeing fewer inconsistencies in the SOC readings."

Amit smiled, feeling a sense of relief. "So we've solved the major issues with powertrain synchronization?"

Vivek nodded, more confident now. "Yes. The tests have been consistent, and I'm confident that we've addressed the concerns we had. The battery life is stable, and the powertrain is delivering the performance we need without overloading the system."

Amit leaned back, satisfied. "That's exactly what I wanted to hear. Reliability has always been our priority, and it sounds like we're finally getting there."

Pooja's Design Focus: Ergonomics, Comfort, and Space Optimization

Next, Amit turned to Pooja, who had been leading the efforts on design and interior comfort. The decision to focus on both driver ergonomics and passenger space had been a cornerstone of the Electric Auto's differentiation in the market.

"Pooja, let's talk about the design changes. We've made significant improvements to the driver's cabin and the passenger space. How are those coming along in terms of real-world testing?"

Pooja smiled, clearly proud of the progress. "We've completed the ergonomic tests with a sample group of drivers, and the feedback has been overwhelmingly positive. The adjustable driver's seat and the new dashboard layout have improved comfort significantly, especially during long shifts. Drivers reported less back strain, thanks to the lumbar support we added."

Amit nodded. "And the dashboard layout—how's the usability there?"

Pooja tapped her tablet, showing the latest ergonomics report. "The redesigned dashboard has been a hit. The control panel is now positioned within easy reach, so drivers don't have to stretch to access critical functions like the battery level monitor or the headlight controls. We've reduced driver fatigue by making sure everything is accessible with minimal movement."

Amit studied the report, feeling reassured by the improvements. "What about the passenger space? The extra legroom and luggage space were key to our differentiation from Zephyr. Have we maintained the structural integrity while optimizing space?"

Pooja nodded enthusiastically. "Yes, we've managed to increase the legroom by 10%, and we've added a dedicated luggage compartment behind the rear seats. This is a game-changer, especially for urban commuters who often carry shopping bags or small suitcases. Despite the space optimization, we haven't compromised the BIW structure. The FEA showed that the new design is just as robust as the previous version."

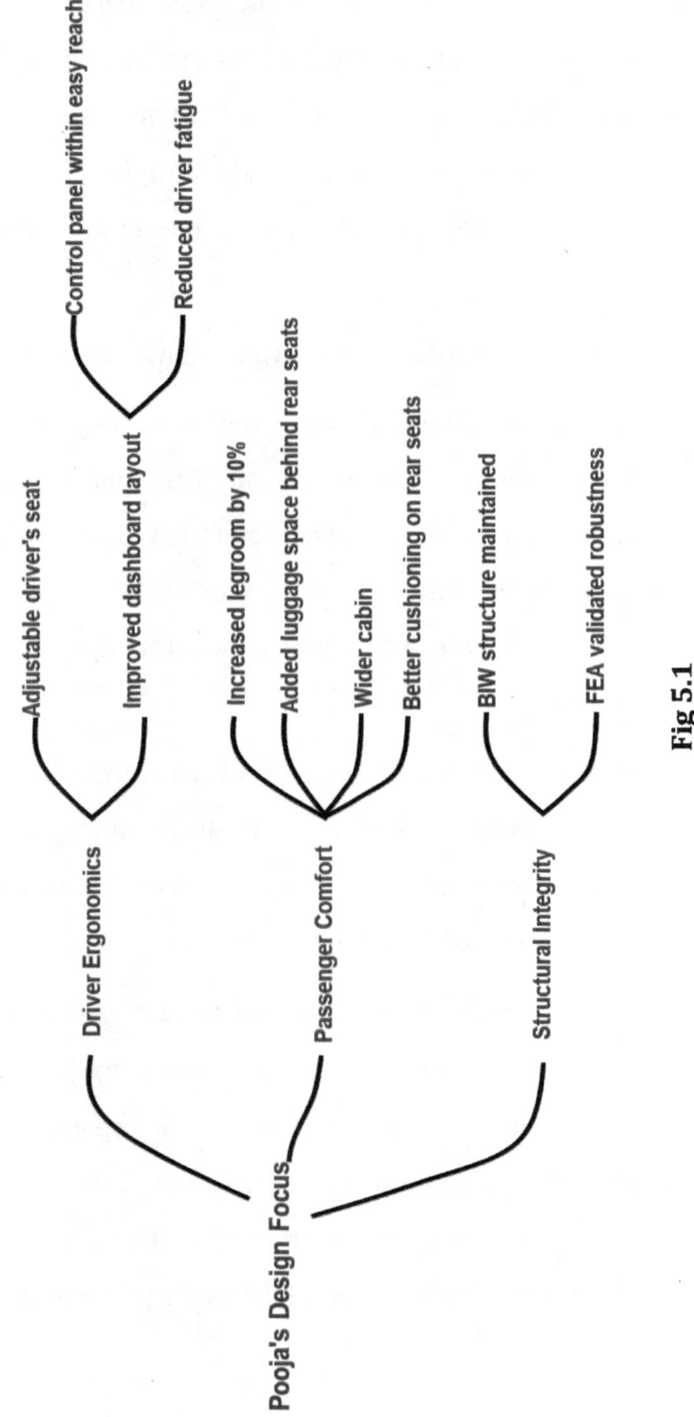
Pooja's Design Focus
Driver Ergonomics
Adjustable driver's seat
Improved dashboard layout
Control panel within easy reach
Reduced driver fatigue
Passenger Comfort
Increased legroom by 10%
Added luggage space behind rear seats
Wider cabin
Better cushioning on rear seats
Structural Integrity
BIW structure maintained
FEA validated robustness

Fig 5.1

Amit was pleased. The focus on comfort and space had been a strategic move to set their Electric Auto apart from the competition, and it sounded like they were on track. "This is excellent, Pooja. We're not just building a reliable vehicle—we're building something that enhances the driving and passenger experience. Zephyr can focus on flashy features, but we're building practical comfort."

Pooja smiled. "Exactly. The feedback we've gathered shows that passengers are noticing the difference. We've even added better cushioning to the rear seats, and the wider cabin has been a huge hit with test groups."

Amit nodded, feeling more confident with each update. "This is the kind of innovation that will speak louder than any marketing campaign Zephyr puts out."

Kiran's Marketing Strategy: Positioning the Product's Strengths

Finally, Amit turned to Kiran, who was busy refining the marketing strategy. The challenge now was to communicate the reality of their product's advantages to counter Zephyr EV's aggressive marketing push.

"Kiran, we need to get the messaging right," Amit said. "Zephyr's dominating the conversation with flashy features, but we know our strengths are in reliability, comfort, and affordability. How do we make sure the market understands that?"

Kiran leaned forward, clearly ready for this conversation. "I've been thinking about that a lot. We don't need to respond directly to Zephyr's marketing—we need to double down on what our product delivers. I've reworked the messaging to focus on three key areas: driver comfort, passenger experience, and total cost of ownership. That's where we beat them, hands down."

Amit raised an eyebrow. "Tell me more."

Kiran tapped on his tablet, bringing up the latest marketing mockups. "First, we lead with driver comfort. Zephyr's auto looks futuristic, but their driver's cabin is cramped. We're going to highlight how our ergonomic design reduces driver fatigue and makes long shifts more bearable. The adjustable seat, the optimized dashboard, and the better lumbar support—that's something drivers will notice immediately."

Amit nodded, impressed. "And for passengers?"

Kiran grinned. "That's our second angle. We push the extra legroom and the luggage space. Passengers don't want to feel cramped, especially in crowded urban areas. We've made their ride more comfortable, and that's a big selling point. The wider cabin and cushioned seats will set us apart. Zephyr's auto might look good in a showroom, but in real-world conditions, passengers are going to prefer ours."

Amit smiled, liking where this was going. "And the cost?"

Kiran's tone became more serious. "This is where we hit them hardest—total cost of ownership. Zephyr's model is more expensive to maintain because they've prioritized flash over substance. We'll emphasize the low maintenance costs of our auto, the longer battery life, and the durability of the vehicle. Fleet operators care about the bottom line, and when they see that our product will save them money in the long run, they'll choose us over Zephyr."

Amit felt a surge of confidence as he listened. Kiran was right— their product was built for the real-world needs of drivers and passengers, not just to look good in a marketing campaign. "This is exactly what we need, Kiran. Let's make sure the market knows that we've built something that lasts."

Kiran nodded. "We'll start rolling out the new messaging in the next few days. We're focusing on real customer testimonials, too. The drivers who've tested our auto are already seeing the benefits, and when that word gets out, Zephyr's flashy features won't matter."

As the meeting came to a close, Amit looked around the room, feeling a renewed sense of unity. Each member of the team had brought their expertise to the table, and together, they had built something that went beyond the competition's noise. The reality was clear: the Electric Auto was designed for comfort, reliability, and cost- efficiency—everything their customers needed.

Amit stood up, addressing the group. "We've faced a lot of noise lately, from both inside and outside the company. But today, we've grounded ourselves in the reality of what we've built. We're not just making an auto-rickshaw—we're making something that drivers and passengers will rely on for years to come. Let's keep pushing forward and show the market what we're really about."

Vivek, Pooja, and Kiran nodded in agreement, their confidence in the project renewed. The perceptions would fade, but the reality of their product's strength would endure.

Key Learnings from Chapter 5: Learn to Deal with Reality, Not Perceptions

1. **Perception vs Reality:** A major takeaway from this chapter is understanding the difference between internal and external perceptions versus the actual progress of a project. While perceptions may cause panic and doubt, grounding oneself in the reality of the situation—what has been achieved and what still needs to be done—is essential for maintaining focus and confidence.

2. **Transparent Leadership:** Amit demonstrated the importance of **transparency** in leadership. By addressing the team's concerns and being open about the challenges they were facing, he reinforced trust within his team and showed that addressing perceptions requires clear communication and alignment with the project's goals.

3. **Product Differentiation Through Substance, Not Hype:** The comparison with Zephyr EV highlighted that while competitors may focus on flashy marketing and surface-level features, real success comes from creating a product that meets the practical needs of the customer. Amit's team prioritized reliability, driver comfort, passenger space and

affordability, showing that substance will win over perception in the long run.

4. **Collaboration to Ground the Team in Reality:** Amit's ability to bring his core team— Vivek, Pooja, and Kiran — together in constructive conversations allowed them to focus on the facts of the project. Each team member contributed critical insights, and together, they were able to counter negative perceptions by reinforcing the strengths of the Electric Auto, from technical reliability to design innovations.

5. **Focus on Customer-Centric Design:** The chapter emphasized the importance of creating a product with real-world usability. The improved driver ergonomics, passenger comfort, and extra luggage space were not just design upgrades—they directly addressed customer pain points, differentiating the Electric Auto from competitors. This focus on customer experience helped the team stay grounded in what mattered most to their market.

6. **Handling Market Pressure:** The external pressure created by Zephyr EV's marketing campaign demonstrated that market perceptions can often be misleading. Amit's response—to stay focused on product development rather than react to the competitor's noise—highlighted the importance of maintaining composure under market pressure and ensuring that the team sticks to the core values of the product.

7. **Strategic Marketing Alignment:** Kiran's approach to repositioning the Electric Auto in the market showed that strategic messaging

plays a crucial role in managing perceptions. By focusing on reliability, comfort and total cost of ownership, the marketing strategy aligned with the actual strengths of the product, ensuring that the external messaging was grounded in reality rather than hype.

8. **Resilience and Confidence in Execution:** Amit's leadership in this chapter underscored the importance of resilience. Despite the internal and external pressures, he remained confident in the team's progress and the long-term vision of the product. This reinforced the need to stay committed to the project's goals, even when faced with doubts and setbacks.

9. **Unity Through Collaboration:** Amit's team exemplified how collaboration can lead to solutions that address both technical challenges and market demands. By involving Vivek in resolving powertrain issues, Pooja in optimizing design, and Kiran in refining the marketing message, Amit ensured that the entire team was aligned with the reality of the project and not swayed by external perceptions.

10. **Leadership Grounded in Facts:** The chapter highlighted the importance of leading with facts and data. Amit's ability to counter both internal gossip and external market noise was rooted in his firm grasp of the technical, financial, and design aspects of the project. He demonstrated that staying grounded in reality—through data-driven decision-making—creates confidence in the face of market perceptions.

These learnings from Chapter 5 emphasize the importance of staying grounded, aligning the team and countering market perceptions with a product that delivers real value to customers.

Chapter 6

There Is No 'Gain' Without 'Pain'

Part 1: The Pressure Builds

The office lights flickered in the late evening, casting long shadows over the workstations. It had been another grueling day at Volt Motors, and as the launch date for the Electric Auto crept closer, the pressure was mounting like a storm about to break. The once lively chatter among the team had been replaced by an oppressive silence, the kind of silence that spoke volumes about the tension everyone was feeling. Reports piled high, technical glitches persisted, and the sense that time was running out loomed over them all.

Amit was in the design lab, leaning over Vivek's workstation. Vivek's eyes were red with exhaustion, but his focus was unbroken as he scanned through lines of code on the screen, trying to find the flaw in the BMS that had plagued them for weeks.

"We're stuck, Amit," Vivek said, frustration clear in his voice. "No matter what we do, we can't get the voltage regulation to stay stable. It fluctuates every time we run the discharge test, and it's impacting the overall range efficiency. We're talking about a potential 5% drop."

Amit rubbed his temples, trying to fight off the headache that had been building all day. The weight of the project sat heavily on his shoulders. "We need that stability, Vivek. Without it, the reliability of the entire system comes into question. We can't afford to lose that much efficiency—our entire pitch is based on long-term durability and performance."

Vivek turned to face Amit, his frustration bubbling to the surface. "I get that, but we're running out of time. The more we push this, the more new problems keep cropping up. We've tried recalibrating the thresholds, adjusting the thermal management system, even tweaking the charge cycles. I don't know what else we can do without a full overhaul, and we don't have time for that."

Amit knew Vivek was right, but there was no room for retreat now. "We have to keep pushing. We've come too far to let this problem break us. I know it's tough, but there's no gain without pain."

Vivek slumped in his chair, the fatigue clearly wearing him down. "It's not just the technical issues, Amit. The team is stretched thin. We're all exhausted. You've seen Pooja and Kiran—they're burning out, just like the rest of us."

Amit crossed his arms, his mind racing for solutions. "I've seen it, Vivek. But the finish line is in sight. Every project hits this point where it feels like everything's falling apart. This is ours. It's painful, yes, but we need to hold it together. This is what separates the successful projects from the failures—the ability to push through when everything seems impossible."

Vivek let out a heavy breath, nodding slightly. "I know. But it's hard not to feel like we're fighting an uphill battle."

Amit placed a hand on his shoulder, his voice softer. "I get it, Vivek. I'm feeling the pressure just as much as you are. But we're not giving up. We'll get through this. We're too close to let it fall apart now."

Vivek leaned back in his chair, staring at the screen for a moment before responding. "Alright. I'll run the simulations again. Let's see if there's something we missed."

Amit gave him a nod of encouragement before heading to check on the rest of the team. The atmosphere was thick with tension, but they had no choice but to keep moving forward. The launch date wasn't going to move, and neither could they.

Part 2: Personal Sacrifice

Late into the night, Volt Motors' headquarters was a stark contrast to the quiet neighborhoods outside. The office was dimly lit, save for the glow of computer screens where a few team members were still grinding away. Amit sat in his office, eyes fixed on the screen, but his mind wasn't on the numbers. His phone vibrated with another message from Rina, his wife:

"The kids were asking about you today. They miss you. We all miss you."

Amit's heart sank. He hadn't been home for dinner in over a week, and every time he talked to Rina, the conversations had become shorter, more strained. It was the price of leadership, he told himself. But lately, the cost felt too high.

Before he could type a response, a soft knock interrupted his thoughts. He looked up to see Pooja standing at the doorway, looking as tired as he felt. Her eyes were heavy, dark circles beneath them telling the story of long hours and restless nights.

"Amit," she said quietly, "do you have a minute?"

Amit motioned her in, gesturing to the chair across from him. "Of course, Pooja. What's going on?"

Pooja sat down slowly, as if the weight of the past few weeks was pulling her down. She sighed, running a hand through her hair. "It's... everything. The dashboard feedback, the design revisions, the constant pressure... I'm at a breaking point, Amit. I don't know how much longer I can do this."

Amit leaned forward, listening intently. He could see the stress etched on her face. Pooja had been an essential part of the team, leading the interior design and user experience aspects, but the burden was clearly starting to wear her down.

Pooja continued, her voice trembling slightly. "The feedback from the test drivers is worse than we expected. The dashboard layout—the one we worked so hard on—isn't working. The drivers are complaining about how difficult it is to read the battery charge indicator while driving, and the placement of the controls is confusing them. I thought we had nailed it, but now... I feel like we're back to square one."

Amit exhaled, absorbing the weight of her words. "How bad is it?"

"It's bad enough that we'll need to redesign the layout," Pooja said, her frustration clear. "The drivers are saying it's not intuitive. We're looking at redoing the entire layout, and that's going to take extra time. Time we don't have."

Amit rubbed his temples, his own fatigue starting to catch up with him. "I get it, Pooja. We're all feeling the same pressure."

She slumped in her chair, staring at the floor. "It's not just the work, Amit. It's everything. I haven't seen my family in weeks. My parents keep calling, asking when I'm going to visit, but I don't have the time. I've barely slept. And honestly... I don't know how much longer I can keep going like this. Every time we solve one problem, three more pop up."

Amit nodded, recognizing the familiar strain in her voice. He knew exactly how she felt. The sacrifices weren't just professional— they were personal. The long hours, the missed family moments, the mental and emotional toll—it all added up.

"I understand, Pooja," Amit said softly. "I'm right there with you. I haven't seen Rina and the kids properly in weeks. I know what it's like to feel like you're missing out on life while you're stuck here, trying to push this project forward."

Pooja looked at him, her expression softening as she realized she wasn't alone in her struggle. "But how do you deal with it, Amit? How do you keep going? I feel like I'm being pulled in a thousand directions, and I'm failing at all of them."

Amit leaned back in his chair, choosing his words carefully. "It's not easy. There's no simple answer to balancing work and life, especially on a project like this. But one thing I've learned over the years is that when you're in the middle of something this big, you have to accept that you won't always have balance. Sometimes, work takes over. Sometimes, you feel like you're failing at everything. And that's okay—as long as you stay focused on the bigger picture."

Pooja frowned slightly, not quite convinced. "But what about family? What about the people waiting for us at home?"

Amit thought about Rina, her patience stretching thin, and the kids who asked about him every night before bed. "That's the hardest part, Pooja. Family is everything, but sometimes, we have to make sacrifices in the short term for the long-term good. It doesn't mean we don't care. It means we're doing this now so that later, we can be there fully. I look at Rina and the kids, and I remind myself that this project—it's part of something bigger. It's not just about us. It's about what we're building for the future."

Pooja's eyes softened as she considered his words. "But it feels like the sacrifices are all-consuming. Like there's nothing left at the end of the day."

Amit leaned forward, his tone serious but empathetic. "I get that. Believe me. But think about what we're building, Pooja. Look at Vivek. He hasn't been home either, but he's here every day, tackling the technical issues head-on. Or look at Suhani—she's been managing the financial chaos, negotiating with suppliers, pushing for cost reductions, all while juggling her own personal commitments. They're all sacrificing something, but they're doing it because they believe in this project, just like you."

Pooja nodded, though her exhaustion was still evident. "But how do you keep going when you feel like you're burning out?"

Amit paused, reflecting on his own struggles. "You find strength in the purpose behind what you're doing. It's easy to get lost in the day-to-day grind, but if you step back and look at the bigger picture, you realize that what we're doing here—it's going to make a difference. We're not just building an Electric Auto. We're building something that could redefine urban transportation, something that could make a real impact in people's lives."

He looked at her directly, his voice filled with conviction. "The pain we're going through right now—the late nights, the stress, the personal sacrifices—it's temporary. It feels unbearable in the moment, but it won't last forever. And when we launch this product, when we see it out there, changing lives, we'll know it was worth it."

Pooja sat silently for a moment, letting his words sink in. "But what if we're too late? What if we make all these sacrifices, and it still doesn't work out?"

Amit smiled, a soft but determined smile. "That's the risk, isn't it? But nothing worth having ever came easy. There's a saying I've always believed in: 'There is no gain without pain.' It's not just a cliché—it's a fact of life. Success, especially on something this ambitious, comes at a cost. But that's what makes it so rewarding when you finally get there."

Pooja nodded slowly, the weight of her exhaustion still heavy but her resolve starting to return. "You really believe this is going to work, don't you?"

Amit met her gaze, his eyes steady. "I do. I believe in this project, and I believe in this team. We've come too far, overcome too many challenges, to let it fall apart now. Yes, we're tired. Yes, we've made sacrifices. But look at what we've already achieved. Every problem we've faced, we've solved.

Every setback, we've pushed through. And we're going to keep pushing until we cross that finish line."

Pooja exhaled, a small smile forming on her lips. "Thanks, Amit.

I needed to hear that."

Amit nodded, a feeling of solidarity between them. "We're all in this together, Pooja. You're not alone. And when we get through this, it's going to be worth every sacrifice we've made."

She stood up, the fatigue still visible but a renewed determination in her step. "I guess I should get back to the design team. We've got a dashboard to fix."

Amit smiled, watching her leave. As the door closed behind her, he looked back at his phone, at the message from Rina. He sighed and typed a response:

"I miss you too. I'll be home soon. Just a little longer."

He knew the pain of being absent from his family wouldn't disappear overnight. But he also knew that the sacrifices he was making now would pave the way for something greater—for his team, his company, and his family.

Part 3: A Breakthrough

The testing lab was bathed in the glow of monitors displaying complex graphs and live data streams. The Volt Motors team had gathered for what felt like the hundredth time to test the latest modifications to the BMS. This round of testing wasn't just another routine diagnostic—this was make- or-break. They needed the system to pass a series of rigorous tests, including voltage stability, thermal regulation, and charge-discharge cycles, all while maintaining a high SOC efficiency.

Vivek was at the testing terminal, surrounded by reams of data. His face, etched with fatigue, remained focused as he entered the final adjustments. Amit stood beside him, monitoring the situation closely. The entire project hinged on the battery's ability to perform under real-world conditions, and up until now, the results had been inconsistent.

"We've tweaked the load variance algorithm to manage those high-current spikes better," Vivek muttered, half to himself. "If this works, we should see a more stable voltage curve during the peak discharge cycle."

Amit leaned over his shoulder. "And how's the thermal regulation?

Are we still seeing heat spikes when the discharge cycle peaks?"

Vivek shook his head, pulling up the thermal management system's (TMS) data. "We've made significant improvements there. The coolant flow rate has been increased by about 15%, and we added a secondary loop for when the battery hits over 85 degrees Celsius. That should prevent those runaway temperature spikes we've seen during the last few cycles."

Amit frowned, considering the implications. "But is it sustainable? Running a secondary cooling loop will increase power consumption, and that's going to affect the overall efficiency rating."

Vivek nodded. "True, but we calculated the trade-off. The secondary cooling loop only kicks in at extreme conditions, and we're talking about a less than 2% hit on the SOC efficiency. It's worth it to keep the battery cells from overheating."

Amit exhaled, trying to weigh the potential benefits. "Alright, let's see how it holds up."

The room was silent as Vivek initiated the test. The battery pack, fully integrated with the BMS, hummed softly as the system began ramping up to simulate a real-world driving scenario. The screens lit up with graphs detailing the voltage, current, battery temperature, and SOC levels. The first few seconds passed smoothly, with the voltage curve holding steady and the battery maintaining a safe operating temperature.

Vivek glanced at the screen, his fingers hovering over the keyboard. "Voltage regulation looks good so far. We're holding steady at 380 volts."

Amit, standing next to him, studied the live data. "What about the discharge rate? Are we still getting that sharp drop during peak acceleration?"

Vivek pulled up the discharge data and squinted at the screen. "Not yet. So far, the current output is staying within range. The BMS is doing a better job managing the load, so we're not seeing those wild fluctuations."

The test moved into the more demanding phase, where the battery would need to simulate a peak acceleration event—the kind that typically caused the voltage to dip and put strain on the battery cells. Everyone in the room braced for the inevitable drop, the red warning lights that had become all too familiar.

And then, it happened.

The voltage dropped—just slightly. A 2% dip, followed by a slight rise. A red warning flickered on the screen but didn't hold.

Vivek's fingers flew across the keyboard. "We've got a slight voltage dip—about 2% under peak load—but the load-balancing algorithm is kicking in. It's compensating for the drop."

Amit's eyes narrowed as he analyzed the data. "Is the algorithm pushing too much current to the cells? If we overcompensate, we risk burning out the system."

Vivek shook his head, watching the numbers settle back into the green. "No, it's holding. The current is within the safe operating range. We've managed to smooth out the drop without overloading the cells. The state of charge is maintaining at 92%, which is a huge improvement."

Amit exhaled. This was the breakthrough they needed—but they weren't done yet.

"What's happening with the thermal management?" Amit asked, glancing at the temperature graph. "We're hitting high current—did the cooling system hold up under the extra strain?"

Vivek flipped to the thermal data. "So far, so good. Temperature's rising, but the secondary loop kicked in right at 83 degrees Celsius. It's brought the battery back down to 78 degrees. No runaway heat spikes this time."

Amit nodded, pleased with the result but still cautious. "And what about the charge-discharge efficiency? Where are we landing?"

Vivek tapped a few keys and brought up the discharge cycle data. "We're at 95% efficiency through the discharge cycle. There's a small loss in the SOC due to the thermal regulation, but it's well within acceptable limits."

Amit allowed himself a small smile. "That's what we needed. A stable discharge cycle, efficient cooling, and no more wild fluctuations. This is the breakthrough we've been waiting for."

But then, just as they started to relax, another warning flashed on the screen—this time on the cell balancing system. The SOC was holding steady, but one of the battery cells had dropped below its minimum voltage threshold.

"What the hell?" Vivek muttered, his fingers flying across the keyboard. "We've got a rogue cell. It's dropping faster than the others."

Amit's eyes narrowed. "Can the BMS compensate? If we let that cell discharge too far, we'll lose efficiency across the whole system."

Vivek's hands moved quickly, adjusting parameters in real- time. "I'm rerouting the current flow to balance the load across the remaining cells. The BMS is recalculating... Okay, we're back within range."

The rogue cell stabilized, and the SOC remained consistent. The battery pack continued running through the final stages of the test, and slowly, the red warning lights disappeared from the screen. The team let out a collective sigh of relief.

"We did it," Vivek said, sitting back in his chair, his face a mixture of exhaustion and satisfaction. "The BMS handled the imbalance. We've stabilized the system."

Amit felt a wave of relief wash over him. They had been battling the voltage regulation, thermal issues, and cell balancing problems for weeks. Each failure had brought them closer to despair, but this breakthrough—this felt like a real win.

He turned to the rest of the team, who had been quietly watching the entire process. Pooja was the first to break the silence.

"Does this mean we've fixed it?" she asked, her voice filled with cautious optimism.

Amit nodded, his smile growing. "Yes, we've fixed it. The system's stable, the voltage is holding, and the thermal management is functioning exactly as we need it to. This is the breakthrough we've been waiting for."

Kiran, standing in the back, let out a breath he hadn't realized he was holding. "Thank God. This changes everything. We can finally go into our final market tests with confidence."

Amit turned to face the group, his voice steady but full of pride. "This wasn't easy. We've been through countless failures, sleepless nights, and more setbacks than I can count. But we pushed through. We kept fighting. And now, we have a battery system that will not only work—it will excel."

Vivek leaned back in his chair, wiping his forehead. "Honestly, Amit, I wasn't sure we'd get here. Every time we thought we fixed one problem, another one showed up. I thought this battery was cursed."

Amit clapped him on the shoulder. "We almost didn't make it. But we did, because we refused to quit. You've been relentless, Vivek. The way you handled the voltage dips and kept tweaking the load- balancing algorithm? That's what got us through."

Pooja smiled, the tension finally easing from her face. "I can't believe it. After everything... we're finally seeing progress."

Amit glanced at her, a knowing smile on his face. "This is just the beginning. The battery was our biggest hurdle, and now that we've crossed it, everything else will fall into place."

Kiran added excitedly, his voice full of enthusiasm. "And now we can shift our focus back to the customer side. This breakthrough will give us a huge advantage in the market. Our message will be clear: Tested under pressure, built to last."

Amit nodded in agreement. "Exactly. We don't just have a product—we have a story. And that's what's going to resonate with our customers."

The room was buzzing with energy again, the earlier exhaustion momentarily forgotten. For the first time in weeks, the team could see the light at the end of the tunnel. They had made it through the darkest moments, and now they stood on the brink of success.

Amit looked around at his team, pride swelling in his chest. "This breakthrough belongs to all of us. Every setback we faced, every problem we solved—it's all led us to this moment. We're not done yet, but this is the turning point. We've proven that the pain was worth it."

The team exchanged smiles, the earlier tension dissolving into a shared sense of accomplishment. They had fought hard for this moment, and now they were finally seeing the gain after all the pain.

Key Learnings from Chapter 6: There Is No 'Gain' Without 'Pain'

1. **Perseverance in the Face of Challenges:** The chapter highlights the importance of resilience. Both Amit and the team experienced intense pressure, repeated setbacks, and moments of near-failure. Their ability to persist through these difficulties, without giving up, was essential to achieving the breakthrough. Success is rarely immediate and often requires enduring prolonged hardship.

2. **The Importance of Incremental Problem-Solving:** The testing process revealed that technical issues—such as voltage regulation, thermal management, and cell balancing—can only be solved through step-by-step problem-solving. The team had to approach each challenge one at a time, breaking down complex problems into manageable parts. This is a key takeaway for handling large, high-stakes projects.

3. **Balancing Trade-Offs:** In technical projects, decisions must often be made to balance multiple conflicting factors. For example, Vivek's team had to trade off between thermal management and state of charge (SOC) efficiency. Understanding and making calculated decisions about which aspects to prioritize—without compromising the core function—was crucial for the team's success.

4. **Team Collaboration and Support:** Throughout the chapter, the success of the project was deeply dependent on the collaborative efforts of the team. The combination of Vivek's technical expertise, Pooja's design insight, and Kiran's market perspective showed the value of a multi-disciplinary approach. Each member contributed their strengths, allowing the team to solve challenges that no one person could have managed alone.

5. **Handling Uncertainty with Calm Leadership:** Amit's ability to remain calm and composed in moments of tension, especially when the team faced a near-failure during testing, was critical. His confidence in the team and in the process helped steady the group during the most uncertain moments. This reinforces the idea that strong leadership is often about managing emotions, staying calm under pressure, and trusting in the team's ability to overcome challenges.

6. **Personal Sacrifice and Professional Dedication:** Both Amit and Pooja, along with the rest of the team, made personal sacrifices—long hours, missed time with family, and high stress levels. This chapter highlights the reality of professional projects at critical stages: personal and professional boundaries often blur. However, their dedication ultimately led to the breakthrough, showing that sometimes sacrifices are required to achieve big goals.

7. **Emotional Support and Empathy:** Amit's conversation with Pooja also emphasized the importance of empathy and emotional support in leadership. By acknowledging the personal toll the

project was taking on Pooja and sharing his own struggles, Amit strengthened the bond within the team. Leadership isn't just about solving technical problems but also about addressing the emotional well-being of the team.

8. **Dealing with Setbacks as Learning Opportunities:** The numerous failed attempts in testing the BMS provided valuable insights into the system's limitations. Each failure brought them closer to the right solution. The team learned to view setbacks not as dead-ends but as critical learning opportunities that refined their approach.

9. **Critical Role of Testing in Product Development:** The rigorous testing of the battery system demonstrated the need for real-world validation of theoretical designs. The system's performance under stress conditions—such as high discharge rates and thermal stress—was vital in ensuring reliability before market launch. This underscores the lesson that thorough testing is indispensable in any product development cycle.

10. **Celebrating Small Wins:** The team's success in stabilizing the battery system was a small but crucial victory. By taking the time to acknowledge and celebrate this breakthrough, Amit reinforced the importance of recognizing progress, even when the larger goal is still ahead. Small wins help maintain momentum and keep the team motivated.

These key learnings from Chapter 6 underline the importance of perseverance, collaboration, technical problem-solving and emotional leadership in driving a complex project toward success. They also emphasize that success is built on a foundation of sacrifices and steady leadership with each small gain contributing to the larger vision.

Chapter 7

'Cost' is Reality and 'Price' is Politics

Part 1: Financial Tightrope

Amit sat in the main conference room at Volt Motors, ready to meet with the sales and marketing team. Kiran was there, along with Rahul, Head of Sales and several other key members of their teams. The agenda for this meeting was clear—Rahul and Kiran were pushing for a price-led strategy to ensure that Volt Motors could gain rapid market share with the new Electric Auto.

The room buzzed with a sense of urgency, but Amit knew the reality: they were cutting it close on production costs, and meeting the sales team's aggressive pricing demands would be a major challenge.

As the meeting began, Rahul kicked things off, his tone confident. "Amit, I've reviewed our competitors, and let's face it—price is going to make or break us in the market. Zephyr EV is positioning their auto at an incredibly competitive price point. They're practically giving it away to fleet operators, and if we don't respond, we're going to lose market share before we even get started."

Kiran, always analytical, nodded in agreement. "He's right. We've run the numbers. We need to launch the Electric Auto with a lower price tag if we want to make a splash in this market. Customers— especially fleet operators—are price-sensitive. They're looking for the lowest upfront costs, and while we have a stronger product, they're not going to see that unless we get our price down."

Amit listened carefully. He understood their perspective, but he also knew the product better than anyone. He glanced down at his notes, filled with production costs and performance data, and prepared for the balancing act he would have to navigate.

"Rahul, I get that price is a critical factor for market entry," Amit began, his tone measured. "But there's more to this equation than just matching Zephyr's price. Our Electric Auto isn't designed to be the cheapest option on the market. It's designed to be the most reliable and cost-effective over time. If we focus solely on upfront price, we risk undermining the value proposition we've spent months building."

Rahul, clearly used to pushing aggressive strategies, leaned forward. "I understand that, Amit. But look at the reality: customers, especially in the fleet market, aren't thinking long-term when they're making purchasing decisions. They want to see an attractive upfront cost. If Zephyr is offering their auto at a 10% lower price than us, we won't even get a second look. They'll close deals before we get a chance to explain our advantages."

Kiran jumped in, pulling up some market research data on his tablet. "We surveyed potential buyers, especially fleet operators. Their number one concern is initial price. Sure, long-term reliability and performance are important, but they're making buying decisions based on what they can afford now, not what they'll save over five years. If we want to grab their attention, we need to lead with price. Once we're in the market, we can start positioning ourselves based on performance and reliability."

Amit nodded, appreciating their strategic thinking, but he knew the engineering constraints and financial realities of the project. He pulled up his own data, showing the bill of materials (BOM) and cost breakdowns for key components, including the battery pack, powertrain, and thermal management system.

"I hear what you're saying," Amit replied, his voice steady. "But here's the reality: we've made certain technical choices to ensure that our Electric Auto stands out in terms of performance and reliability. The battery pack alone is one of the most expensive components, but it's also what gives us a competitive edge—longer range, better charge-discharge cycles, and more consistent performance under heavy loads. If we drop the price too much, we'll have to start cutting corners on components like the battery, and that's going to lead to higher maintenance costs, downtime, and ultimately, dissatisfied customers."

Rahul wasn't ready to back down. "I understand that. But, Amit, the sales cycle doesn't always allow for those nuances. Zephyr is putting out flashy ads, promising the cheapest and most 'advanced' auto on the market. If we come in at a higher price point, we'll have to work twice as hard to even get in the door with potential customers. It's a brutal market."

Amit nodded but held firm. "And what happens when those fleet operators start seeing higher failure rates and shorter battery lifespans because they chose a cheaper product? Our value proposition is different. We offer reliability and low total cost of ownership (TCO). Our battery will last longer, our auto will require fewer repairs, and drivers will experience less downtime. That's what makes our product worth more."

Rahul exchanged a glance with Kiran, who spoke next. "I get your point, Amit, but here's where we need to think strategically. Customers won't see the long-term value until they've already bought the product. Right now, they're focused on the sticker price. If we want to capture the market, we have to at least meet Zephyr somewhere close on price—just to get our foot in the door."

Amit leaned back, thinking for a moment. He understood the sales team's argument. The market was undeniably competitive, and Volt Motors was going up against giants like Zephyr, who could afford to take losses to dominate market share. But Amit wasn't willing to sacrifice the integrity of the product just to match Zephyr's aggressive pricing.

"There's a middle ground here," Amit said finally, his voice calm but firm. "We can adjust the price, but we're not going to compromise on critical components like the battery or the powertrain. I'm not willing to risk the reliability of the product to chase a short-term price war with Zephyr."

Rahul frowned, clearly frustrated. "So, what's your solution, Amit? We can't go to market with a higher price and expect to compete."

Amit glanced at Kiran. "We'll have to focus on market segmentation. Position the base model with a competitive price point, but keep our high-performance variants at a higher price. We can cut some non-essential features from the entry-level model—may be reduce some of the connectivity options or interior upgrades—to get the price down, but without sacrificing the key performance elements that define our product."

Kiran nodded, understanding Amit's approach. "So, we offer a stripped-down version for price-sensitive customers but highlight the long-term benefits of the full version?"

"Exactly," Amit said. "And we lead with our key strengths— reliability, low maintenance costs, and long battery life. Once fleet operators see the TCO, they'll realize that our product offers far better value than Zephyr's cheaper, less reliable alternative."

Rahul leaned back in his chair, mulling it over. "It's a compromise, but I can work with that. We'll have to make sure the sales pitch focuses on the lifetime savings rather than just upfront price. But it's doable."

Kiran smiled slightly, tapping his tablet. "And we can spin this in our marketing. 'More miles, less downtime. Built to last.' It'll resonate with fleet operators once they see the bigger picture."

Amit nodded, feeling the tension in the room start to ease. "Great. I'll talk to Suhani and the engineering team. We'll look at what we can adjust in the entry-level model without compromising performance. But I need you both to understand—price is important, but it's not the whole story. Cost is reality—we can't ignore that. And if we play the price game too aggressively, we risk sacrificing the long-term stability of the product."

Kiran and Rahul exchanged glances and nodded in agreement. Amit stood up, knowing that the conversation with his core team was about to get even more challenging.

Amit's Conversation with His Core Team

Later that day, Amit gathered his core team—Suhani, Vivek, and Pooja—in his office to discuss the outcomes of the meeting with the sales team.

Suhani was the first to speak, already sensing the difficulty of the conversation. "Let me guess—they want us to cut costs even further?"

Amit smiled wryly. "Of course they do. They want to lead with price, but I pushed back. We're not going to compromise on critical components like the battery or powertrain. But we need to look at the non-essential features. If we strip down the base model, we might be able to hit a competitive price point without destroying our margins."

Vivek, who had been quiet until now, frowned. "So, what are we cutting? The battery pack is non-negotiable. We need the full capacity to meet our range requirements. The thermal management system is another big cost, but without it, we'll be facing overheating issues. We've already seen how fragile Zephyr's system is—if we start cutting corners, we'll end up with the same problems."

Amit nodded. "I know, Vivek. We're not cutting those. But may be we can look at things like the infotainment system—do we really need all the features we've planned for the base model? We could reduce the connectivity options, may be use simpler materials for the interior without affecting safety or performance."

Suhani pulled up the BOM on her laptop, scanning through potential cost-saving areas. "We could save around 2% if we go with a simpler BIW design for the base model. Nothing that would compromise the structure, but it would be less feature-heavy than the premium version."

Pooja, who had been listening quietly, spoke up. "That's doable. We can keep the interior ergonomics intact but cut back on some of the high-end features. No leather seating, for example, and we could use a standard dashboard layout instead of the advanced digital one. It'll still be functional but more cost-effective."

Amit looked at each of them, feeling the pieces of the puzzle coming together. "Alright. Let's make those adjustments. We'll present a competitive entry-level model without sacrificing the core reliability. But we're going to keep our focus on long-term value. The sales team will push price, but we're sticking to the story of reliability and low total cost of ownership."

Vivek nodded, more relaxed now. "As long as we don't touch the performance side, I'm on board."

Suhani smiled, her fingers flying across the keyboard. "I'll run the numbers. It'll be tight, but we can make it work."

Pooja leaned back in her chair, her expression thoughtful. "We'll have to make sure the messaging is clear—customers need to understand that they're getting what they pay for. Reliability isn't something you can see on a spec sheet, but they'll feel it in their day-to-day operations."

Amit stood up, feeling a sense of satisfaction. The team had found a way to balance cost and price, ensuring the Electric Auto would hit the market competitively without compromising its long- term performance.

"We've done it before," Amit said with confidence, "and we'll do it again. Cost is our reality, but the price—that's how we navigate the market. Let's make sure we're telling the right story."

Part 2: Balancing Act

The next morning, the executive boardroom at Volt Motors was filled with key stakeholders. Nisha Mehta, the CEO, stood at the front of the room, calm but sharp, ready to lead what would be one of the most important discussions around the Electric Auto's future. Alongside her were heads from various departments—Suhani from finance, Kiran from marketing, Rahul from sales, Vivek from engineering, and Amit, who was there to represent the entire project team.

The goal was clear: to balance cost and price for the Electric Auto, ensuring it would be competitive enough to capture market share without compromising on the core product values—reliability, performance, and long-term cost efficiency.

Nisha opened the meeting, her gaze steady as she surveyed the room. "We're at a critical junction," she began. "The launch of our Electric Auto is not just about hitting a price point—it's about positioning Volt Motors as a serious player in the EV market. Our competitors, particularly Zephyr, are pushing aggressive pricing strategies to dominate the mass market. We need to respond, but we can't sacrifice our product's integrity. Today, I want us to engage in a deep conversation about how we can find the right balance between cost and price. Let's hear your thoughts."

Rahul spoke first, his voice confident but slightly edgy. "Nisha, I've been saying this from the start. The sales team is on the ground, talking to fleet operators and urban drivers. They're all focused on price. Zephyr is hitting them hard with offers that are, frankly, unsustainable in the long term, but that's what's getting attention right now. We need to be in that same price bracket, or at least close, or we'll lose these customers before we even get a chance to show them the benefits of our product."

Nisha nodded, acknowledging his point. "I understand, Rahul. But what about the long-term picture? How do we convince the market that our higher upfront price leads to lower total ownership costs and fewer headaches over time?"

Kiran, ever the strategist, weighed in. "Nisha, from a marketing standpoint, I agree with Rahul. The initial push needs to get our foot in the door. We can talk all we want about reliability and low total cost of ownership, but those aren't the metrics that grab attention in a competitive market like this. Price gets us noticed; reliability keeps us there."

Suhani, who had been listening intently, leaned forward and spoke next, her voice measured. "I get it. Price opens the door, but we have to face the reality of what we're working with. Our BOM is already tight. We can't lower the price too far without eroding our margins. As it stands, we're at risk of pushing too close to breakeven if we make deep cuts. That's a problem for the company's long-term viability."

Nisha nodded thoughtfully. "Let's talk specifics. Vivek, from an engineering standpoint, what can we adjust without compromising the product's performance?"

Vivek, always analytical, looked at the data on his laptop. "There are some areas where we could consider trimming costs, like simplifying the interior features for the base model or reducing the complexity of the infotainment system. But, Nisha, I want to be very clear—any cuts to the battery pack, powertrain, or thermal management system would be a serious risk. Those components define the vehicle's reliability and range. If we start cutting costs in those areas, we'll lose what makes the product stand out."

Nisha's expression was neutral but thoughtful as she processed the input from each department. She paused for a moment before speaking again. "So, we're looking at a situation where the sales team is telling us that price is critical for market entry, but our finance and engineering teams are warning that if we drop too low, we risk either sacrificing our margins or compromising the core performance of the product."

She turned to Kiran. "Kiran, how do we bridge this gap? How do we create a message that emphasizes long-term value while still being competitive on price?"

Kiran straightened up in his chair, his mind racing. "We need to lead with the idea of smart investment. We'll position our product as not just another electric vehicle, but one that provides better value over time. Zephyr is offering flashy, low-cost options that look good on the surface, but we'll highlight the hidden costs—higher maintenance, shorter battery life, more downtime. Our messaging will emphasize that while our auto might cost more upfront, it will save customers money in the long run."

Rahul nodded, though still cautious. "That's fine for a long-term strategy, but how do we sell that message to a price-sensitive market right now? Fleet operators care about cash flow, not just long-term value. If we can't make it financially viable for them today, they're not going to care about the long-term savings."

Nisha raised her hand slightly, signaling for a pause. "We're in a classic cost vs. price scenario, and this is exactly the kind of challenge that defines businesses in competitive industries like ours. Let's take this in stages. Amit, what are your thoughts?"

Amit, who had been listening intently to the various perspectives, finally spoke. "The way I see it, we can't ignore the financial constraints. Cost is reality—we know what our production costs are, and we can't push the price down too far without serious consequences. But we also can't ignore the market reality. Price is what draws customers in the short term, but we have to find a way to sell the long-term value."

He turned to Nisha, choosing his words carefully. "I think the middle ground lies in segmentation. We create a base model that's stripped down to meet the market's price sensitivity, but without compromising on the key aspects that define our product—battery life, reliability, and low maintenance. At the same time, we offer higher- end variants with all the bells and whistles for customers who are willing to invest more."

Nisha nodded, listening carefully. "That makes sense. So, a two-pronged approach—one that meets the immediate price demands while keeping our core values intact."

Amit continued. "Exactly. We position the base model competitively, but we'll maintain the performance standards that set us apart from Zephyr. We can cut back on some of the non-essential features, like the infotainment system or interior luxury, but we don't touch the core components like the battery or powertrain."

Suhani nodded, jumping in. "That could work. If we cut costs in areas like the interior materials or infotainment, we could bring down the price without cutting into our margins too much. I'll need to rework the numbers, but I think it's doable."

Nisha turned to Rahul. "Rahul, do you think we can sell that? A base model that's price-competitive but focused on long-term savings?"

Rahul's head dipped slowly. "It'll take some work, but I think it's the right move. We'll need to educate the sales teams on how to push the long-term value proposition to customers, but if we're close enough on price, we'll have a shot."

Nisha leaned back in her chair, seemingly satisfied with the discussion so far. "Alright, I think we're starting to form a strategy here. But before we wrap this up, I want to make sure we're all aligned. We're not going to get dragged into a price war with Zephyr. That's not how we win. We win by offering a better product that delivers more value over time. We'll be smart about cost-cutting, but we won't compromise on the elements that make our product superior."

The team nodded in agreement, but Nisha wasn't finished. "Amit, stay behind after the meeting. I want to discuss a few details with you."

One-on-One with Amit and Nisha

Later, the room had cleared out, and Amit remained seated as Nisha closed the door. She sat down across from him, her expression softer but still focused.

"Amit, I wanted to take a few minutes to talk through some of the strategic decisions we're facing," Nisha began. "You're in the thick of this project, and I know it hasn't been easy. But I need your help in making sure we balance these trade-offs correctly."

Amit nodded. "I've been thinking a lot about it. We've already pushed the product to its limits in terms of performance. If we start compromising on quality, it'll undo everything we've built."

Nisha leaned forward, her voice calm but firm. "Exactly. But at the same time, we can't ignore the market pressures. We're walking a tightrope between maintaining the product's integrity and responding to external realities. That's where we need to be strategic. I agree with your suggestion—segmentation is the way to go. We can't afford to be too rigid in our approach, but we also can't chase Zephyr into a pricing race that erodes our margins."

Amit exhaled, relieved to hear her alignment with his thinking. "So, we focus on the base model to meet the price-sensitive market but keep our core product strong."

Nisha smiled slightly. "Yes, but more than that. You need to make sure that every decision we make—whether it's cutting costs or pricing adjustments—stays true to the long-term vision. We're not here to win a quick race. We're here to build a sustainable business that competes on quality and performance. Every trade-off you make needs to keep that in mind."

Amit appreciated her clarity. "Understood. I'll work with the team to finalize the adjustments, but we won't touch anything that compromises the product's reliability or long-term value."

Nisha nodded, standing up. "Good. Because at the end of the day, cost is reality. It's the foundation of everything we do. But price— that's where the politics come in. It's a game we have to play, but we have to play it on our terms. Make sure we don't lose sight of that."

Amit stood as well, feeling more confident now. "I will. Thanks, Nisha."

As he left the office, Amit felt a renewed sense of direction. He knew what needed to be done: balance the reality of costs with the political demands of pricing. The strategy was becoming clearer, and now it was time to put it into action.

Part 3: Strategic Decisions and Actions

Amit walked back to his office after the meeting with Nisha Mehta, feeling more focused than he had in weeks. Nisha's clear- headed approach had helped crystallize the strategy: they would balance the financial reality of the Electric Auto's cost structure with a market-sensitive price, while protecting the product's core strengths. Now, it was time to turn this strategy into action.

He gathered his core team—Vivek, Suhani, Pooja, Kiran, and Rahul—for a meeting to lay out the plan. Everyone knew the stakes were high, and tensions still lingered from the earlier discussions. The challenge was enormous: cut costs without sacrificing quality, and position the Electric Auto competitively without being dragged into a price war.

As they settled into the conference room, Amit began by addressing the team, his tone steady but energized. "Alright, everyone, we've had a lot of tough discussions about costs and pricing. I just came from a meeting with Nisha, and we've solidified our strategy. The goal is clear—balance cost and price, but without compromising on the essential elements that make this product stand out."

He paused for a moment, letting his words sink in. "Nisha's given us the direction, but now it's on us to work through the specifics, and that means making some tough trade-offs. But I want us to be clear on one thing—we are not going to sacrifice the integrity of the product. We're going to protect our core strengths: reliability, performance, and long-term value. Now, let's figure out how to execute this strategy."

Suhani, always quick to focus on the numbers, was the first to speak. "Amit, the financial reality is that we're close to breakeven on the BOM. If we need to reduce costs, we'll have to make some very specific decisions about what stays and what goes. We can't afford to make sweeping cuts."

Amit nodded. "Exactly, Suhani. We'll be targeted in our cost reductions. We're going to focus on the non-essential components for the base model—things that won't compromise performance or reliability. But I also want to look at how we can optimize our existing supply chain and vendor relationships. There's room for negotiation and realignment."

Vivek, as the head of engineering, had concerns that needed addressing. "Amit, I understand the need for trade-offs, but my biggest worry is that we're going to push too far on the non-essential cuts. The battery pack, powertrain, and thermal management systems—they're the heart of this product. Any reduction in quality there, and we risk introducing failure points that will ruin our market reputation."

Amit raised a hand, acknowledging Vivek's concerns. "Don't worry, Vivek. We're not touching the battery system or powertrain. Those are non-negotiable. Our long-range capability and reliability are our biggest selling points, especially against Zephyr. But we will be making adjustments in other areas—like reducing interior materials and connectivity features for the base model. I need your team to work on integrating these simplified designs without impacting core performance."

Vivek leaned forward, thinking. "That's manageable. We can downgrade some of the infotainment systems and use more cost- effective materials for the bodywork on the base model. As long as the mechanical integrity and driving performance stay intact, we can make it work."

Kiran was next. "Amit, if we're going to position the base model as a more affordable option, we need to make sure the marketing communication is clear. We'll need to highlight the long-term savings—how our autos have lower maintenance costs and better performance over time. We'll also need to ensure the premium model's features—like enhanced connectivity and comfort—are clearly differentiated, so customers know what they're paying for."

Amit smiled, appreciating Kiran's focus on messaging. "Exactly, Kiran. The key is to sell the value over time. We might not be the cheapest upfront, but customers need to understand that they'll be saving more in the long run. Your team's job will be to craft that narrative—how our reliability and lower total cost of ownership make this a smarter choice."

Kiran nodded thoughtfully. "We'll focus the marketing strategy on fleet operators and urban commuters—they'll be our primary targets. We'll emphasize mileage per charge, low breakdown rates, and reliability during long hours of operation. If we can position ourselves as the reliable workhorse of the EV market, we'll beat Zephyr on reputation, even if we don't match them on price."

Amit turned to Pooja, who had been taking notes quietly. "Pooja, we're going to need your team's help with the design trade-offs. We'll be simplifying the interior materials for the base model—less luxury, more practicality. I need you to work with Vivek on this, making sure that whatever changes we make, they still align with our brand promise of durability and comfort."

Pooja thought for a moment before responding. "We can definitely scale back some of the premium features—things like the dashboard electronics, infotainment, and luxury seat materials—and still maintain a strong interior experience. But we need to ensure that the ergonomics and driver comfort don't take a hit. If the base model feels too cheap, it'll hurt the brand."

Amit nodded, appreciating the balance she was proposing. "Exactly. It's about reducing costs where we can, but without making the product feel like a downgrade. Fleet operators are tough customers, but they appreciate comfort during long hours of driving. Let's keep that in mind."

The conversation turned to supply chain realignment, with Amit addressing both Suhani and Vivek. "We need to start looking at our supplier network. The goal is to renegotiate with key vendors, especially for electronics and mechanical aggregates. Suhani, I need you to start reaching out to our suppliers and see where we can push for better pricing—particularly on body components and interior electronics. Vivek, can your team work with the vendors on cost- effective redesigns without compromising on reliability?"

Suhani nodded, already thinking ahead. "I'll start with the smaller suppliers and work my way up. There's definitely room for renegotiation, especially with the volumes we'll be committing to once production ramps up."

Vivek, ever pragmatic, responded. "We'll work with our tier-one suppliers on redesigns. I'll get the engineering team involved to ensure we don't compromise any critical systems. But we'll definitely push for simplifications in the body electronics—things like the sensor modules and infotainment systems. That's where we can shave off some cost."

Amit leaned back, satisfied with the direction the conversation was taking. "Good. We'll also need to look at our mechanical aggregates—like the chassis and braking systems. See if we can negotiate better pricing by consolidating orders with fewer vendors. The more we can streamline, the better our margins will be."

Rahul, who had been relatively quiet, jumped in. "From a sales perspective, Amit, we're going to need clear messaging about these changes. We can't have customers thinking they're getting a 'lesser' product just because we've made some cost reductions. We need to communicate that the core value of the Electric Auto is still intact."

Amit nodded, fully understanding the stakes. "Exactly, Rahul. The messaging needs to reflect that while the base model is more affordable, it's still built on the same foundation of reliability and long- term value. That's where you and Kiran come in—craft the narrative that speaks to the market, focusing on how we're delivering a smarter, more practical solution."

Kiran added, "We'll emphasize the practicality and reliability of the base model while still showcasing the premium options for those who want more luxury or tech features. It'll be a tiered messaging strategy—so customers understand the choices they have."

The team was now fully engaged, the initial doubts giving way to clarity and a shared sense of purpose. The conversation moved forward with increasing energy as they outlined specific actions for the coming days.

Specific Actions and Key Trade-Offs

1. **Cost Reduction Areas:**
    - Electronics: Simplification of infotainment systems, using more cost-effective modules for the base model while maintaining higher-end features for premium versions.
    - Mechanical Aggregates: Renegotiation of contracts with chassis and bodywork suppliers to streamline orders and reduce unit costs. Consider bulk orders to leverage pricing.
    - Interior Materials: Downgrade from premium to standard materials for seats and dashboard components in the base model, while maintaining driver ergonomics and comfort.
    - Sensor Modules: Reduce the complexity of sensor and body electronics for non-critical functionalities, ensuring cost-effectiveness without impacting safety or performance.

2. **Supply Chain Realignment:**
   - Vendor Negotiations: Suhani to renegotiate with suppliers, focusing on securing better pricing for body electronics and interior components. Focus on volume discounts for larger production runs.
   - Tier-1 Suppliers: Vivek's team to work with tier-one suppliers on redesigning mechanical aggregates, ensuring cost reductions without compromising reliability.
   - Logistics Optimization: Review supply chain logistics to minimize transportation costs and delays, particularly for battery components and powertrain systems.

3. **Marketing and Sales Strategy:**
   - Two-Tiered Product Offering: Base model positioned as a practical, affordable solution for price-sensitive customers, with the premium model offering enhanced features for those seeking luxury and advanced tech.
   - Messaging: Kiran and Rahul to craft a targeted marketing campaign highlighting the long-term value, low maintenance, and reliability of the Electric Auto. Emphasize total cost of ownership savings and fewer breakdowns compared to competitors like Zephyr.
   - Fleet Operators Focus: Focus sales messaging on fleet operators, showcasing the benefits of reduced downtime and increased reliability over cheaper alternatives.

4. **Engineering and Product Adjustments:**

    - Simplified Designs: Vivek and Pooja's teams to simplify non-essential features without affecting core performance—like interior materials, dashboard design, and connectivity features in the base model.
    - Long-Term Product Development: Continue to refine the premium model to include enhanced features for higher-end customers, while keeping the base model practical and robust.

As the meeting drew to a close, the mood in the room had shifted from uncertainty to confidence. The team had engaged in a deep, detailed conversation, with each member raising valid concerns and contributing solutions. The strategy was now clear, and specific actions had been outlined. They had found the balance between cost and price, while staying true to the integrity of the product.

Amit stood up, addressing the team one last time. "We have a solid plan. We've made the tough trade-offs, but we've done it without compromising the core of what makes this product special. Now, it's time to execute. Let's make this happen."

The team nodded in agreement, feeling a renewed sense of purpose. They knew the path ahead was still challenging, but they were confident in their strategy and their ability to bring the Electric

Auto to market—strong, reliable, and competitive.

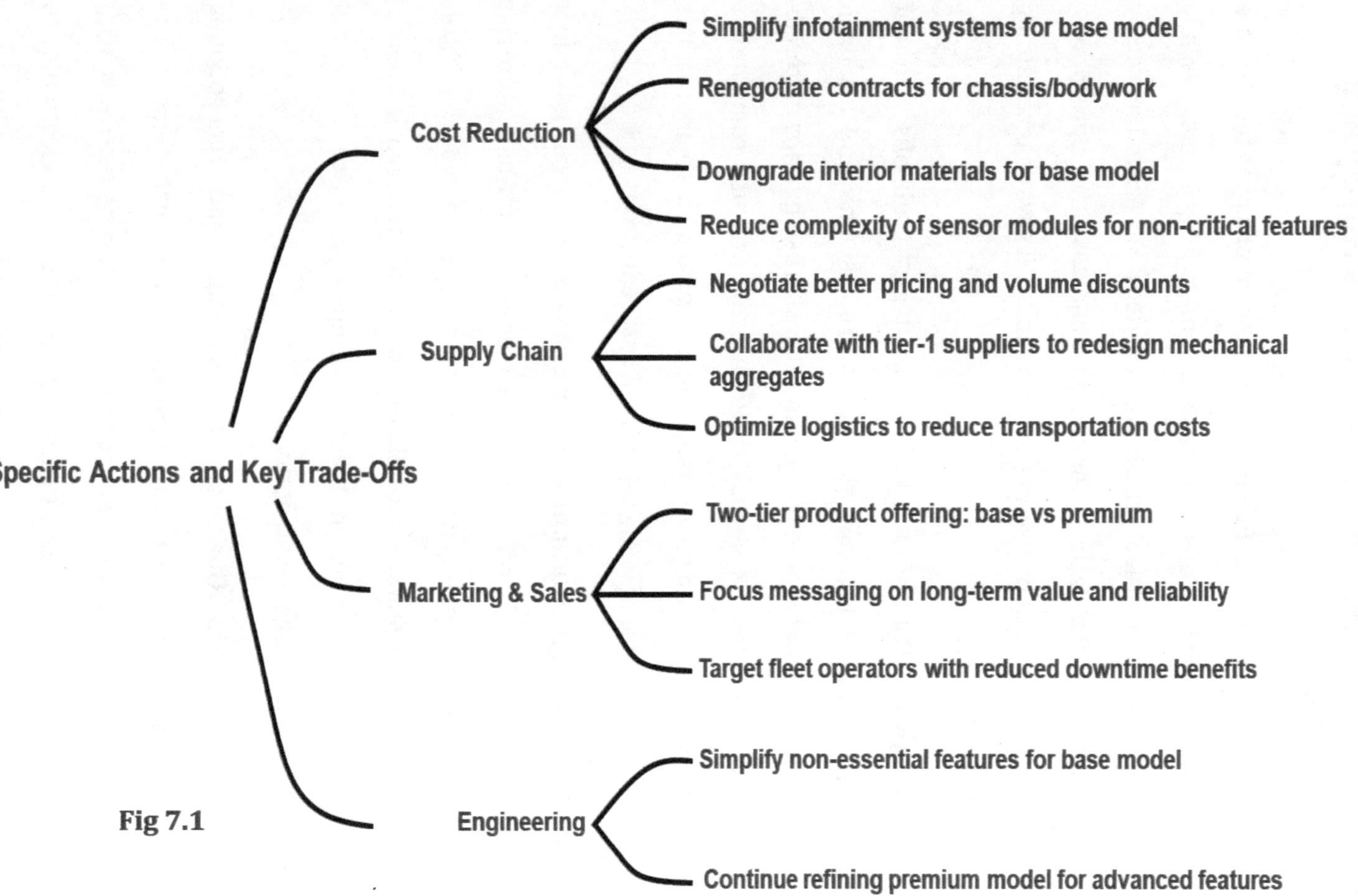
Specific Actions and Key Trade-Offs
Cost Reduction
Simplify infotainment systems for base model
Renegotiate contracts for chassis/bodywork
Downgrade interior materials for base model
Reduce complexity of sensor modules for non-critical features
Supply Chain
Negotiate better pricing and volume discounts
Collaborate with tier-1 suppliers to redesign mechanical aggregates
Optimize logistics to reduce transportation costs
Marketing & Sales
Two-tier product offering: base vs premium
Focus messaging on long-term value and reliability
Target fleet operators with reduced downtime benefits
Engineering
Simplify non-essential features for base model
Continue refining premium model for advanced features

Fig 7.1

Key Learnings from Chapter 7: 'Cost' is Reality and 'Price' is Politics

1. **Balancing Cost and Price:** The chapter emphasizes the delicate balance between cost management and pricing strategy. While cost is a non-negotiable reality, pricing decisions are influenced by external market factors, competition, and customer perceptions. Success requires navigating these complexities while maintaining product integrity.

2. **Strategic Trade-Offs:** Making strategic trade-offs without compromising the core product is critical. Amit and his team identified areas where they could cut costs (like interior materials and infotainment systems) while ensuring essential components like the battery and powertrain remained intact. This demonstrates the importance of being selective in cost reductions.

3. **Product Segmentation:** A key takeaway is the power of product segmentation. By offering a base model with fewer features at a lower price point, while retaining a premium model with all features, Volt Motors was able to address different market needs. This approach allowed them to compete on price while still showcasing higher-end options.

4. **Supply Chain Optimization:** Realigning and renegotiating with suppliers is a crucial strategy for cost management. The team recognized the importance of securing better deals with vendors, particularly on mechanical aggregates and electronics, to streamline production costs without compromising quality.

5. **Importance of Long-Term Value:** While price is an immediate factor for customers, emphasizing the long-term value—such as low total cost of ownership, reliability and reduced maintenance — can differentiate a product in the market. The team focused on crafting a message that highlighted these benefits, especially for fleet operators.

6. **Collaboration and Cross-Department Alignment:** Effective collaboration between sales, marketing, engineering and finance is vital for addressing complex challenges. Each department contributed insights, raised concerns, and provided solutions, leading to a more holistic and aligned strategy.

7. **Vendor and Supplier Management:** The chapter underscores the importance of strong relationships with vendors and suppliers. By engaging in renegotiations and exploring bulk order discounts, the team aimed to optimize supply chain costs, showing that external partnerships play a key role in cost control.

8. **Clear Communication in Marketing:** Crafting the right marketing message is essential when balancing cost and price. Kiran's focus on positioning the product as a reliable, long-term investment that saves customers money over time highlights the need for clarity in communication, particularly when facing price-sensitive customers.

9. **Focus on Core Product Integrity:** A consistent theme is the importance of protecting the core strengths of the product. Even when making cost reductions, the team was careful to ensure that

the reliability, performance and durability of the Electric Auto remained intact. This shows that strategic compromises should never undermine the key value propositions.

10. **Leadership in Trade-Off Decisions:** Amit's leadership in guiding his team through tough trade-offs, while maintaining focus on the long-term vision, shows the importance of steady decision-making. Leaders must balance competing pressures from different departments while staying true to the company's core values and objectives.

These key learnings illustrate how cost management, pricing strategy and cross-functional collaboration are essential to successfully bringing a product to market without sacrificing quality or long-term viability.

Chapter 8

The Giving-Getting Equation in Life

Part 1: Office Politics

The mood at Volt Motors was tense. The Electric Auto project had progressed significantly, but the undercurrent of dissatisfaction among the departments was growing. As the launch date neared, different teams began to compete for recognition, resources, and credit for the project's success. The whispers of frustration were growing louder, and Amit knew he needed to address it before it became a bigger issue.

Vivek, the head of engineering, was one of the key figures feeling the weight of the project's pressures. He had been leading the charge in resolving critical issues like battery stability and thermal management, and yet, he felt that engineering's contributions were being overlooked. One afternoon, he came into Amit's office, frustration evident in his eyes.

"Amit, I need to talk," Vivek began, settling into a chair. His voice was tight with frustration, but he was trying to keep his composure. "I'm feeling like my team is doing the bulk of the heavy lifting— solving the toughest problems—but we're not getting the recognition we deserve. The battery management issues, the thermal system overheating, all of that—we've fixed it. But it's sales and marketing that seem to be getting all the attention."

Amit listened patiently, nodding as he let Vivek express his frustration. "I hear you, Vivek. I know you and your team have been putting in countless hours, and I've seen the results first-hand. But before we dive into the recognition piece, let's step back for a moment. I want you to think about something—what do you believe is the bigger picture here?"

Vivek frowned slightly, unsure of where Amit was going. "The bigger picture? Well, obviously, it's about launching the product and

making sure it's the best in the market. But it's hard to focus on that when you feel like you're being side-lined."

Amit nodded again, then leaned forward slightly, his voice calm but firm, taking on a coaching tone. "Exactly. The bigger picture is the product, right? Now, let's talk about the challenges you've been dealing with—the BMS, the thermal management, and stabilizing the voltage regulation during discharge cycles. These were big, critical issues that, if unresolved, would have derailed the entire project. You and your team solved that. And that's a huge win."

Vivek relaxed slightly, but his frustration hadn't entirely dissipated. "Yeah, we did. But it doesn't feel like anyone cares. I hear more about how sales is setting up deals with fleet operators and how marketing is getting all this attention for their campaigns. It feels like we're doing all the hard work, and they're just... riding the wave."

Amit leaned back in his chair, giving Vivek space to reflect. "I get that. But let me ask you this—are we really solving the hardest problems right now? Think about the bigger picture again. The battery is critical, yes, but is that the only challenge we're facing?"

Vivek looked confused for a moment, then sighed. "Well, no. I know we've had issues with the OTA (Over-the-Air) software updates. The ECU integration has been a headache, and it's causing delays in synchronizing the autonomous driving features. But that's more of a software team issue."

Amit smiled slightly, sensing an opportunity to help Vivek see the broader scope of the project. "It's not just software, Vivek. The ECU issues are impacting the vehicle's ability to receive critical updates. That directly affects performance, especially with the safety systems. And let's not forget the front fork design—the excessive vibration at higher speeds is a serious issue. If we don't fix that, we'll compromise ride stability and safety, which will affect the customer experience and potentially sales down the line. These aren't just 'other' problems— they're all interconnected."

Vivek blinked, clearly starting to see what Amit was getting at. "So, what you're saying is that while we've solved the battery issue, there's still a lot more we need to address. We can't just focus on one part of the project."

Amit nodded, his voice steady. "Exactly. The project's success depends on all these systems working together. The battery and thermal management systems are one part of the puzzle, but we can't ignore the OTA, the ECU, or the front fork design. It's all connected, and solving one problem without addressing the others isn't going to lead to a successful product launch."

Vivek sat back, clearly processing what Amit was saying. "I guess I hadn't thought about it like that. I've been so focused on what my team is dealing with, I didn't see the other issues as being just as critical."

Amit smiled warmly, leaning forward slightly. "That's understandable, Vivek. It's easy to get tunnel vision when you're working through tough problems. But here's what I want you to think about—engineering's role isn't just about solving the immediate technical challenges. It's about seeing the whole vehicle and how everything connects. Yes, marketing and sales may be louder right now, but they're working on their pieces of the puzzle too."

Vivek frowned again, still holding on to some of his frustration. "But doesn't it feel unfair? We're dealing with the tough stuff, and they get the attention."

Amit's expression softened, sensing this was where the real issue lay. "I get it. It can feel that way sometimes, but that's where we need to change our perspective. Corporate life—especially in projects like this—isn't always about getting recognition in the moment. Sometimes you're the one who's giving more than you're getting. That's part of the give-and-get equation. The reality is, your contributions are the foundation. Without the engineering team's work, there's no product for sales to sell or marketing to promote. But the payoff comes later."

Vivek looked at him, still unconvinced. "Later? When?"

Amit leaned in, his voice taking on a more coaching tone. "Think about it. When the Electric Auto hits the market and customers start giving feedback—when they talk about how reliable the battery is, how smooth the ride handling is, and how well the software updates work—who do you think they'll thank? Who will they credit for the long-lasting performance and stability?"

Vivek paused, then smiled faintly. "Engineering."

Amit nodded, smiling back. "Exactly. The recognition comes when the results speak for themselves. You may not be front and center in the marketing campaign, but trust me, when the product performs, everyone will know where the success came from. You're not just building a product—you're building trust and reliability that will last far beyond this launch."

Vivek exhaled slowly, the tension leaving his body. "You're right. I've been too focused on the immediate. I guess I just needed to hear that."

Amit leaned back, his voice more relaxed now. "And remember this, Vivek—your team is looking to you for leadership, not just in solving technical problems, but in navigating these frustrations. They're feeling the pressure too, and they need to see that you understand the bigger picture. Share this with them—let them know that we're all working toward the same goal. Sales, marketing, engineering—we all have different roles, but we're all part of the same machine."

Vivek nodded, the frustration in his eyes replaced with a clearer sense of purpose. "I'll talk to the team. We'll keep pushing forward, but with a better understanding of how everything fits together."

Amit smiled, standing up and offering a handshake. "That's what I need to hear. Keep me updated on the front fork issue and work with the software team on the ECU. We'll get through this, one problem at a time, as a team."

As Vivek left the office, Amit sat back, feeling a sense of satisfaction. He had helped Vivek see the broader picture, not just as an engineer, but as a leader. The give-and-get equation wasn't about immediate recognition—it was about the long-term impact, the eventual payoff of a job well done. Amit knew the road ahead was still challenging, but with the right mindset, the team would push through.

Part 2: Balancing Expectations

Amit had just finished his conversation with Vivek, and though that discussion had been intense, it felt constructive. Now, as he prepared to meet with Pooja, he sensed the upcoming conversation would require a different approach. Pooja had been unusually quiet in recent meetings, and it was clear that the relentless workload was taking a toll on her.

Pooja was responsible for balancing the technical constraints of the Electric Auto with user experience and aesthetics. As they pushed through the final stages of development, the constant revisions to the design, the pressure of simplifying the interior without sacrificing comfort, and the endless rounds of feedback had started to wear her down.

When she walked into Amit's office, she looked tired—her usual energy dimmed by exhaustion. She offered a small smile, but it didn't reach her eyes.

"Pooja, come in," Amit said gently, gesturing for her to sit. "I've been meaning to catch up with you. You've been carrying a lot on your plate recently."

Pooja nodded, sinking into the chair across from him. "I have, Amit. And to be honest, it's getting to me. I've been working late nights, redoing the dashboard layout, adjusting the interior materials, making sure the design meets the cost targets we talked about. But sometimes it feels like no matter how much I do, it's never enough. I'm just... tired."

Amit could see the strain on her face, and he knew this conversation needed a more personal, empathetic approach. "I understand, Pooja. The amount of work you've been doing, especially with all the redesigns, hasn't gone unnoticed. I can see how much effort you're putting in, but I also know how overwhelming it can feel when the workload doesn't seem to ease up."

Pooja gave a small nod, her eyes downcast. "I know, but it feels like I'm always behind. I've redone the seating ergonomics three times now because of new feedback. And with the cost cuts, I'm constantly trying to balance keeping the design functional without making it look too basic. I just feel like I'm putting in so much, but it's never quite good enough."

Amit sat forward, his voice calm but filled with empathy. "Pooja, you've been giving so much, and it's completely normal to feel overwhelmed when the demands keep piling up. But let's take a step back for a moment. You've been focused on the immediate challenges, but I want you to think about the long-term impact of what you're doing."

Pooja looked up, her brow furrowed slightly. "Long-term? I don't know if I can even think that far right now."

Amit smiled softly. "I get that. But hear me out. Right now, it feels like you're just putting out fires, one after the other. Redesigning, tweaking, responding to feedback. But what you're actually doing is laying the foundation for a product that will be remembered for its user experience. The seating comfort, the dashboard layout, the interior space—these are all things that drivers and passengers will feel every day. Your work might feel like it's in the background right now, but once the product hits the market, it will be front and center."

Pooja's expression softened slightly, but the exhaustion was still there. "I know, but it's hard to see the big picture when I'm stuck in the weeds, dealing with all these constant changes."

Amit leaned forward, his tone more gentle now. "Let me tell you something, Pooja. I've been having conversations with Vivek, Kiran, Suhani—all of them are feeling the same way. Everyone is giving so much right now, and I understand the frustration that comes when you feel like you're giving more than you're getting. But I want you to think about the long-term benefits—not just for the company, but for you personally."

Pooja looked curious now, her eyes more engaged. "What do you mean?"

Amit leaned back slightly, choosing his words carefully. "Look, this project is tough, but it's also a career-defining moment for all of us. You're not just working on any ordinary product. This Electric Auto is going to set a new standard in the market. When it's successful—and it will be—everyone who contributed is going to be recognized for their role. Think about what this means for your career. You've been leading the design. When customers start talking about how comfortable and practical the auto is, that's a direct reflection of your work."

He paused, letting the thought sink in. "I know it feels like the work is endless right now, but the long-term rewards will follow. Whether it's recognition within the company, future opportunities, or even just the personal satisfaction of knowing you helped create something that impacts people's lives—those rewards are coming."

Pooja's eyes softened, but there was still a lingering tension in her expression. "I hear you, Amit, but it's hard to keep going when I feel like I'm just burning out. I've been missing dinners with my family, staying late at the office, and it's starting to feel like I'm sacrificing too much."

Amit's voice softened, sensing the deeper emotional strain. "I know that's tough, Pooja. And I know you've got a lot going on at home too. Your family is important, and it's hard to balance everything. I've been there—trying to juggle work and home life, feeling like you're stretched too thin."

Pooja looked down for a moment, her voice quieter now. "Yeah... my son's been asking why I'm not around as much. And my husband has been really supportive, but I can tell he's worried about how much I'm pushing myself."

Amit gave her a reassuring smile. "I understand. And it's important that you don't lose sight of what matters most—your family. But here's the thing, Pooja. The sacrifices you're making now, the late nights, the extra effort—they're not just for the project. They're for you, your family, and your future. Think about the example you're setting for your son. He's seeing how hard his mom is working to achieve something big, something meaningful."

Pooja looked up, her eyes reflecting both the exhaustion and the clarity starting to break through. "I guess I hadn't thought about it that way."

Amit continued, his tone more encouraging now. "And remember, you don't have to do it all alone. Part of this process is leaning on your team, and if you need to take a step back, even just for a bit, that's okay. We're all in this together. The long-term benefits will be worth it, but you have to pace yourself. You've been doing incredible work, and I don't want you to lose sight of that."

Pooja gave a small nod, her tension easing just slightly. "It's hard to see the long-term when you're so deep in the day-to-day, but I appreciate what you're saying. I guess I've been so focused on getting everything perfect that I haven't taken a moment to step back and see the bigger picture."

Amit smiled. "That's natural, Pooja. We're all in that mindset right now—pushing to get everything done. But sometimes, it's okay to take a breath and remember why we're doing this. You're making a massive contribution, and it's going to have a lasting impact. Just don't lose sight of the fact that the getting comes after the giving. What you're giving now will pay off—may be not immediately, but in ways you'll see down the road."

Pooja looked more reflective, the exhaustion still there but tempered with a renewed sense of purpose. "Thanks, Amit. I think I needed to hear that. It's easy to forget why we're pushing so hard when it feels like the work just keeps piling up."

Amit leaned forward, his tone warm but resolute. "I get it. And I'm here to support you, just like the team is here to support each other. Don't hesitate to reach out if you need to take a step back. We'll keep pushing forward, but I want you to know that you're not alone in this. We'll get through it together, and when the product is out there, making a difference, you'll look back and know that it was all worth it."

Pooja smiled more genuinely this time, the heaviness in her expression starting to lift. "Thanks, Amit. I'll keep that in mind."

As she left his office, Amit felt a deep sense of responsibility. Pooja wasn't just a team member—she was a person trying to balance work, family, and the pressure of a demanding project. The give-and-get equation wasn't just about corporate politics or recognition; it was about people, their contributions, and the sacrifices they made for something bigger than themselves. And it was Amit's job to remind them of that every step of the way.

Part 3: The Power of Reciprocity

Amit knew it was time to address the entire core team. The individual conversations with Vivek and Pooja had been necessary to re-energize them, but the team as a whole needed alignment. There had been subtle tensions, unspoken frustrations, and the feeling that some were giving more than they were getting. But the project was nearing a critical stage, and he needed everyone to see the bigger picture—what they had achieved, what was left to be done, and most importantly, how they could rally together for the success of the Electric Auto.

He called a meeting with his core team: Vivek, Suhani, Pooja, Kiran and Rahul from sales. As they settled into the conference room, he could feel the weight of the months of hard work and late nights hanging in the air. Each of them had been working tirelessly, and Amit knew that the weariness could easily turn into discontent if not addressed properly.

He stood at the head of the table, waiting for everyone to quiet down before he began.

"First, I want to start by acknowledging something that I think we all need to hear—what we've accomplished so far is nothing short of remarkable."

Amit looked around the room, making sure to meet each of their eyes.

"Think about where we were when we first started. We had ambitious goals, but we knew this project wasn't going to be easy. Every one of you has faced massive challenges, and I've seen first- hand how hard you've worked to overcome them."

He turned to Vivek first. "Vivek, your team has solved some of the toughest problems we've faced. From the battery management system to the thermal regulation, you stabilized systems that would've derailed the entire project if not handled properly. And now, we're looking at a vehicle that's capable of performing in ways our competitors can't even match."

Vivek nodded, the fatigue still on his face but a flicker of pride in his eyes. "Thanks, Amit. But we've still got issues with the ECU and the OTA updates. The integration isn't as seamless as we need it to be, and that's going to be a major focus going forward."

Amit smiled. "I know, and you're right. But let's not lose sight of what's been done. You've taken us through the hardest technical challenges, and I have full confidence that you and your team will handle the next set of issues with the same dedication. The ECU integration and the front fork stability will be solved because you've already proven you can tackle the toughest problems."

Then, Amit turned to Suhani, the head of finance. "Suhani, I know the financial strain this project has put on your team. We've had to balance aggressive cost targets with maintaining product integrity, and that hasn't been easy. But you've been instrumental in helping us find that balance. We're close to hitting our financial goals, and that's a testament to your leadership."

Suhani, ever pragmatic, nodded. "Thanks, Amit. But we still have some cost overruns, especially on the supply chain side. If we're going to meet our margins, we need to renegotiate with a few more vendors and cut down on unnecessary spending in the final production stages."

Amit agreed, "Absolutely. That's one of the next priorities, and we'll work closely with the suppliers. But again, let's not forget that we're on track because of your team's diligence in managing costs without compromising on quality."

He shifted his attention to Pooja, whose role had been particularly tough with the constant redesigns. "Pooja, I know the workload has been immense. You've had to revise the dashboard layout, adjust the interior materials, and make sure the design stays within cost parameters while still delivering on comfort and user experience. What you've done isn't easy, and it often goes unnoticed. But believe me, when this product hits the market, the feedback from customers will be a direct reflection of your hard work."

Pooja, still looking tired but more relaxed after their one-on-one conversation, smiled. "Thanks, Amit. I just hope that all the changes we've made will resonate with the customers. I've been worried that with all the compromises, we might lose the user-friendly touch we were aiming for."

Amit shook his head. "You've maintained the core of what we set out to do—make this auto practical, comfortable, and affordable. The ergonomics and driver comfort are still there, and that's going to make a huge difference in how this vehicle is received. Your team has done an incredible job."

He then turned to Kiran, who had been quietly observing. "Kiran, you've crafted a marketing strategy that perfectly captures what this product is all about—reliability, long-term value, and how it's built to last. Your team has been the voice of this project, creating a narrative that highlights the strengths of the Electric Auto in a market that's crowded with competitors. And I know you've got some exciting campaigns lined up."

Kiran smiled, always the strategist. "We do. But we'll need to make sure that the product launch aligns with the messaging. Customers are looking for something reliable, especially fleet operators. If the product reliability doesn't match the story we're telling, it could hurt us."

Amit nodded in agreement. "You're right. And that's why it's so important that we continue to focus on performance testing in the final stages. The product will back up the story you're telling because we're building something reliable. We've got a few hurdles left, but the foundation is strong."

Finally, he turned to Rahul. "Rahul, you've been leading the charge with potential buyers, particularly the fleet operators. I know you've had to fight for competitive pricing while maintaining the value proposition, and you've positioned us well. But we still need to secure those deals. What's your take on where we stand?"

Rahul leaned forward, thoughtful. "Amit, the interest is there, but we need to close. Fleet operators are looking at Zephyr's pricing, and while we've got a better long-term value story, they need to be convinced. We need to make sure that the fleet testing results are rock solid. If they see reliability, we're in. But if there's any question, it could cost us."

Amit nodded, appreciating Rahul's insight. "That's why the final testing phase is crucial. We'll focus on the areas that matter most to fleet operators—reliability, maintenance costs, and mileage per charge. Once they see the numbers, they'll understand why our product is the smarter investment. And you've done a great job in laying the groundwork for that."

He paused, looking at the team collectively. "Now, let me be honest with all of you—we've come a long way, but we're not done yet. There are still challenges ahead. We need to tackle the ECU integration, finalize the supply chain negotiations, and ensure that our marketing and sales strategies are perfectly aligned with the product's performance. But I have no doubt that we'll get there, because we've proven time and again that we can solve tough problems."

Amit's tone shifted slightly, becoming more reflective. "This journey hasn't been easy, and I know many of you feel like you're giving more than you're getting. That's natural in projects like this. But let me remind you—the recognition doesn't always come immediately.

It comes when we deliver a product that exceeds expectations, when customers see the value, and when the market acknowledges the work that's gone into this."

He paused, letting his words settle before continuing. "Think about the stages we've gone through—conceptualization, design, prototype testing, and now we're in the final push before launch. Each of you has played a critical role in every one of these stages, and the success of this product will be the sum of all those contributions."

Pooja raised her hand slightly. "Amit, it's been tough to keep sight of that sometimes, especially with all the changes we've had to make. How do we stay motivated when the finish line keeps shifting?"

Amit smiled, his tone thoughtful but reassuring. "It's a fair question, Pooja. The truth is, projects like this are marathons, not sprints. The finish line might feel like it's moving, but every step we take gets us closer. And remember, the long-term impact of what we're building will last far beyond the launch date. It's not just about finishing—it's about finishing strong, knowing that the work you've done will resonate with customers for years to come."

Suhani nodded in agreement. "I agree with Pooja. It's been hard, especially when you're juggling short-term pressures with long-term goals. But I guess that's the reality of what we're doing."

Amit nodded. "Exactly. And this is where we need to support each other. The give-and-take within the team is what keeps us moving forward. Sometimes you give more than you get, but it comes full circle. We're building something that's going to make a difference, and when the product is out there, performing well in the market, the recognition will follow. The rewards—both personal and professional— will come. But right now, we focus on finishing the job."

The room fell silent for a moment as the team absorbed his words. The challenges ahead were still daunting, but there was a renewed sense of purpose in the air.

Amit looked around, his expression resolute but hopeful. "We're not done yet, but we're close. Let's keep pushing forward, support each other, and remember that everything we've given will come back to us in the end. We're building something we'll all be proud of."

With that, the meeting ended, and the team left the room with a sense of direction and unity. Amit had reinforced the idea that while the journey had been long and difficult, the reciprocity—the balance of giving and getting—would come, just as long as they stayed committed to the vision they had all worked so hard to achieve.

Key Learnings from Chapter 8: The Giving-Getting Equation in Life

1. **The Importance of Acknowledging Achievements:** Amit begins the meeting by recognizing each team member's individual contributions, showing that acknowledging accomplishments, even before a project is complete, boosts morale and reinforces the value of everyone's hard work.

2. **Seeing the Bigger Picture:** Throughout the chapter, Amit emphasizes the importance of looking beyond immediate frustrations and focusing on the long-term impact of their efforts. This helps the team understand that while individual recognition might not be immediate, their contributions are part of a greater success that will eventually pay off.

3. **Balancing Short-Term and Long-Term Thinking:** Amit guides the team through the reality that there's often a delay between the work done and the recognition or reward received. In projects of this scale, short-term sacrifices often lead to long-term rewards—both for the team and for the individual.

4. **Team Collaboration and Interdependence:** Amit reminds the team that different departments—engineering, finance, design, marketing, and sales—are all interconnected. The success of one relies on the success of the others. He emphasizes the power of collaboration and how it contributes to the overall success of the project.

5. **The Value of Emotional Support:** Amit's conversations with Vivek, Pooja, and the entire team highlight the importance of emotional support. A project isn't just about technical work; it's about understanding personal challenges and offering empathy and encouragement to ensure that people stay motivated.

6. **The Power of Reciprocity:** Amit explains that the giving- getting equation in corporate life is not always balanced in the short term, but reciprocity eventually plays out. When team members give

their best efforts, they build a culture of trust and support that ultimately leads to collective success and individual recognition.

7. **Overcoming Burnout by Understanding Purpose:** Amit addresses Pooja's feelings of burnout by helping her reconnect with the purpose behind her work. He reminds her that the sacrifices she's making now will have long-term personal and professional benefits. This insight can help employees push through fatigue by keeping their larger goals in mind.

8. **Recognition Comes with Results:** The chapter illustrates that recognition often follows the delivery of results. For the team, the recognition they seek will come when the Electric Auto is successfully launched and the market acknowledges the vehicle's reliability and performance.

9. **Leadership as a Balancing Act:** Amit's role as both a coach and a manager shines through in this chapter. He maintains a balance between empathy and accountability, ensuring the team understands that while their frustrations are valid, they still have responsibilities to meet. This balanced leadership approach builds trust and keeps the team focused.

10. **Fostering a Culture of Mutual Support:** Amit underscores the importance of fostering a culture where team members support one another. By reinforcing that their success depends on everyone working together, he helps the team move past personal frustrations and toward a common goal, ensuring that the team remains cohesive and motivated.

These key learnings highlight how leaders can guide teams through challenging stages of a project by fostering emotional resilience, long-term thinking, and a spirit of collaboration.

Chapter 9

Knowing-Doing Gap

Introduction: The Pressure to Deliver

The alpha testing phase for Volt Motors Electric Auto was now in its most critical phase, and the results would dictate the company's next steps. After months of design, testing, and countless revisions, the moment of truth had arrived: whether to invest more than `100 crore in tooling and production—the largest financial commitment the startup had ever made.

Nisha Mehta, the CEO, sat across from Amit Gupta, project lead, in her office. Stacks of reports from the test track, road trials, and simulation tests lay in front of them. The investment decision hinged on the vehicle's ability to prove its reliability, and Nisha wasn't about to approve any tooling unless the vehicle performed beyond question. The biggest issues revolved around core components: mechanical systems, software, and BIW integration.

"Amit, I've gone through the initial test results," Nisha began, her voice steady but serious. "I see improvements in some areas, but others are still a concern—particularly the chassis and BIW integration, and issues with panel alignment and door fitting."

Amit nodded, already expecting this line of questioning. "I know. The front and rear panels and the door panels are creating alignment issues that are affecting aerodynamics and structural integrity. Vivek's team has already identified the problem, but it's going to require precise adjustments to ensure the fit during production."

Nisha looked through the reports, then glanced up. "Amit, the tooling investment we're considering hinges on getting the BIW right. If the panels aren't aligning properly now, how can we be sure this won't turn into a larger issue once we scale production? Tooling costs are massive—if we get this wrong, it'll be catastrophic. You're asking me to commit to over `100 crore, and I need to be certain."

Amit leaned forward. "I understand, Nisha. The issue with the panels is related to slight misalignments in the chassis framework, which affects the way the panels fit. We're going to make targeted adjustments to the jig fixtures used for alignment during assembly. Once that's done, we'll retest to make sure everything locks into place. It's a solvable issue, but it needs immediate action."

Nisha tapped her fingers on the desk, her mind clearly working through the implications. "I'm hearing a lot of fixes, Amit. But are we just patching problems? The BIW integration isn't just cosmetic misalignments affect aerodynamics, wind noise, and ultimately structural strength. If this carries over to mass production, we'll face warranty claims and recalls. That's not something we can afford."

Amit kept his tone calm but firm. "No, it's not cosmetic. The adjustments we're making will ensure the BIW panels fit perfectly in production. The tooling will be designed based on the final, corrected prototypes. We're reworking the front and rear panel mouldings to improve the way they attach to the frame, and the door panels will be retooled to guarantee smooth closing without misalignment."

Nisha pressed on, shifting the conversation to another critical area. "Alright. Now, what about the chassis itself? The crash test simulations showed that the crumple zones didn't perform as expected under high-impact scenarios. We're going to need the tooling to accommodate those changes as well, right?"

Amit nodded. "Yes. We found that the front crumple zone absorbed impact well, but the rear wasn't dispersing energy as efficiently. We're modifying the crossmembers and reinforcement bars in the rear, which will enhance the structural integrity during a rear impact. Once we finalize these modifications, the tooling will reflect those changes."

Nisha's eyes narrowed. "So, this means additional delays in getting the tooling right."

Amit was ready for this. "There will be some extra testing, but not major delays. The critical thing is making sure these adjustments are built into the tooling design. It's about spending the time now to get it right, so we don't face higher costs in the future."

Nisha leaned back, considering his words. "What's the status on the powertrain? I saw issues with torque output during high-speed runs."

"That's linked to the gear ratio mismatch in the final drive," Amit explained. "We're recalibrating the gear ratios for better torque distribution at higher speeds, which will smooth out acceleration. Vivek's team is already on it, and we'll need to run a few more tests, but I'm confident we can fix this quickly."

Nisha continued; her voice sharp as she moved to the battery systems. "What about the battery cooling system? We've seen temperature spikes during testing. That's not acceptable, especially in India's climate. If we can't guarantee stable performance under extreme heat, this product won't survive."

Amit sighed. "We've traced the issue to the ECU's communication with the cooling system. It's not triggering cooling fast enough when temperatures rise. We're working on a software patch to ensure the thermal management system reacts more quickly to temperature changes. It's fixable, but it's critical we resolve it before the next phase of testing."

Nisha leaned forward, her voice low and measured. "Amit, this is all coming down to whether we can fix these problems before we move to tooling. I need to be convinced that we're not going to face production delays, massive reworks, or, worse, a flawed product launch. The tooling investment is huge—it'll lock us into certain design decisions. Are you confident we can resolve these issues before the next round of testing?"

Amit met her gaze steadily. "Yes, I'm confident. But we need to close the knowing-doing gap that's been holding us back. My team knows what needs to be done—we've known for weeks—but we've been slow to act. I'm going to address this immediately. We'll prioritize the critical areas—chassis, BIW, powertrain, and battery—and make sure every one of these systems is ready for tooling."

Nisha nodded, though the tension in her expression remained. "Good. Because if we don't fix these issues now, we won't be able to justify moving forward with this investment. You have my support, Amit, but we need results, not just plans."

Amit stood up, ready to take action. "I'll get the team together and close the gaps. We'll get this done."

Part 1: Knowledge vs. Action

After his tense meeting with Nisha, Amit felt the weight of the looming tooling decision more acutely than ever. With over `100 crore at stake, Volt Motors couldn't afford any mistakes. The vehicle's chassis, BIW, powertrain, and battery systems had to be flawless before they moved into production. And right now, they weren't.

Amit decided to see the performance issues first-hand. The test track would tell him more than any report could.

When he arrived, the Electric Auto was already being put through its paces. The engineers were monitoring the vehicle as it took laps around the track, but even from a distance, Amit could see the subtle dips in acceleration as the vehicle struggled to maintain speed. He narrowed his eyes, focusing on the vehicle's torque output. The issue was exactly what had been reported—the gear ratios were still off, causing a noticeable loss in torque after the vehicle hit 40 km/h.

He walked over to the engineers stationed near the monitoring station, watching the real-time data flow across the screens.

"Is the torque loss consistent across all runs?" Amit asked, his tone calm but authoritative.

One of the engineers, Ankit, nodded. "Yes, sir. The issue shows up every time the vehicle crosses 40 km/h. The final drive gear ratios are too conservative. We're not getting the torque we need at higher speeds. Vivek's team is working on recalibrating them, but it's still a few days out."

Amit stared at the screen, watching as the data continued to confirm the problem. "Alright, we'll need those recalibrations faster. Every delay here pushes us back on tooling."

His attention shifted to another screen displaying battery temperature data. The thermal spikes were visible, even to the untrained eye. The battery cooling system wasn't reacting fast enough, allowing temperatures to climb dangerously high before the system engaged.

"How are we handling the cooling system issue?" Amit asked, his voice tinged with concern.

Another engineer, Ravi, stepped forward. "The problem's with the ECU communication, sir. The cooling system isn't being triggered fast enough to respond to the temperature spikes. We're working on a software patch to improve the ECU-BMS communication, but it's going to take some time."

Amit frowned. Time wasn't something they had. He watched the Electric Auto complete another lap, still struggling with the same issues.

"Let's push forward with that patch. We can't move into final testing until this is sorted. The vehicle's thermal performance is critical, especially given the climate conditions we're targeting."

With that, Amit took a deep breath, made his notes, and headed back to the headquarters. It was time to gather the team for a serious conversation about the state of the project.

Later that afternoon, Amit called for an urgent meeting with his core team. The stakes were too high to allow the current issues to drag on, and it was time to address every problem head-on. Vivek, Pooja, Suhani and Kiran gathered in the conference room, sensing the seriousness in Amit's tone.

"Thanks for coming on short notice," Amit began, wasting no time. "I've just come from the test track, and we've got significant issues with the alpha prototype. Nisha has reviewed the reports, and we're not where we need to be. If we don't fix these problems, the tooling decision—and the `100 crore investment that comes with it—will be delayed. We can't afford that."

He looked around the room, making sure he had everyone's attention.

"Let's start with the chassis and BIW integration," Amit continued, turning to Vivek. "The front and rear panels are misaligned, and that's affecting both aerodynamics and structural integrity. What's the plan for fixing the jig fixtures?"

Vivek shifted in his seat, pulling up the data on his tablet. "The misalignment is caused by slight deviations in the chassis framework. We're making adjustments to the jig fixtures to ensure the panels align perfectly during assembly. The challenge is getting the tolerances tight enough for mass production. If we don't get it right now, it'll create major problems once we scale."

Amit nodded. "What about the door panels? They're not closing smoothly, and that's a major issue. If the doors don't align properly, it's going to affect both the safety and user experience."

Vivek took a breath. "We've already begun reworking the door panel moldings to improve the fit. The BIW tooling for the doors will be recalibrated to eliminate these issues. But we need at least a week of testing to make sure the adjustments work across all prototypes."

Amit's gaze was steady. "I'll give you the time, but we need those tests completed as soon as possible. The BIW alignment is non- negotiable. Misaligned panels and doors are dealbreakers for tooling."

He shifted focus to the powertrain. "Now, let's talk about the gear ratios. I saw the torque drop firsthand at the test track. What's causing the mismatch?"

Vivek tapped his screen, pulling up more data. "The current gear ratios in the final drive were optimized for low-speed urban driving, but they're choking at higher speeds. We've identified the ratios that will give us better torque output at higher speeds without sacrificing too much efficiency at low speeds. The recalibrations are in progress, but we need another round of testing before we can lock them in."

Amit frowned but kept his tone focused. "We need those adjustments sooner rather than later. Torque loss at higher speeds isn't just a performance issue—it'll affect the overall driving experience, and we can't have that."

Next, Amit turned to Pooja, who had been quietly listening. "Pooja, the material issues with the interior design are still causing problems during stress testing. We need to address those now before we finalize anything for tooling. What's the plan?"

Pooja straightened up. "The materials we're using for the dashboard and seats aren't performing as well as expected under high stress. We're looking into alternative materials that can handle the stress without increasing costs too much. I'll work with Vivek's team to ensure that the materials are both durable and cost-effective."

Amit gave a slight nod of approval. "Good. But I need those tests done quickly. The interior materials are critical to the user experience, and we can't afford to overlook any part of it."

He then turned to the battery and thermal management system, his voice firm. "The battery temperature spikes are still an issue. I saw the data—thermal regulation is inconsistent, and that's a dealbreaker in our target markets. What's the status on the ECU patch?"

Vivek cleared his throat. "We've identified the issue—like I mentioned earlier, the ECU isn't communicating with the cooling system efficiently. The patch is being developed, but we're running into delays with testing."

Amit's gaze hardened. "We don't have time for delays. This cooling system needs to work flawlessly under all conditions. I want the patch tested and ready before the next round of road tests."

Finally, he turned to the rest of the team. "This isn't just about knowing what the issues are. We've all known the problems for weeks. But knowing and doing are two different things. We need to execute— and we need to do it fast. There's no more time to wait for 'next week' fixes. We need immediate action on every issue."

The room was silent for a moment, the gravity of the situation sinking in. Then Vivek nodded, determination settling in. "We'll get it done, Amit. I'll push my team harder to meet these deadlines."

Pooja added promptly. "I'll expedite the material testing and get everything finalized."

Amit met each of their eyes, knowing they understood the stakes. "Good. Let's get to work. I expect updates on every one of these issues by the end of the week."

With that, the meeting ended. The knowing-doing gap was closing, but the team had no time to lose. They needed results, and they needed them fast.

Part 2: Accountability Shift

The urgency of the project had reached a new level after Amit's meeting with his core team. The knowing-doing gap was now clear to everyone, but identifying the problem was only the first step. The next move was to implement a system of accountability that ensured every idea, every solution, and every action was executed without delay. To achieve this, Amit called for a critical meeting with the Project Management Team—the group responsible for tracking each component's progress and ensuring all timelines were met.

As the team gathered in the conference room, the atmosphere was noticeably different. The casualness that once characterized their meetings had evaporated, replaced by a sense of urgency. Amit was not looking for more discussions about theory or abstract solutions; he was here for concrete, actionable progress.

Mathew, the head of the Project Management Office (PMO), brought up the project tracking report on the large screen in front of the team. The detailed dashboard showed the current status of every component and aggregate of the Electric Auto—each marked either green, yellow, or red based on their progress.

Amit stood at the front of the room, his gaze sweeping across the group. "Alright, team, we're in a situation where every day counts. We've already identified the technical issues holding us back, but now it's time to act. I'm not interested in hearing more about what needs to be done I want to know who is doing what and by when. We need to close the gap between knowing and doing, and that starts with clear accountability."

He turned to Mathew. "Mathew, I want a detailed component-wise and aggregate-wise breakdown. Let's go through this line by line. Where are we with the powertrain recalibration?"

Mathew nodded and clicked on the powertrain section of the dashboard. "The gear ratio recalibration for the final drive is currently in progress. According to Vivek's team, the recalibration is 70% complete. The testing phase will begin in three days, and full results should be ready by the end of next week."

Amit frowned slightly but remained composed. "Three days? Vivek's team mentioned the recalibrations could be fast-tracked. I want this moved up to two days. This needs to be a priority."

Rohit, one of the senior engineers on Vivek's team, spoke up. "We can push the recalibrations faster, Amit, but that'll require overtime from the team. I can speak to Vivek and get the green light."

Amit nodded. "Do it. This is a critical issue—torque loss at high speeds can't be something we take lightly. I expect the recalibration results in two days, and we'll review the performance data immediately after."

Mathew moved on to the next section. "The battery cooling system is currently being patched with updated software to improve the communication between the ECU and the cooling system. The patch is 50% complete, and testing is scheduled for next week."

Amit shook his head. "That's too slow. The battery cooling system is non-negotiable. If we can't control temperature spikes, this vehicle won't survive in real-world conditions, especially in markets like India. Suhani, what resources do we need to accelerate the software patch?"

Suhani, who had been listening closely, responded quickly. "We can allocate more resources from the software development team, but it'll mean pulling people from the body electronics project."

Amit thought for a moment. "Do it. The ECU patch takes priority over body electronics right now. We can't move forward with tooling if the thermal management system is still experiencing delays. I want to see the patch completed and tested in the next five days."

Mathew nodded, updating the status on the dashboard. "Got it, Amit. I'll inform the software team immediately."

The next item was the BIW integration, specifically the door panels and the front and rear panel alignment.

Mathew clicked on the status report. "The panel misalignment is being addressed with jig fixture adjustments. Pooja's team has been working with Vivek's group to recalibrate the alignment during assembly, but we've only completed 40% of the adjustments so far. The testing phase hasn't started yet."

Amit's voice was sharper now. "We're too far behind on this. The BIW integration is a foundational part of the vehicle. Misaligned panels affect not only the aerodynamics but also the structural integrity of the auto. This needs to be pushed through faster. Pooja, what's holding us back?"

Pooja shifted in her seat. "The jig fixture adjustments are more complex than we initially thought. We're recalibrating the machinery to account for slight shifts in the panel dimensions, and it's taking longer than expected. But I can push my team to accelerate the adjustments. We should be able to finish recalibration within five days, and testing can begin immediately after."

Amit gave a firm nod. "That's the kind of action we need. Push your team, Pooja. Get the recalibrations done, and have the alignment tested thoroughly. I don't want any more surprises down the line with the door and panel fittings."

Mathew moved on to the next section of the report. "The interior material testing is ongoing, but we've run into issues with the durability of some of the materials under stress. We've tested alternatives, but the current material choices don't hold up under extended heat exposure."

Amit turned to Pooja again. "This is another area we can't afford to delay. The interior materials need to be finalized before we can commit to tooling. The testing has to move faster."

Pooja nodded, looking determined. "I'll coordinate with the materials team to expedite testing. We'll also start testing some backup materials we've identified, just in case the current options don't hold up."

"Good," Amit said. "But I want to see a clear plan by the end of the day on how we're going to fast-track these tests."

Mathew moved to the final item on the agenda: software and OTA updates. "The integration of the OTA updates and software syncing with the vehicle's control systems is 60% complete. However, we've identified bugs with the sensor integration that are causing miscommunication between the body electronics and the vehicle control unit."

Amit's expression tightened. "We can't move forward with unreliable OTA updates. The moment we release the vehicle, any software glitches will damage our reputation. The sensor issues need to be fixed immediately. Who's responsible for this?"

Pranav, from the software team, spoke up. "It's on my team, Amit. We've isolated the bugs, and the developers are working on a patch. It'll take about a week to roll out the fix."

Amit's voice was firm. "We don't have a week, Pranav. Can we allocate more developers to this?"

Pranav looked at Suhani, who nodded. "We can shift resources from non-critical areas. I'll free up more developers to handle this, and we'll prioritize the OTA fixes."

"Good," Amit said, his tone decisive. "I want the OTA issues resolved and tested within five days. Anything less than that is going to push us off schedule."

With the major issues reviewed and accountability established, Amit turned back to the entire team. "Here's the bottom line: Every one of these issues needs to be addressed immediately. From this point on, I want clear ownership of each problem. If something is delayed, I want to know why, and I want to know who's responsible for getting it back on track."

He paused, letting his words sink in. "Ideas and plans mean nothing if we don't execute them. I've set timelines for each critical area, and I expect everyone to meet those deadlines. This is where we close the knowing-doing gap—by holding ourselves accountable and delivering results."

The team sat in silence for a moment, absorbing the seriousness of Amit's words. There was no room for complacency anymore.

"Let's get to work," Amit said, closing the meeting. "I expect daily updates on progress, and if any issue arises, bring it to me immediately."

The atmosphere had shifted. The sense of urgency was palpable, and the team knew there was no turning back. Amit had made it clear—every team member was now accountable for turning knowledge into action. The transition from theory to practice had begun.

Part 3: Overcoming the Gap

The weeks following Amit's push for accountability were marked by a distinct shift in the atmosphere at Volt Motors. The sense of urgency had taken root, and the team had begun moving faster, closing the knowing-doing gap that had once been a source of frustration. Execution, no longer a distant goal, was becoming the driving force behind their work.

Amit had instituted a weekly project review meeting with the core team and the Project Management Office (PMO), ensuring that no issue was left to linger. Every delay was addressed, and every problem had a clear owner. It was this level of focused action that was slowly turning things around.

The first review meeting after the accountability shift was a critical moment. Amit wanted to see not just ideas and plans, but tangible progress.

The team gathered in the conference room. The large project tracking screen that had been a source of tension in earlier meetings now felt like a scoreboard, reflecting how far they had come in closing the gap between knowing and doing.

Amit started the meeting with his usual calm but firm tone. "Alright, team. We've been pushing hard to close the knowing-doing gap. Today, we're here to see what progress we've made in the past week. Let's go through each component and review where we stand. We're moving from theory to practice now, and the results need to show that."

He turned to Mathew, who had the project tracking report ready. "Mathew, let's start with the powertrain recalibration. Where are we?"

Mathew clicked on the powertrain section, bringing up the latest data. "The gear ratio recalibrations were completed on schedule. Vivek's team finished the testing two days ago, and the results show a significant improvement in torque output at higher speeds. The vehicle is now maintaining consistent torque levels up to 60 km/h."

Amit smiled slightly, a rare show of satisfaction. "That's what I like to hear. Vivek, any additional testing needed?"

Vivek, looking more confident than he had in previous meetings, shook his head. "No, Amit. We've optimized the gear ratios, and the tests confirm that the torque issue has been resolved. We'll continue to monitor it during the next few track tests, but I'm confident we've got it right."

Amit gave a nod of approval. "Great work, Vivek. Let's keep monitoring, but it sounds like we've cleared one major hurdle."

Next, Amit moved to the battery cooling system. "What's the status on the ECU patch for the battery cooling?"

Mathew clicked to the next section. "The ECU software patch was completed two days ago, and initial tests show that the cooling system is now responding to temperature spikes in real-time. The thermal management system is engaging immediately when temperatures rise, and we've eliminated the overheating issues during extended high-load runs."

Amit exhaled in relief. The battery cooling system had been one of the most critical and complex issues and knowing that it was finally under control gave him confidence in their progress. "That's a big win. Vivek, we'll need to stress-test this in various conditions, but if we've eliminated the thermal spikes, we're on track."

Vivek nodded. "We're already planning stress tests in high-temperature conditions, simulating the heat extremes the vehicle will face in markets like India. But so far, everything's working as expected."

Amit smiled again, feeling momentum building. "Good. Keep pushing those tests and let me know if anything changes."

He turned to Pooja, ready to review the next critical area. "Pooja, where do we stand with the BIW integration—particularly the panel misalignments?"

Pooja pulled up the latest data, her voice clear and confident. "We've completed the jig fixture adjustments, and the misalignments have been corrected. The front and rear panels now fit perfectly with the chassis, and we've run tests to confirm that the aerodynamics and structural integrity are holding up. We've also resolved the issues with the door panel alignments. Everything is closing smoothly, and there are no further gaps in the fit."

Amit's eyes lit up. This was another major issue that had been holding them back, and hearing that it was now fixed was a huge relief. "That's excellent news, Pooja. The panel misalignment had the potential to cause serious delays, but it sounds like we've got that under control now."

Pooja nodded, smiling slightly. "It took some time, but the adjustments worked, and we've already started prepping for the next round of testing. We're confident the BIW integration will hold up in mass production."

Amit's voice carried a note of approval. "Great work, Pooja. Let's keep moving forward. We'll continue monitoring during the alpha testing phase, but it sounds like we've finally crossed a major milestone."

Next, Amit moved on to the interior material testing. "Pooja, how are the interior materials holding up?"

Pooja clicked on the section related to material testing. "We fast-tracked the tests, as you asked. We've finalized a material that can handle the heat exposure and stress we've been concerned about. It's slightly more expensive than our original choice, but it's still within budget, and it performs better under stress."

Amit nodded, impressed. "That's good to hear. The durability of the interior is a key factor in customer satisfaction, and we can't compromise on that. I'm glad we've found a material that works."

Mathew then moved to the final section: OTA updates and sensor integration. "The OTA software bugs have been fixed, and we've rolled out the patch. The sensors are now communicating seamlessly with the vehicle control unit. We've run several tests, and the miscommunication issues have been resolved."

Pranav reported. "The OTA fixes were a challenge, but we pushed the team to work overtime and get it done. We've synced everything, and the sensors are responding as they should. We've also optimized the updates to ensure that future patches won't disrupt the system."

Amit felt a wave of relief. "That's what I needed to hear. The OTA and sensor integration were critical—if that hadn't been fixed, we would've had serious post-launch problems."

He turned to the entire group, taking a deep breath before speaking. "I can't emphasize enough how important it is that we've made this progress. We've gone from identifying issues to actually fixing them. This is what it means to close the knowing-doing gap— we're not just talking about what needs to be done, we're doing it."

He looked at each of them, his expression serious but filled with pride. "The shift from theory to action is what's going to make this project successful. We still have a long way to go, and there will be more challenges, but we're building momentum. I want to keep this level of urgency and focus as we move forward."

Amit leaned back slightly, letting the weight of his words sink in. "It's easy to get stuck in planning mode, to think that knowing the answer is enough. But the truth is, execution is what makes the difference. It's not what you know, it's what you do that determines success. And right now, we're finally doing what needs to be done."

The team nodded; the room filled with a quiet but palpable sense of accomplishment. The progress was real, and they had learned the hard way that knowing wasn't enough—it was acting on that knowledge that mattered.

Amit closed the meeting with a smile. "Let's keep up the momentum. We're not just closing the knowing-doing gap—we're crossing it. Keep pushing, keep executing, and let's get this product to market."

As the team left the room, Amit felt a sense of pride and satisfaction. They were no longer stuck in theory; they were moving decisively toward action. And that was what would make the difference.

Key Learnings from Chapter 9: Knowing-Doing Gap

1. **Urgency Drives Execution:** One of the key takeaways is that knowing what the problem is and having solutions is only half the battle. Urgency in execution is critical to move from theory to

action. Without a sense of urgency, even the best ideas and plans remain ineffective.

2. **Accountability is Essential:** By instituting a system of clear accountability, Amit was able to ensure that each team member had ownership over specific tasks and timelines. This shift from shared responsibility to individual accountability created a sense of focus and drive to meet deadlines.

3. **Bias for Action:** The team learned the importance of having a bias for action. Moving quickly from identification of issues to their resolution ensured that they were progressing in real time, which ultimately led to fewer delays and a more focused approach to problem-solving.

4. **Collaboration Between Departments:** Progress accelerated once the team began working more closely across departments—whether it was engineering, software, or design. The ability to align mechanical, electronic, software and material testing simultaneously was critical to overcoming major roadblocks.

5. **Continuous Monitoring:** Amit emphasized the importance of continuous testing and monitoring, ensuring that fixes were not just implemented but also tested rigorously. This reduced the likelihood of issues re-emerging later in the project lifecycle.

6. **The Importance of Progress Reviews:** Regular progress reviews and close tracking of each component helped the team stay aligned and focused. Weekly check-ins allowed Amit to course-correct quickly and hold everyone accountable for their part of the project.

7. **Closing the Knowing-Doing Gap:** The biggest lesson of the chapter was the importance of closing the gap between knowing and doing. The team realized that knowledge without action is useless. What matters is turning that knowledge into tangible results through decisive action.

8. **Execution Over Theory:** Amit's leadership highlighted the value of execution over theory. While ideas and solutions are necessary, the real success lies in making those ideas happen. Action is the foundation of progress and results.

9. **Adaptability and Resource Reallocation:** The chapter showed how the team learned to adapt by reallocating resources—shifting developers from lower-priority projects to critical areas like the ECU patch and OTA updates. This ability to adapt resources based on urgency contributed to faster resolution of critical issues.

10. **Momentum is Key:** Once the team began to act decisively, momentum started to build. Amit emphasized the need to maintain that momentum by continuing to push for timely execution and avoiding slipping back into the comfort of discussing plans rather than implementing them.

The overall lesson from the chapter is that success hinges on execution, not just on knowledge or ideas.

Chapter 10

Guys Have Tremendous Capability but Low Self-Belief

Part 1: The Team's Capability

Amit sat at his desk, mulling over the progress the team had made so far. They had come a long way, closing the knowing- doing gap, addressing technical issues, and pushing the Electric Auto project towards the next critical milestone. Yet, despite their undeniable technical skills, Amit sensed a deeper issue: self-doubt. His core team was immensely capable, but they lacked the self-belief to fully take ownership of their work.

He noticed this hesitancy during meetings. When someone proposed an idea or solution, there was often a sense of uncertainty in their voices, as if they were waiting for approval or bracing for criticism. This had to change, especially with the next phase of the project—a critical tooling investment decision—on the horizon. Amit knew his team had the talent to succeed, but they needed to believe it themselves.

A Conversation with Vivek

Later that afternoon, Amit scheduled individual conversations with each of his core team members, starting with Vivek, the engineering lead. Vivek had been instrumental in resolving many of the technical issues with the powertrain and thermal management system, but Amit had noticed his tendency to hesitate before making final decisions.

Vivek entered Amit's office, looking focused but somewhat guarded. Amit gestured for him to sit.

"Vivek," Amit began, "I've been thinking about how far we've come, and I want to acknowledge that your technical leadership has been critical. The work your team did on the gear ratio recalibrations and fixing the ECU patch has been top-notch."

Vivek smiled slightly, but Amit could see the hint of uncertainty behind it. "Thanks, Amit. We're getting there, but there's always more to be done."

Amit leaned forward, his voice calm but direct. "That's true, but here's the thing—I've noticed something in the way you approach decisions. You often wait for confirmation, even when it's clear that you know what needs to be done. Why do you think that is?"

Vivek shifted in his chair, looking thoughtful. "Honestly, Amit, it's the stakes. The decisions we're making—especially with the powertrain and thermal management—are critical. If we make the wrong call, it could set us back or even jeopardize the project."

Amit nodded, understanding the weight of Vivek's concerns. "I get that. But let me ask you something—how many times have you been wrong when you've made a technical decision? Think about the major calls you've made over the past few months."

Vivek frowned slightly, clearly reflecting on the past. "Not many,

I guess. The major decisions have worked out."

"Exactly," Amit said, leaning back in his chair. "You have a strong track record, Vivek. You've proven yourself capable time and again, but I feel like you don't trust yourself as much as you should. You don't need to wait for validation or approval—you've earned the right to make these decisions with confidence."

Vivek seemed to absorb Amit's words, his posture relaxing slightly. "I hadn't really thought about it that way. I guess I've been too focused on avoiding mistakes rather than just trusting my instincts."

Amit smiled. "You're capable, Vivek. I trust your judgment, and you need to trust it too. We're heading into a critical phase, and we need every leader to take full ownership of their work. You have the capability—now you just need to believe in it."

Vivek nodded, a look of determination crossing his face. "Thanks, Amit. I'll work on that. You're right—I need to stop second-guessing myself."

A Conversation with Pooja

Next on Amit's list was Pooja. She had been instrumental in refining the BIW integration and fixing the panel alignment issues. However, Amit had noticed her hesitancy when it came to pushing bold ideas or taking risks with the vehicle's design.

"Pooja, come in," Amit said as she entered his office. "I wanted to have a quick chat about your role in the project."

Pooja sat down, her demeanor always professional but somewhat cautious. "Sure, Amit. What's on your mind?"

Amit smiled. "First, I want to tell you how impressed I am with the work you've done on the BIW integration. Fixing those alignment issues was no small feat, and the way your team handled the jig fixture adjustments was impressive. We're in a much better place because of your efforts."

Pooja smiled, but Amit could sense her holding back. "Thanks.

I'm glad it's working out."

Amit leaned forward. "But there's something I've been noticing, Pooja. When you present ideas or make suggestions, you do it with hesitation, almost as if you're waiting for someone else to validate your thoughts. Why is that?"

Pooja looked slightly uncomfortable but thoughtful. "I think it's because I don't want to push too hard on things that might not work out. I've seen ideas get shot down before, and I don't want that to happen with mine."

Amit nodded, understanding the fear of rejection. "I get that. But here's the thing—your ideas are good. The improvements you've made in the interior materials and design ergonomics are already making a difference. You've got the technical skill and creativity to push this project forward, but you're holding back. Why do you think that is?"

Pooja paused for a moment. "I guess I'm worried about making a wrong call or proposing something that doesn't work. It's easier to play it safe."

Amit smiled gently. "I understand the hesitation, but you're limiting yourself by playing it safe. This project isn't about perfection— it's about progress, and sometimes that means taking risks and pushing boundaries. You've got the capability to make bold design decisions, Pooja, and I trust you to do that."

Pooja nodded, looking thoughtful. "I hadn't really seen it that way. I guess I've been focusing too much on what could go wrong."

Amit leaned back. "Exactly. But what could go right? You've already shown your capability—now it's time to back yourself. Don't be afraid to push those ideas forward. You're in this role because I believe in your ability to make a difference. Now, you need to believe in it too."

Pooja smiled, this time with more confidence. "I'll work on that, Amit. Thanks for the push."

A Conversation with Suhani

Suhani was next. She had been a rock for the project, keeping budgets tight and ensuring that cost overruns were managed effectively. But even she, in moments of high pressure, had a tendency to doubt the aggressive financial decisions she made.

"Suhani," Amit said as she sat across from him, "I want to talk about how well you've been managing the budget. Your work has kept this project financially viable, especially with the tooling investment decision looming."

Suhani agreed, though a hint of caution lingered in her eyes. "Thanks, Amit. But there are still a lot of moving parts, and I'm worried about cost overruns, especially when we're making fast decisions."

Amit smiled slightly. "That's exactly what I wanted to talk about. You've been incredibly cautious, which has helped us avoid unnecessary costs, but I've noticed that sometimes you hold back on certain decisions because you're worried about overspending."

Suhani nodded, looking concerned. "It's just that we're operating on tight margins, and the tooling investment is going to stretch us even further. I don't want us to make a financial mistake that we can't recover from."

Amit leaned forward, his tone firm but supportive. "Suhani, you've managed this project brilliantly so far. But you need to trust your judgment more. You know the numbers inside and out, and you've already proven that you can keep us on track. Don't let fear of what could go wrong stop you from making the right decisions. Sometimes we need to invest aggressively to ensure long-term success."

Suhani tilted her head slightly, her expression thoughtful "You're right. I guess I've been holding back because the stakes are so high. But I do know what we need to do."

Amit smiled. "Exactly. I trust your judgment, Suhani, and you need to trust it too. The tooling investment is huge, but it's necessary, and I know you can guide us through it."

Part 2: Mid-Year Appraisal Feedback Sessions

The mid-year appraisal was a critical moment for Amit and his team. It wasn't just about checking boxes or going through performance metrics—it was about giving each of his team members feedback that would help them grow both professionally and personally. Amit knew that beyond their technical skills, the team struggled with self-doubt. Despite their talent, they hesitated, often seeking validation before making decisions. This had to change, especially with the next phase of the Electric Auto project looming.

Amit decided to approach these appraisal sessions not just as a manager but as a mentor and coach, guiding his team to overcome their internal doubts. He wanted to help them understand that confidence comes from doing the work, thinking things through, and achieving small successes that build trust in their abilities.

Vivek's Appraisal Session

Vivek had been a crucial player in fixing the technical issues with the powertrain and battery systems, but he often hesitated, doubting his decisions even when the data clearly supported him. Amit had noticed this pattern and wanted to address it.

As Vivek entered the meeting room, Amit greeted him warmly.

He gestured toward a seat and began the session.

"Vivek, let's start with your performance so far. You've done an excellent job leading the engineering team, especially when it came to resolving the ECU issues and gear ratio recalibrations. Your work has been critical to keeping the project on track."

Vivek smiled, though it was the guarded smile Amit had seen many times before—one that hid lingering doubts. "Thanks, Amit. But there's still a lot left to do, and I feel like we could've caught some of these issues earlier."

Amit leaned forward, his tone more personal now. "Vivek, I want to talk about that. I've noticed that even when you've made the right call—like with the torque output fix—you hesitate. You second-guess yourself, even though your decisions are almost always backed by the data. What's going on there?"

Vivek shifted in his seat, clearly uncomfortable. "I guess... I'm just worried about making the wrong decision. The stakes are high, and I don't want to be the one who makes a mistake that costs us time or money."

Amit nodded, understanding his concern. "I get that. But here's the thing—you've already proven that you know what you're doing. You've led your team through some of the most complex issues we've faced, and every time, your decisions have been solid. Yet, you still doubt yourself. Why?"

Vivek sighed, thinking it over. "I guess it's the pressure. I feel like if I don't double-check or get someone else's input, I might miss something."

Amit smiled gently. "That's natural. But Vivek, confidence doesn't come from having all the answers upfront. It comes from doing the homework, thinking through the problem, and then making a decision based on the best information you have at the time. And you've done that consistently."

Vivek looked up, still unsure. "But what if I make the wrong call?

What if something slips through?"

Amit paused, letting the question settle before responding. "Here's the thing, Vivek—no one gets everything right all the time. But you've put in the work. You've done the analysis, you've run the tests, and you've thought through the solutions. That's all we can ask for. The rest is about execution, and execution doesn't happen if you're hesitating at every step."

Vivek nodded slowly, starting to grasp Amit's point.

"You know, small successes build confidence," Amit continued. "You've already had several of those, even if you don't see it. The fix you implemented for the thermal management system—that was a win. The recalibration of the gear ratios—another win. But you need to start recognizing those wins and trusting yourself more. Each success, no matter how small, adds up. They're your proof that you can handle this."

Vivek seemed to brighten at this, the weight of his self-doubt lifting slightly. "I guess I just need to focus on those wins and not the what-ifs."

Amit smiled. "Exactly. You've got the capability. Now, focus on doing the work, taking ownership, and building on those small successes. That's how you turn doubt into confidence."

Pooja's Appraisal Session

Next, Amit met with Pooja. She had always been meticulous and creative in her work, but like Vivek, she often hesitated to push forward bold ideas, fearing rejection or failure.

"Pooja, come in," Amit greeted her warmly. "Let's talk about how things have been going on your end."

Pooja sat down, looking a little more comfortable than usual. "I've been working on the final touches for the interior design and the adjustments we made to the BIW integration. So far, it's looking good."

Amit nodded. "I've seen the results. The way you handled the panel realignments was fantastic. It's made a huge difference in both the look and functionality of the vehicle."

Pooja smiled, though, again, it was tinged with that same hesitancy. "Thanks, but I wasn't sure about the adjustments at first. I had a couple of different ideas, and I didn't want to make the wrong choice."

Amit raised an eyebrow. "Pooja, that's what I wanted to talk to you about. I've noticed you're often hesitant when it comes to making bold design decisions, even though your ideas are always well thought out. What's holding you back?"

Pooja sighed, clearly uncomfortable with the question. "I guess... I just don't want to propose something that won't work out. I've seen ideas get rejected in the past, and I don't want to push too hard if there's a chance it might fail."

Amit leaned forward, his tone more like a mentor now. "Pooja, let me ask you something—how many of your ideas have failed so far? Really think about it."

Pooja thought for a moment. "Not many, actually. Most of them worked once we tested them."

"Exactly," Amit said. "You're holding back because you're afraid of something that's barely happened. You've already proven that you can solve complex design issues. But here's the thing—confidence isn't about knowing you'll succeed every time. It's about trusting the process. Do the work, think through your designs, and then push forward with conviction."

Pooja looked thoughtful. “But what if I do fail? What if something doesn’t work?”

Amit smiled. “If something doesn’t work, we fix it. That’s what we do. But you can’t let the fear of failure stop you from taking bold steps. Confidence comes from knowing that, no matter what, you’ll figure out a way forward. And you’ve already proven that you can do that.”

Pooja nodded, starting to understand. “I guess I’ve been focusing too much on the possibility of failure and not on the fact that I can solve the problems if they come up.”

“Exactly,” Amit said. “Take small steps. Get a few more wins under your belt. Each time you take ownership of a problem and solve it, that’s a win. And with each win, you’ll build more confidence. It’s a process.”

Pooja smiled, this time more genuinely. “Thanks, Amit. I’ll work on that. I think I just need to push myself a little more and not be afraid of what could go wrong.”

Suhani’s Appraisal Session

Last was Suhani. She had kept the project on track financially, but her cautious approach sometimes led to delays in decision-making, especially when it came to allocating resources or approving costs.

“Suhani,” Amit began, “I’ve been meaning to talk about how well you’ve managed the project’s finances so far. Without your efforts, we wouldn’t have been able to keep things under control with the budget, especially with the tooling investment decision coming up.”

Suhani smiled, though, as always, there was a trace of worry in her eyes. "Thanks, Amit. I've tried to be careful, especially with all the moving parts. But the tooling investment... it's going to be tight."

Amit leaned in. "That's what I wanted to talk about. You've been careful, and that's great. But I've also noticed that sometimes you're hesitant to approve certain investments or allocate resources because you're worried about cost overruns. What's causing that hesitation?"

Suhani sighed, looking down at her notes. "I just don't want to make a mistake. The tooling investment is huge, and if we overspend or make the wrong call, it could really hurt us."

Amit nodded, understanding her concern. "I get that. But Suhani, you've already proven that you know how to manage the budget. You've made the right calls every step of the way, and we're in a strong financial position because of that. You need to trust your judgment more."

Suhani looked up, surprised. "But what if I approve something that leads to an overrun? What if we run out of resources?"

Amit smiled. "Suhani, part of being a leader is making those tough calls. You've done the work, analysed the numbers, and made careful decisions up to this point. You've shown that you can manage this project's finances effectively. But if you let fear of overspending stop you from making the right investments, we'll end up in a worse position. You've got the capability—now it's time to act on it."

Suhani nodded slowly, starting to absorb his point. "I guess I just need to trust that I've thought everything through."

"Exactly," Amit said. "You've done the work, and you've made the right calls. Now, start building on those small wins. Each time you make a decision that pays off, that's a win. And with every win, your confidence will grow."

Suhani smiled, her posture relaxing. "Thanks, Amit. I'll work on being more decisive. You're right—I've done the homework, and I need to trust that."

After spending time with each team member during the appraisal sessions, Amit felt a renewed sense of optimism. His team was talented, capable, and hardworking, but they had been held back by their own self-doubt. Through these conversations, Amit had begun the process of helping them recognize their own strengths and trust in their abilities. He emphasized the importance of focusing on small successes—each win, no matter how small, would build their confidence and strengthen their self-belief.

The tooling investment decision was fast approaching, and Amit needed his team to be fully behind him, confident in their abilities and decisions. He could see the shift happening already small but noticeable changes in the way his team members approached their work. They were beginning to trust themselves more, and that, more than anything, would be the key to their success.

Part 3: Confidence Grows – Moving Toward the Tooling

Investment Decision

The atmosphere in the conference room was markedly different from just a few weeks ago. As the team gathered for their final review meeting before the tooling investment decision, there was a palpable shift in energy. The team, once hesitant and cautious, now sat with a sense of purpose and quiet confidence. Amit's work during the mid-year appraisal sessions had clearly paid off—his team members had started believing in their capabilities, and it showed in their interactions, decision-making, and overall approach to the project.

Amit sat at the head of the table, watching as his team settled in. This meeting was critical—it was the last review before the official decision to invest over `100 crore in tooling, a make-or-break move for Volt Motors' Electric Auto project. But now, instead of seeing hesitation or second-guessing, Amit saw a group of professionals who were not only ready but eager to move forward.

As the meeting began, Mathew brought up the project tracking report on the large screen. Amit had asked for a detailed status update on every critical area—mechanical systems, powertrain, battery and thermal management, BIW integration, and interior design—to ensure they were in the best possible position to finalize the tooling investment.

Amit glanced around the room. His core team was present— Vivek, Pooja, Suhani, Kiran, and Pranav—each prepared to give a final report on their respective areas. But this wasn't just another review meeting. Amit had spent weeks building their confidence, helping them take ownership of their decisions, and now it was time to see that confidence in action.

He leaned forward, his voice calm but firm. "Alright, everyone. This is it. We're at the point where we need to lock in the tooling investment decision. Today, we'll go through each component and make sure we're ready to move forward. I want to hear where we stand, what progress we've made, and if there are any last-minute concerns."

Amit looked at Vivek first. "Vivek, let's start with the powertrain.

How's the recalibration holding up after the last round of tests?"

Vivek, who had been notably more decisive in recent weeks, nodded confidently. "We've completed the final round of gear ratio tests for the final drive, and I'm happy to report that the torque output is consistent across all speed ranges now. We ran additional stress tests at both low and high speeds, and the vehicle is performing exactly as expected. No further adjustments are needed."

Amit nodded, satisfied. "Good. That's a major hurdle cleared.

Anything else we need to monitor?"

Vivek shook his head. "We're ready. I've already briefed the team on what needs to be done during the beta phase, but from a powertrain perspective, we're locked in."

Amit gave Vivek a small smile, recognizing the confidence behind his words. "Excellent work, Vivek. Let's keep that momentum going into the next phase."

Next, Amit turned to Pooja. "Pooja, where do we stand with the BIW integration and the interior materials?"

Pooja had grown more assertive in her role since their one-on-one discussions, and her confidence was evident as she spoke. "We've completed all the jig fixture adjustments, and the front and rear panels are now perfectly aligned with the chassis. We've also run multiple stress tests on the door panels to ensure they close smoothly and maintain their structural integrity. The aerodynamics have improved significantly, and we've confirmed there are no alignment issues."

Amit raised an eyebrow. "And the interior materials? Are we satisfied with their performance?"

Pooja nodded; her voice steady. "Yes. We finalized the material testing last week, and the new options we've chosen are performing well under heat stress and extended use. We had to make a slight cost adjustment, but everything is within budget, and the materials will hold up long-term."

Amit leaned back slightly, clearly impressed. "Good to hear. We're going to rely on those improvements to make a strong impression during beta testing. Excellent work, Pooja."

He then turned to Suhani. "Suhani, we've talked a lot about the financial implications of the tooling investment. Where do we stand?"

Suhani, who had previously been hesitant to make aggressive financial decisions, now spoke with calm assurance. "Amit, I've reviewed the budget projections based on the final material costs and tooling estimates. We're on track to manage the `100 crore investment without overshooting. I've also built-in contingencies in case any unexpected expenses come up during the beta phase. We're in a strong position to make the investment now."

Amit nodded, pleased with her confidence. "You're sure there won't be any issues with cash flow once we make the investment?"

Suhani smiled slightly. "Positive. We've allocated the necessary funds, and with the contingencies in place, we have enough buffer to handle any surprises."

Amit gave her a nod of approval. "Great. That's exactly what we need."

Finally, Amit turned to Pranav. "Pranav, how's the OTA update and sensor integration going? Are we fully synced?"

Pranav, who had always been diligent but sometimes overly cautious, now spoke with newfound confidence. "The OTA patch has been fully tested and rolled out. We've resolved the sensor miscommunication issues, and the vehicle control unit is now responding perfectly to real-time inputs. We've run multiple simulations, and everything is functioning as it should. We're ready to move forward."

Amit took a moment to absorb everything. Each team member had delivered their updates with confidence, and the results were clear: they were ready. The technical issues had been addressed, the financial risks managed, and the vehicle was performing well in all critical areas.

Amit leaned forward; his tone serious but encouraging. "This is the moment we've been working toward. We've overcome a lot of challenges, and we've closed the knowing-doing gap. Now it's time to take the next step. We're ready to move forward with the tooling investment."

He glanced around the table, making eye contact with each team member. "I want everyone to be clear—this decision isn't just about the money. It's about us backing the work we've done so far and believing in our ability to execute during the beta phase. We've put in the work, we've solved the problems, and now it's time to take full ownership."

The team nodded, fully aligned and ready to move forward.

Suhani raised her hand slightly, a smile on her face. "So, Amit,

I assume you're asking for a final vote of confidence?"

Amit chuckled. "I am. So, do I have everyone's buy-in to proceed with the tooling investment?"

Around the room, one by one, the team members voiced their agreement.

Vivek nodded. "We're ready. Let's do it." Pooja smiled. "Absolutely. We've got this."

Suhani added confidently. "The finances are in order. We're good to go."

Pranav raised his hand in agreement. "Software is ready. Let's move forward."

Amit leaned back, satisfaction washing over him. His team—once hesitant and plagued by self-doubt—had grown into a confident, capable unit, ready to take on the next phase of the project. He had worked hard to build their confidence, and now they were not only willing but eager to take ownership of their decisions.

"Alright, then," Amit said, smiling. "Let's make it official. We move forward with the tooling investment. This is a huge step for us, but I know we're ready."

The team left the room with a sense of accomplishment, their confidence growing with every decision they made. The Electric Auto project was about to enter its most critical phase, and Amit knew they had the talent, the plan, and now the belief to see it through to success.

As the door closed behind the last team member, Amit sat back in his chair, feeling a deep sense of pride. His team had come a long way—not just in technical capability, but in their belief in themselves. The tooling investment was only the beginning. With the team's confidence solidified, there was no limit to what they could achieve.

Key Learnings from Chapter 10: Guys Have Tremendous Capability but Low Self-Belief

1. **Self-Belief is Crucial for Success:** A team can have all the technical capability in the world, but without self-belief, they will hesitate and second-guess themselves, which can slow down progress. Developing confidence is as important as developing skills.
2. **Mentorship Builds Confidence:** Amit's approach as a mentor and coach helped his team members recognize their strengths and build confidence. Providing constructive feedback in a supportive way allows people to overcome self-doubt.

3. **Small Successes Lead to Greater Confidence:** By focusing on small wins, Amit helped his team build momentum. Small successes reinforce the idea that they can handle larger challenges, boosting overall confidence in their abilities.

4. **Homework and Preparation Lead to Confidence:** Amit emphasized that confidence isn't just about natural ability—it comes from doing the homework, thinking through decisions, and preparing thoroughly. Once the team did this consistently, their confidence grew.

5. **Ownership of Decisions is Key:** Taking ownership of decisions helps build self-belief. When team members are empowered to own their ideas and actions, they become more committed and confident in their roles.

6. **Confidence is Contagious:** As Amit's team members started to believe in themselves, their confidence spread throughout the team. Once key individuals showed more self-assurance, others followed, creating a positive, motivating atmosphere.

7. **Coach-Manager Approach is Effective:** Amit's blend of being both a manager and a coach—giving technical direction while offering emotional support—helped his team overcome internal barriers, allowing them to make bolder decisions.

8. **Clear Communication Builds Trust:** By engaging in open conversations about doubts and fears, Amit built trust with his team. This allowed them to feel safe in discussing their weaknesses and led to more authentic engagement and growth.

9. **Confidence Supports Critical Decisions:** The decision to move forward with the `100 crore tooling investment was a significant one, but it was made possible by the growing confidence of the team. They believed in their own execution plan, which made them more willing to commit to high-stakes decisions.

10. **Progress is the Result of a Confident Team:** Once the team overcame their self-doubt and built confidence, they began delivering results faster, with more accuracy, and moved forward with conviction.

The key takeaway from Chapter 10 is the critical role that self- belief plays in driving both individual and team success. While technical skills and knowledge are important, it is the confidence to act on that knowledge that truly enables progress. Through Amit's mentorship, his team overcame their self-doubt by focusing on small wins, doing the necessary preparation and taking full ownership of their decisions. This approach not only empowered them to trust their abilities but also fostered a culture of confidence and accountability.

As their self-assurance grew, so did their ability to make critical decisions, culminating in the team's unanimous commitment to the high-stakes tooling investment. The chapter illustrates that a capable, confident team can move forward decisively, delivering results and pushing a project toward success.

Chapter 11

All Successes Are Yours, All Failures Are Mine

Introduction: The Final Testing Phase

The Electric Auto project had reached a pivotal point. After months of development, revisions, and countless hours of testing, the beta phase had begun. The tooled parts had arrived, and the first batch of beta vehicles was now undergoing rigorous testing. This phase would determine the fate of the entire project—whether Volt Motors could move forward with full-scale production or face further delays and potential setbacks. It was a make-or-break moment for the team.

Amit Gupta, having led the project from the start, understood the weight of the situation. The performance of the beta vehicles would either confirm that months of hard work had paid off or reveal flaws that could derail the entire launch schedule. The success of the Electric Auto was crucial not only for Volt Motors' future but also for Amit's career.

Standing alongside Nisha Mehta, the company's CEO, Amit watched closely as the vehicles were tested in real-world conditions— high-speed runs, thermal stress, and battery performance under load. This was the ultimate test of the engineering, design, and management decisions that had been made along the way.

But as Amit observed the data streaming in, his thoughts weren't just on the technical results. He knew that his leadership was also being tested. Over the past few months, Amit had worked hard to instill a culture of ownership and accountability in his team. He had adopted a leadership philosophy that he believed in deeply: all successes belong to the team, and all failures are his to bear. This wasn't just a management style—it was a reflection of how he saw leadership.

As the beta tests progressed, Amit's resolve was clear. He would support his team through any obstacles they faced, taking responsibility for every setback and empowering them to claim their successes. This was more than just a test of the Electric Auto—it was a test of Amit's leadership.

Part 1: Amit's Leadership Philosophy

The beta vehicles had been through several rounds of testing, and now it was time for the most critical discussion—the review of the test results. The room was filled with anticipation as Amit gathered his core team to go over the data that would determine the Electric Auto's readiness for full-scale production. Vivek, Pooja, Suhani, Pranav and Kiran sat around the table, their eyes on the large screen displaying the results.

As the beta phase progressed, the data had been streaming in—performance under stress, battery endurance, thermal management, powertrain stability, body integrity, and software integration. This was where everything would come together or fall apart. Each part of the vehicle had been pushed to its limits, and the results were now in front of them for analysis.

Amit stood at the front of the room, laser focused. He knew his team had worked tirelessly to get the Electric Auto to this point, but now, the pressure was on. The tooling investment decision hung in the balance, and the results of these tests would dictate whether they could move forward with production.

"Let's go through the key metrics one by one," Amit began, his voice calm but authoritative. "I want to hear your thoughts on each area. If there are any concerns, let's address them now."

Vivek took the first step. He had been closely monitoring the powertrain and torque output. "The powertrain performed well overall, but I'm seeing some variance in torque distribution during sustained high speeds. It's minor, but enough to affect efficiency. We're getting less torque above 60 km/h than we initially projected."

Amit nodded; his expression serious but not alarmed. "Let's dig into that. Vivek, do you think this is something that requires an adjustment to the gear ratios again, or are we looking at a software calibration issue?"

Vivek paused, pulling up more data on his tablet. "I'm leaning toward a software recalibration. The gear ratios are optimized for urban speeds, but at higher speeds, we're seeing some loss of torque that could be fixed through the control software. I don't think we need to retool any mechanical components at this point."

Amit took a moment to absorb the information, then nodded. "Good call. Let's prioritize that software patch. Torque performance is critical, but if we can handle this through software, we avoid delays in production. Vivek, get your team on this immediately."

Vivek looked relieved. "We'll have a patch ready within 48 hours.

That should stabilize torque distribution across all speed ranges."

Amit moved on to Pooja. "Pooja, how are we looking on the BIW and panel alignments?"

Pooja, who had overseen the BIW integration and the interior materials testing, looked up from her notes. "The panel alignments are holding up well. We've eliminated all the earlier issues with the door fittings, and the aerodynamic integrity is intact. However, I did notice a slight increase in wind noise during highway tests."

Amit raised an eyebrow. "Is it significant enough to affect the user experience?"

Pooja shook her head. "It's noticeable but not critical. The noise increase is within acceptable limits for most vehicles in this class, but we can work on reducing it in the next batch of beta vehicles by adjusting the seal structure around the doors."

Amit thought for a moment before responding. "Let's not ignore that. Even if it's within acceptable limits, we want to exceed expectations wherever we can. Make those adjustments to the seals, and let's see if we can bring that noise level down."

Pooja nodded, grateful for Amit's attention to detail. "Understood. I'll coordinate with the materials team to get that done before the next round of testing."

Next, Amit turned to Pranav, "Pranav, I'm seeing a couple of error codes from the VCU (Vehicle Control Unit) during sustained testing. What's going on there?"

Pranav, always meticulous with his data, pulled up the report. "The error codes are coming from the BMS. During prolonged high-speed runs, there's a slight miscommunication between the BMS and the VCU. It's not causing a major failure, but the system is flagging it as a potential risk."

Amit frowned slightly, understanding the potential impact. "Is this a hardware issue or a software glitch?"

Pranav took a breath before answering. "I believe it's a software issue. The communication protocol between the BMS and the VCU needs fine-tuning. We're not seeing this issue at lower speeds, but once the vehicle hits highway conditions, the communication lag triggers the error codes."

Amit nodded, deep in thought. "Let's address that immediately. We can't afford any miscommunication between the BMS and VCU, especially at high speeds. Safety and reliability are our top priorities. Get your team on it, and I want this fixed before we move to the next phase."

Pranav looked determined. "We'll handle it. I'll have the fix ready in time for the next test cycle."

As the discussion continued, Suhani spoke up, her role as the finance lead always keeping an eye on the budget. "Amit, I've been reviewing the impact of these adjustments on our cost projections. The software patches and material adjustments shouldn't add much to our overall cost, but we're cutting it close. The tooling investment is significant, and any further delays could push us over budget."

Amit nodded, appreciating Suhani's vigilance. "Understood. We'll move quickly on these fixes to avoid any delays. Suhani, keep tracking the costs, but I'm confident we can stay within the budget if we act swiftly."

Suhani gave a slight nod. "I'll keep a close watch. But I agree—we need to move fast and stay focused."

Amit turned to the whole team; his voice steady but filled with conviction. "Look, I know there are still some concerns, but I believe we're on track. These issues are manageable, and we have the talent in this room to solve them. I need each of you to stay focused and trust in your ability to execute. We've come too far to let minor setbacks shake us."

Pooja spoke up, her tone slightly hesitant. "Amit, are we cutting it too close with these final fixes? I mean, what if something else pops up?"

Amit looked at her directly, his expression calm but confident. "Pooja, we've faced setbacks before, and we've overcome them. This isn't any different. I know it feels like the pressure is mounting, but we've built something solid here. Every time an issue has come up, we've handled it. And we'll handle this too. I believe in the work you've done and the team we've built. Trust me when I say we're going to make it."

There was a moment of silence as the team absorbed Amit's words. Slowly, nods of agreement spread around the room.

"Let's not forget," Amit continued, "we're not just here to pass tests—we're here to build a product that will set a new standard. We're nearly there. The tooling investment is within reach, and once we clear this phase, there's no turning back. So, let's put these last issues to bed and move forward with confidence."

Vivek, always practical but cautious, nodded. "We're with you, Amit. We've made it this far, and I believe we can get these final issues resolved quickly."

Pooja, now more assured, added, "You're right. We can't let small doubts hold us back. I'll get the noise issue resolved."

Pranav added confidently, "Same here. We'll take care of the communication glitch with the BMS and VCU. We've got this."

Suhani, always the financial realist, smiled slightly. "As long as we stick to the timeline, we'll be fine. Let's move fast and keep pushing."

Amit smiled, feeling a sense of pride wash over him. His team was stepping up, ready to face the final hurdles with confidence and determination. The Electric Auto was nearly there, and Amit knew that with this group behind him, they would succeed.

"Alright," Amit said, his voice filled with confidence. "Let's get to work. We've got a few final fixes to make, but I believe in each of you. We're going to make it."

The team dispersed, energized and ready to tackle the final challenges. As they left the room, Amit stood for a moment, reflecting on how far they had come. All successes belong to the team, he reminded himself. All failures are mine to carry. It was a philosophy that had guided him through the project, and it was paying off. His team was stronger than ever, ready to move forward with full confidence in their abilities.

Part 2: Taking Responsibility

The Electric Auto project had been progressing well through the beta phase, but just as the team prepared to shift gears toward full-scale production, an unexpected issue hit—one that could delay the entire project by a month. The tooled BIW parts, crucial to the vehicle's structure, arrived with significant alignment flaws. Issues with the door hinges, front, and rear panels meant that retooling would be necessary, a process that could potentially delay production by several weeks.

This setback was serious, especially given the competitive pressure Volt Motors faced in the market. Amit knew that this delay would affect the project timeline and, possibly, the launch window.

But he also knew that the situation needed to be addressed with clarity, responsibility, and action. Before speaking to Nisha Mehta, the CEO, Amit called for a series of critical review meetings with the Vendor Development, Sourcing, Operations, and Quality Systems teams to ensure that every aspect of the supply chain and production readiness was addressed.

Vendor and Sourcing Review

Amit started his review with Rajesh, head of Vendor Development, and Meera, who led Sourcing. The key issue at hand was ensuring that the suppliers were ready to meet production demands, especially in light of the BIW retooling problem. They needed to know if their battery module supplier, BIW vendor, and other critical components would still be able to deliver within revised timelines.

"Rajesh, let's start with the BIW supplier," Amit began, as the team gathered around the table, reports and charts spread before them. "We've identified the issues with the door hinges and panel misalignment. How quickly can we get this retooled?"

Rajesh, looking over his notes, was visibly tense. "Amit, I've been in contact with the BIW vendor. The retooling will take at least three to four weeks, may be five if there are complications. They've assured me that they'll expedite the process, but realistically, we're looking at a month's delay."

Amit's expression remained calm, though the news was troubling. "And what's the root cause? Why did these alignment issues only come up now?"

Rajesh shifted in his seat. "The prototype parts we used in the alpha phase were manually adjusted, which hid some of the minor alignment issues that didn't show up until we scaled up tooling for mass production. The tooled dies weren't calibrated perfectly, and the material flex during assembly wasn't accounted for. That's what led to the misalignment."

Meera, who had been quiet until now, spoke up. "We're already working with the BIW vendor to correct the dies, and I'm exploring secondary suppliers for critical components like the battery management systems and electronics to ensure that we don't face further delays from any other vendors."

Amit nodded, processing the information. "Good. But I want us to be aggressive on this. Meera, push the BIW vendor for daily updates. I don't want any further slippage on this timeline. Rajesh, make sure the tooling corrections are precise this time. We can't afford another batch of flawed parts once we retool."

Both Rajesh and Meera nodded in agreement.

Meera added, "I've also been in touch with our battery supplier. They're dealing with delays from their own subcontractor in China, which is affecting our BMS delivery. I'm preparing a backup supplier, but we might need to split the order to keep production moving."

Amit's tone grew firmer. "Let's not wait on this. Start the onboarding of the backup supplier immediately. I don't want to be caught off guard if the primary supplier slips further. Make sure the quality checks are in place for both suppliers. We can't afford any more issues."

Operations and Quality Systems Review

With the vendor and sourcing issues addressed, Amit turned his attention to the Operations and Quality Systems teams. He needed to ensure that, aside from the BIW setback, the production line was ready to go as soon as the corrected parts arrived.

"Asif," Amit said, turning to the head of operations, "where do we stand with the production line setup? Are we ready to handle the transition from beta to full-scale production once the parts are here?"

Asif, known for his attention to detail, was quick to respond. "We're nearly there, Amit. The assembly stations are fully equipped, and the chassis integration and battery installation processes are solid. But we're still finalizing the calibration for the body electronics. The issue we're facing is the communication between the VCU and the BMS, especially during assembly."

Amit raised an eyebrow. "Is this a software problem or a hardware alignment issue?"

Asif checked his notes before responding. "Mostly software. Pranav's team is working on fine-tuning the communication protocol between the systems, but it shouldn't hold us up much longer. We'll have it resolved before we get the new BIW parts."

Amit nodded, satisfied for the moment. "Good. I want to make sure we're not facing any further integration issues when the corrected parts arrive."

He then turned to Jennifer, the head of Quality Assurance (QA) "Jennifer, what's our status on quality assurance? Can we catch these types of alignment issues in the future before they cause delays?"

Jennifer, always composed and direct, spoke clearly. "We've already enhanced the inspection protocols for incoming parts, particularly for critical components like the BIW, battery modules, and powertrain systems. Our new three-stage inspection process—covering incoming parts, mid-line checks, and final assembly—should catch any significant defects early. The main issue we faced with the BIW parts was that the tools themselves were out of spec, which wasn't something we caught early enough. We'll adjust our tolerance levels to ensure this doesn't happen again."

Amit considered this, then said, "I need these systems fully calibrated before we start full production. No more surprises."

Jennifer nodded. "We're running mock tests on the inspection system now. It'll be ready."

The Conversation with Nisha

After the intense series of reviews, Amit knew he couldn't delay the conversation with Nisha Mehta any longer. The BIW delay was serious, and she needed to be informed before it impacted the broader business timeline. Taking a deep breath, Amit entered Nisha's office, ready to explain the situation.

Nisha glanced up from her desk, immediately sensing the weight of what Amit was about to say. "Amit, what's going on? You don't look like you're here to deliver good news."

Amit sat down, his tone calm but serious. "Nisha, we've encountered a problem with the tooled BIW parts. The alignment on the door hinges and front and rear panels is off. It's bad enough that we'll need to retool the dies, which could set us back by a month."

Nisha's expression tightened, but she didn't speak right away. She let the silence hang for a moment before finally responding. "A month? That's a significant delay. How did this happen?"

Amit didn't flinch. He had prepared himself for this question. "The prototype parts were hand-fitted, which masked some of the alignment issues that didn't show up until we moved to full- scale tooling. The dies were slightly out of spec, which caused the misalignment. I should have anticipated this and put more checks in place during the initial tooling process."

Nisha frowned, leaning back in her chair. "Amit, this is a serious setback. We were aiming for production in a few weeks, and now we're looking at a month's delay. How are we going to recover from this?"

Amit remained composed. "We're already working with the BIW vendor to retool the dies. I've also initiated backup plans with the battery supplier to ensure no further delays in other critical areas. We're pushing the vendors hard, and the team is working around the clock to minimize the impact. I'll personally oversee the progress and make sure we catch up where we can."

Nisha considered his words, her expression softening slightly. "I appreciate your taking responsibility for this, Amit. But a month's delay could put us in a difficult position with the board. You'll need to be prepared to answer some tough questions."

"I understand," Amit replied, his tone resolute. "This is on me. I'll take full responsibility for the delay, but I'm confident we can recover from this. I'll ensure we're ready for production as soon as the corrected parts arrive."

Nisha gave him a long look before nodding. "Alright, Amit. I trust you to manage this. Keep me updated daily on the progress, and make sure there are no further setbacks. We can't afford to lose any more time."

Amit stood, feeling the weight of her trust and the burden of responsibility. "I'll keep you in the loop, Nisha. We'll get this done."

As he left her office, Amit knew the road ahead would be tough, but his team had rallied around him before, and he was confident they would do it again. The BIW delay was a challenge, but with the right focus and leadership, they would overcome it.

Part 3: Shared Success

The journey to this point had been anything but smooth. The Electric Auto project had faced its share of challenges, from supplier delays to critical alignment flaws in the tooled BIW parts. Yet, despite all the setbacks, Amit's leadership and the collective efforts of his team had carried them through the tense moments of the beta testing phase. Now, with the final test results in, the Electric Auto had passed the necessary checks, and they were officially cleared for production. The team had made it.

The test track reports, which had been a cause of anxiety for weeks, now displayed positive results. The issues with the BMS communication were resolved, the torque distribution had been stabilized through software patches, and the BIW alignment issues had been corrected. There were no more technical roadblocks. The Electric Auto was now ready to go into full-scale production.

In the conference room, the core team—Vivek, Pooja, Suhani, Pranav and Kiran—sat around the table. The tension in the room that had once been palpable had now turned into a quiet, collective sigh of relief. Everyone knew what this moment meant.

Amit stood at the front, his posture calm but purposeful. He had called this meeting not just to go over the final details, but to discuss the next phase—production. Now that they had cleared the beta stage, they needed to ramp up quickly to meet the initial batch of launch vehicles that would fulfill the company's first orders. The stakes remained high, but today was a moment to acknowledge what they had accomplished.

"We've done it," Amit began, looking at each team member in turn. "The Electric Auto has passed all critical tests. We've cleared the last major hurdle, and now we move to full-scale production. Before we get into the logistics of production, I want to take a moment to say something."

The room fell silent, and the team looked at Amit expectantly.

"This success is yours," Amit said, his voice steady but full of emotion. "Each one of you has worked tirelessly to get us to this point. We faced delays, setbacks, and moments where things looked uncertain, but you kept pushing forward. The solutions you found, the problems you fixed—that's what got us here."

Amit paused, letting the words sink in. "I want you all to know that I take full responsibility for every challenge we faced. But every success belongs to you. I'm proud of this team, and I'm honoured to have worked alongside all of you."

The team exchanged glances, visibly moved by Amit's words. This was more than just a professional acknowledgment—it was a recognition of the personal sacrifices, late nights, and intense problem-solving that had gone into making the Electric Auto a reality.

Pooja smiled at Amit. "We couldn't have done it without your leadership, Amit. You kept us steady through all the ups and downs."

Vivek nodded in agreement. "There were moments when I thought we wouldn't make it, but you always found a way to keep us focused and moving forward."

Amit smiled back. "I may have kept us moving, but it was your work that kept us on track. And now we have a new challenge ahead— production."

Discussion on Production and Launch Vehicles

Amit turned to the production schedule displayed on the screen. "Now that we've cleared the beta phase, we need to move quickly. The initial batch of launch vehicles needs to be ready to fulfill our first orders. We're already delayed by a month due to the BIW retooling, and we need to find ways to make up for lost time."

Asif, jumped in. "We've streamlined the assembly process for the tooled parts, especially after the alignment corrections. The production line is ready, but the delay means we'll have to push harder to meet the initial order volume. We can cover some of the time, but not all of it."

Amit nodded. "I understand. We'll need to be strategic about how we allocate resources. Suhani, where do we stand financially? Can we afford to scale up overtime to speed up production?"

Suhani, always on top of the numbers, replied confidently. "We can manage the extra costs for overtime and expedited logistics for the first batch, but we'll need to closely monitor our budget for the second round of production. If we catch up on the first orders, we'll stabilize financially."

"That's what we'll aim for," Amit said, turning to Pranav. "How's the software integration? Can we ensure smooth OTA updates for the vehicles in the field while keeping the production software stable?"

Pranav gave a firm nod. "We're ready. The VCU and BMS software are stable, and we'll have the OTA system fully operational. We've run multiple test cycles, and everything's syncing up well. No major issues on that front."

With each department head confident in their respective areas, Amit then shifted his focus to Nisha Mehta, the CEO, who had been monitoring the project closely. Amit knew they needed to align with the sales team to prepare for the market launch.

That afternoon, Amit had a detailed discussion with Nisha and Rahul. Nisha had been following the project's developments closely and understood the pressure they were under, especially with the month-long delay. "Amit," Nisha said, as the meeting began, "now that we're cleared for production, we need to prepare for the launch. Rahul, what's our plan for the first orders?"

Rahul pulled up his sales projections. "We've got commitments from several key markets for the first batch of Electric Autos. But the delay in production means we're going to be under pressure to meet those deadlines. Customers are expecting delivery within the next two months."

Amit nodded. "We're aware of the timeline. We'll be pushing the production schedule hard to meet it. The team has already identified areas where we can make up time."

Nisha looked at both men. "This launch is critical for Volt Motors. We're entering a competitive market, and the Electric Auto needs to make a strong first impression. Amit, I trust you and your team to get the production on track."

Amit, with full confidence in his team, replied, "We're ready. We'll meet the launch targets and make sure the product hits the market without further delays."

Celebration of the Milestone

Later that evening, Amit gathered his team for a small celebration. The office, which had been a place of intense work and late nights, now had a lighter atmosphere. They had crossed the most important milestone in the project, and it was time to acknowledge the hard work that had gotten them here.

Amit raised a glass, addressing his team one more time. "Today, we celebrate not just the fact that we've cleared beta testing, but the journey we've all been on together. You've put in the work, the effort, and the dedication to bring this product to life. And now, we're on the verge of launching it to the world."

The team clinked glasses, smiles and laughter replacing the tension that had filled the office for weeks.

"You've all earned this success," Amit continued, looking around at the group. "I couldn't be more proud to be part of this team. The Electric Auto is just the beginning, and I know we're going to accomplish even greater things together."

The team exchanged smiles, clearly feeling a deep sense of pride and ownership over the project. This wasn't just a win for the company—it was a personal victory for each person who had poured their heart and soul into the project.

As the night went on, Amit stood back for a moment, watching his team celebrate. This was their success, and they deserved every bit of recognition. But in his mind, he knew there were more challenges ahead. The launch phase, production, and meeting customer expectations were all looming. Still, for now, they had earned the right to celebrate a job well done.

The road to success had been paved with challenges, but today, it was clear—they had overcome them.

Key learnings from Chapter 11, "All Successes Are Yours, All Failures Are Mine":

1. **Leadership Through Accountability:** Amit adopts a leadership philosophy where he takes full responsibility for the team's failures while giving them credit for their successes. This builds trust, motivates the team, and fosters a sense of ownership.

2. **Critical Importance of Team Communication:** Throughout the beta testing phase, each department provides critical input on the Electric Auto's performance. Open communication between team members ensures that potential issues are addressed promptly, leading to effective problem-solving.

3. **Addressing Challenges Head-On:** Amit's team encounters issues with powertrain torque, BIW alignment, and battery management system communication. Instead of avoiding the problems, Amit encourages a collaborative approach to addressing each challenge with specific solutions.

4. **Vendor and Supply Chain Management:** The chapter highlights the role of vendor readiness and supply chain reliability in ensuring timely production. Delays in parts or alignment flaws can derail project timelines, necessitating agile management and backup planning with alternative suppliers.

5. **Responsibility in Managing Delays:** When the BIW parts arrive with flaws, Amit does not shy away from owning the delay. He actively reviews vendor processes and discusses corrective actions while also keeping the company leadership informed, demonstrating mature handling of setbacks.

6. **Handling Pressure with Focus:** Amit's calm and collected manner under pressure sets an example for his team. He instills confidence by prioritizing issues, such as software patches for the powertrain and communication between the BMS and VCU, to minimize delays.

7. **Continuous Improvement and Quality Control:** The team implements enhanced quality assurance protocols to catch alignment issues early in production. This proactive approach highlights the importance of continuously improving processes and learning from past mistakes.

8. **Team Morale and Recognition:** Amit's leadership emphasizes recognizing the team's hard work and sacrifices. His gratitude towards the team's collective effort, and his willingness to share the success, boosts morale and drives further commitment from the group.

9. **Balancing Financial Considerations with Performance:** Suhani's constant vigilance over the project's budget serves as a reminder of the financial realities that accompany large-scale projects. Managing costs while ensuring performance is a key learning, especially when dealing with unexpected delays.

10. **Celebrate Milestones to Sustain Momentum:** After passing the beta testing phase, the team celebrated their success, marking a critical point in their journey. Recognizing and celebrating such moments helps sustain energy and focus for future challenges.

These learnings demonstrate how leadership, accountability, and teamwork are crucial in navigating technical, operational, and financial challenges in large-scale projects like the development of the Electric Auto.

Chapter 12

If the Organization Could Speak, It Would Express True Emotions

Part 1: Organizational Strain

Amit sat in his office, the soft hum of the Electric Auto development floor outside his door. The project had finally passed its beta phase and was heading into production, but Amit knew that the journey had taken a toll. If the organization itself could speak, Amit thought, it would be carrying an emotional burden of its own—a voice weighed down by the exhaustion and frustration that had slowly accumulated over the past few months. The delay in the project, the pressure of the launch, the strain on resources—everything had pushed the team and the company to its limits.

Volt Motors had been built on ambition and drive, with a mission to disrupt the EV industry with cutting-edge products. But the relentless pace, the technical challenges, and the unexpected delays had left their mark. There was a visible fatigue among the employees. It wasn't just the engineers who felt it, but also the supply chain, quality assurance, and sales teams. Each delay in production and each extra hour spent troubleshooting or recalibrating added to the tension that simmered beneath the surface.

Amit often wondered what it would sound like if Volt Motors could express its true emotions. Would it voice its frustration with the constant delays? Would it acknowledge the investment risks and the financial strain that had come with fixing the tooling and BIW issues? More than that, would it speak to the fatigue of its people, who had been working late nights and weekends, pushing through mental and physical exhaustion to keep the project on track?

In his meetings with different departments, Amit could see the signs of wear—people were growing short-tempered, mistakes were creeping into the workflow, and there was a collective sense that they were running on fumes. Even though the project was moving forward, the human cost was becoming more apparent. People were starting to feel stretched too thin, and Amit knew that if he didn't address this soon, it could affect not just the launch, but the long-term health of the organization.

It was time to step back and take a hard look at the company's culture. Amit had always believed that for a product to succeed, the organization that created it needed to be healthy—both operationally and emotionally. But right now, Volt Motors was showing signs of strain, and if they didn't take action soon, the cracks in the foundation could widen.

Part 2: Leadership Reflection

Later that evening, Amit sat down for a private conversation with Nisha Mehta in her office. Nisha had been keeping a close eye on the project's progress, but like Amit, she was aware of the growing emotional strain within the company. As the CEO, she was not only focused on the technical and financial success of the Electric Auto but also the well-being of the people who were driving it forward.

"Amit, I've been thinking," Nisha began, her tone reflective. "We've come a long way, but it feels like the team is burning out. I'm sensing a lot of frustration in the office. People are tired, emotionally drained. We've been pushing them hard for months now, and I'm worried about the toll it's taking."

Amit nodded, relieved that Nisha had noticed the same things he had. "I've been feeling that too. If the organization itself could speak, I think it would tell us it's reaching its breaking point. Everyone's doing their best, but the delays, the setbacks—it's worn them down. And if we don't address this, it's going to hurt us in the long run."

Nisha leaned back, thoughtful. "What do you think we should do? We're under pressure to deliver, but we can't afford to have our people collapse under the weight of it all."

Amit paused for a moment, gathering his thoughts. "I think we need to take a step back and look at the bigger picture. Product, people, process, and technology—they're all interconnected. We've been so focused on getting the Electric Auto into production that we've neglected the emotional health of the team. We need to make sure that we're not just building a product, but also a sustainable organization."

Nisha looked intrigued. "Go on."

Amit continued, "Right now, the team feels like they're running on empty. If we don't rebuild morale, we're going to see more mistakes, more burnout, and ultimately, lower performance. We need to improve communication, recognize the hard work that's already been done, and give people a reason to feel connected to the bigger mission. It's not just about meeting deadlines—it's about creating a company culture that values the people behind the product."

Nisha nodded, seeing the importance of Amit's words. "You're right. But how do we turn things around? How do we give people that sense of purpose again?"

Amit thought for a moment before responding. "We need to be more transparent with the team. People need to understand why certain decisions are being made, and they need to feel that their work is valued. We should bring the leadership closer to the employees—let them see that we're in this together. Small gestures, like acknowledging individual contributions or giving people more time to recover from intense periods, will go a long way."

He paused and then added, "But more than that, we need to listen. If people are feeling overwhelmed or frustrated, they should be able to express that without fear of judgment. An organization that listens to its people is one that can adapt and grow."

Nisha was silent for a moment, then she smiled. "I knew I could count on you to bring this up, Amit. You've always had a strong sense of how to lead, not just from a technical perspective, but also from an emotional one. I agree—we need to focus on the well-being of the organization as a whole. I'll work with HR and the department heads to start implementing these changes."

Amit smiled back, feeling a sense of relief. "Thanks, Nisha. I think this will make a big difference, not just for the Electric Auto launch, but for the company's future."

Part 3: Turning a Corner

Amit and Nisha had spent weeks reflecting on the emotional and physical strain that had taken a toll on Volt Motors' employees throughout the Electric Auto project. The pressure to deliver, the unexpected delays, and the relentless pace had left many team members feeling exhausted and stretched thin. Now that the Electric Auto was moving toward full-scale production, they knew it was time to address the organizational fatigue before operations hit full swing. They needed a plan, and that required the expertise of Neha Joshi, the company's HR Head, who had a deep understanding of workplace dynamics and culture building.

Amit and Nisha sat down with Neha in a quiet meeting room, the hum of the busy office just outside the door. Neha, with her years of experience in managing people and organizational development, knew that the company's emotional health was just as important as its financial and operational performance. Together, they were about to map out a comprehensive plan that would focus on employee well- being, motivation, and creating a more supportive organizational culture.

Nisha began, setting the tone for the discussion. "Neha, we've seen how hard the team has been working over the past few months, and while we've passed major milestones with the Electric Auto, it's becoming clear that the organization is feeling the strain. People are tired, and some are reaching their breaking points. We can't ignore this anymore—especially with operations going into full swing post- launch."

Neha nodded; her face thoughtful. "You're absolutely right, Nisha. I've seen the signs too—employees coming in early, staying late, the increase in mistakes due to fatigue. If we don't intervene now, this will affect not only productivity but also long-term retention and morale. People need to feel valued beyond just their work output."

Amit, who had been quietly listening, leaned forward. "We need to build a culture that's sustainable. The team has given everything to get this project off the ground, but now we need to give something back. Motivation, well-being, and a sense of purpose—these are the areas we must focus on. If Volt Motors is going to succeed, it can't just be about pushing people to their limits."

Neha agreed and began to outline some ideas. "We have to think holistically about this. It's not just about giving people time off, though that's important. It's about creating an environment where employees feel supported, recognized, and connected to the company's broader mission. There are a few pillars we need to address: communication, recognition, work-life balance, and leadership visibility. These will help lift morale and rebuild trust within the organization."

Culture Building: A Holistic Approach

Nisha nodded, intrigued. "Let's break it down further. What specifically can we do in each of these areas?"

Neha pulled up a document on her tablet, outlining a comprehensive program for improving the company's culture and addressing stress and fatigue.

"First," Neha said, "we need to improve communication across all levels of the organization. Right now, people are feeling disconnected from the leadership. They're not always aware of why certain decisions are made or what's happening at the top. We need to create transparency. Regular town halls, where leadership shares updates and listens to employee concerns, will make a huge difference. If people feel like they're part of the decision-making process, they'll be more engaged."

Amit agreed. "I've noticed that gap too. We've been so focused on delivering the product that we've neglected to communicate openly with the team about the challenges we're facing. We can't expect people to give their best if they don't feel like they're in the loop."

Nisha added, "We also need to make sure that communication is a two-way street. It's not just about us sharing information—it's about listening to what our employees are going through. We need to know what's causing their stress and address those issues directly."

Neha nodded and moved on to the next point. "Second, we need to focus on recognition. People have worked incredibly hard, but many of them feel like their efforts haven't been fully acknowledged. Small wins need to be celebrated, and individual contributions should be recognized publicly. We can implement an employee recognition program, where managers highlight team members who've gone above and beyond. It doesn't have to be complicated—something as simple as a weekly shout-out can make a huge difference."

Amit smiled. "Recognition doesn't just boost morale; it also builds trust. When people feel appreciated, they're more likely to stick around and continue to contribute at a high level."

Work-Life Balance and Leadership Visibility

Neha then addressed one of the most pressing issues—work-life balance. "Third, we have to give people more flexibility. Right now, everyone's been working long hours, and it's not sustainable. We need to encourage people to take breaks, to disconnect after work hours, and to use their vacation days without guilt. We could also look into more flexible working arrangements, especially for those who have been putting in the most overtime. Giving people the space to recharge is essential if we want to avoid burnout."

Amit reflected on this. "It's true. We've been running at full speed, and it's starting to show. But if we don't let people recover, we'll see diminishing returns in the long run. We need to build in recovery time, especially now that we're moving into full-scale production. There's going to be even more pressure once the vehicles start rolling off the line, and if our team isn't at their best, it'll show in the quality of the product."

Nisha agreed. "Amit's right. We need to ensure that employees have the time and resources to maintain a healthy work-life balance. That also means being proactive about mental health support. We should offer counselling services and workshops on stress management."

Neha nodded again, then moved on to the final point. "The fourth pillar is leadership visibility. Right now, people feel like leadership is somewhat distant—like decisions are being made in isolation. We need to be more present in the day-to-day operations. Leadership needs to be on the floor, interacting with employees, and showing that we're all in this together. This kind of visibility makes a big difference, especially when people feel like they're carrying the weight of the project themselves."

Amit leaned in, enthusiastic about this idea. "I completely agree. We can't lead from behind closed doors. I'll start spending more time on the production floor and encourage other leaders to do the same. When employees see that we're right there with them, it builds trust and camaraderie."

Formulating the Comprehensive Plan

By the end of the meeting, Amit, Nisha, and Neha had put together a comprehensive plan to address the strain the organization was feeling and to rebuild morale as Volt Motors transitioned into full-scale production.

The plan included:

- **Regular Town Hall Meetings:** To increase transparency and open up communication between leadership and employees.
- **Employee Recognition Program:** A weekly or monthly program to highlight and reward individual contributions, both big and small.
- **Flexible Working Arrangements:** Offering more flexibility in schedules and encouraging employees to take time off to recover.
- **Mental Health Support:** Introducing counselling services and workshops on stress management to address emotional well-being.
- **Leadership Visibility:** Encouraging leaders to be more present and engaged on the production floor, fostering a sense of shared responsibility and support.

Neha and Amit took the lead in implementing the initiatives. Within weeks, there were noticeable changes in the atmosphere at Volt Motors. The town hall meetings were well-received, with employees feeling more connected to the company's direction. The recognition program boosted morale, as team members saw their contributions being celebrated openly. And with more flexible work arrangements, employees began to feel like they had a better balance between their professional and personal lives.

Amit made it a point to spend time on the production floor, engaging with the engineers, assembly workers, and quality control staff. His presence reassured them that their hard work was seen and valued. The emotional strain that had been building for months began to lift, replaced by a renewed sense of purpose and motivation.

The changes weren't just about making people feel better; they were about creating a healthier, more sustainable organization. Amit felt confident that by addressing the emotional well-being of the team, Volt Motors would be better equipped to handle the demands of full-scale production and beyond. The Electric Auto was just the beginning—now, the company itself was on the path to long-term success.

Key Learnings from Chapter 12: If the Organization Could Speak, It Would Express True Emotions

1. **Organizational Well-Being is Crucial for Success:** The emotional health of the organization is just as important as its operational and financial health. Fatigue, stress and burnout can undermine long-term success, and leaders must address these issues proactively.

2. **Open Communication Builds Trust:** Transparency between leadership and employees is essential. Regular updates, open conversations and town hall meetings can bridge the communication gap, making employees feel more connected to the company's mission and direction.

3. **Recognition Boosts Morale:** Recognizing and celebrating individual and team contributions, no matter how small, significantly improves motivation and employee engagement. Employees feel more valued when their hard work is acknowledged openly.

4. **Work-Life Balance is Key to Sustainable Productivity:** Pushing employees to their limits may yield short-term results, but it's unsustainable. Flexible work schedules and promoting mental health support ensure that employees can maintain high levels of productivity without burning out.

5. **Leadership Visibility is Powerful:** Amit's increased visibility on the production floor demonstrated that leadership engagement at the ground level enhances trust, camaraderie, and shared purpose. Employees feel more valued when leaders are accessible and empathetic.

6. **Holistic Organizational Health Matters:** Amit, Nisha, and Neha implemented initiatives addressing communication, recognition, work-life balance, and leadership visibility. Focusing on people, processes, and emotional well-being created a healthier, more resilient organizational culture.

7. **Building a Culture of Listening:** An organization that listens to its employees' concerns, frustrations, and needs will be more adaptable and better equipped to face future challenges. Feedback loops should be established to continuously improve both the work environment and employee satisfaction.

8. **Team Motivation Requires Connection to Mission:** Employees worked tirelessly for the Electric Auto project but felt disconnected from the bigger picture. Amit's efforts to reconnect them with the company's mission reenergized their sense of purpose and motivation.

9. **Shared Responsibility Strengthens Bonds:** Amit fostered a sense of shared responsibility by acknowledging the challenges faced across departments and encouraging collaboration. This approach unified the team and created a supportive workplace.

10. **Emotional Health Supports Operational Success:** The chapter demonstrated that addressing emotional well-being leads to improved operational outcomes. A healthy, motivated workforce is better equipped to handle demands and ensure high-quality results.

By focusing on these areas, Volt Motors was able to create a more supportive, engaged, and emotionally healthy workplace, preparing the company for sustained success as it moved into full- scale production.

Chapter 13
Cash is King

Introduction: The Reality of Financial Pressure

The Electric Auto project had been a beacon of hope for Volt Motors. The product was innovative, the team had rallied together to overcome every technical challenge, and the company was poised to disrupt the electric vehicle market. But beneath the surface of this progress lay a sobering reality: cash flow was becoming a serious issue. Volt Motors was a start-up, fueled by external funding, and every decision had financial consequences.

While the engineers, designers, and operations teams focused on perfecting the product and preparing for full-scale production, the company's financial health was hanging in the balance. Volt had faced unexpected costs—tooling rework, delays caused by supplier issues, and increased spending to fix critical problems. The rapid pace of spending meant that the company's cash reserves were dwindling faster than anticipated. It was a critical juncture—without immediate action, the project and the company could be at risk.

For Suhani, Volt's financial lead, the warning signs were clear. No matter how impressive the Electric Auto was, without the financial resources to back it, the entire project could unravel. She had been flagging the issue for weeks—reminding the leadership team that cash is king in the business world. A brilliant product with no cash to support its production could sink the company.

As the financial pressure mounted, Amit found himself learning an important lesson: innovation, vision, and technical success were only part of the equation. The real challenge was ensuring that Volt Motors had the financial backing to survive. It was no longer just about developing a product—it was about securing the future of the company. And to do that, Volt Motors needed cash, and they needed it fast.

Part 1: Financial Pressure

The conference room was unusually quiet as Nisha Mehta, Volt Motors' CEO, prepared to address the senior leadership team. The Electric Auto project had brought the company closer to its goal of disrupting the EV market, but the financial pressure was becoming too great to ignore. Amit, Suhani, and the other department heads gathered around the table, all aware that today's meeting would not be about technology or product performance—it would be about the company's financial survival.

Nisha looked around the room, her expression serious but composed. She had led companies through tough situations before, but Volt Motors was in a precarious position. While the team had done incredible work developing the Electric Auto, they were burning through cash reserves at an alarming rate. It was time to have a frank conversation about cash flow, financial discipline, and what it would take to keep Volt Motors afloat.

"Let's talk about cash," Nisha began, her voice clear and direct. "We've made great progress with the Electric Auto, but I need all of you to understand something very important: cash is king. Without cash, all the hard work we've done means nothing. Innovation doesn't matter if we can't fund production. You can't launch a product if you can't pay your suppliers, your employees, or keep the lights on."

The team listened intently, knowing that Nisha was about to give them a lesson in financial survival. She had seen companies crumble because they hadn't managed their cash reserves properly, and she was determined not to let Volt Motors fall into that trap.

"We're a start-up," she continued. "That means we don't have the luxury of a large, established company with deep pockets. We don't have the ability to absorb mistakes or delays easily. Right now, every rupee we spend is crucial, and we're spending faster than we should. Our cash reserves are depleting faster than projected because of the additional costs—tooling rework, vendor delays, and production challenges."

Suhani, seated next to Amit, nodded in agreement. She had been tracking these costs and raising concerns for weeks. "We've been spending heavily to resolve the issues we've faced," Suhani added. "But we're getting dangerously close to the point where we won't be able to cover our expenses unless we bring in more funding or start generating revenue quickly."

Nisha nodded, acknowledging Suhani's input. "Exactly. That's why I want to talk to all of you about the importance of managing our cash flow. We need to be incredibly disciplined. From this point forward, we must only spend on what's essential to get us through to production and beyond. No more discretionary spending, no unnecessary expenses."

She paused for a moment, letting her words sink in before continuing. "We need to bridge this gap between where we are now and when we start generating revenue from the Electric Auto. Once we move into full-scale production and sales, cash will start flowing in. But until that happens, we have to make sure we don't run out of resources before we get there. If we don't manage this carefully, we could run out of cash before we ever sell a single vehicle."

Nisha moved to the whiteboard at the front of the room and began outlining the cash-to-cash cycle—a concept that was critical for start-ups like Volt Motors. She drew a simple diagram showing the flow of cash through the business, from the moment they purchased materials and paid vendors to the moment they sold vehicles and received payments from customers.

"Here's what we're dealing with," Nisha explained, pointing to the different stages of the cycle. "Right now, we're operating with a negative cash-to-cash cycle. That means we're paying out more than we're bringing in. Our suppliers are getting paid, we're covering production costs, but we don't have revenue coming in yet. That puts us in a vulnerable position."

Amit looked at the diagram, understanding the gravity of the situation. While he had been focused on the technical challenges of getting the Electric Auto ready for launch, the financial side of the business was just as critical. Without cash, none of their progress would matter.

Nisha continued, her voice steady but urgent. "The goal is to shorten this cycle. We need to get to the point where we're bringing in cash from sales faster than we're spending it. That's how businesses survive—by managing their working capital effectively. And for us, managing our cash means running as lean as possible."

She turned to the group, her eyes sharp. "This means we need to focus on two things: keeping our costs down and delaying cash outflows where we can. We need to negotiate better payment terms with our suppliers. If we can push out payments by 30 or 60 days, that gives us more breathing room. At the same time, we need to bring in revenue from our customers faster—whether that means asking for advance payments or offering incentives for early payment."

Suhani, who had been instrumental in managing the company's finances, added. "I've already started having those conversations with some of our suppliers. The key is to get them on board with longer payment terms without compromising the quality or delivery timelines. But it's going to require careful negotiation."

Amit spoke up, realizing the importance of these financial strategies. "So, essentially, we're trying to create a buffer. We need to stretch our cash until we start generating revenue from the Electric Auto."

"Exactly," Nisha replied. "And that's where nimble financial management comes in. We're going to be frugal—every expense needs to be justified. Every department needs to be aware of what they're spending and why. There's no room for waste. If we manage this right, we'll survive until the revenue starts flowing. If we don't, we risk running out of cash before we ever see a return on our investment."

She leaned forward, her expression serious but determined. "And this isn't just about cutting costs—it's about being smart with how we use the cash we have. We need to invest in the areas that will get us to market quickly and ensure that our product is ready for customers. But we can't spend a rupee more than necessary."

The room was silent for a moment as everyone absorbed the weight of Nisha's words. The message was clear: managing cash wasn't just the finance department's responsibility—it was everyone's responsibility.

"We're a challenger brand," Nisha continued, her voice growing stronger. "We're up against companies with far more resources than we have. But what we lack in cash, we make up for in agility. We can move faster, be more efficient, and adapt quicker than the bigger players. That's our advantage. But only if we manage our cash flow carefully."

Amit felt a deep sense of responsibility as he listened. He knew that the Electric Auto project was crucial to Volt Motors' future, but without the financial stability to see it through, all their hard work could be for nothing.

Nisha wrapped up the session by reiterating the key points. "From this point on, every decision we make has to factor in cash. We need to ask ourselves, 'Is this essential to the business right now?' If the answer is no, then we don't spend. Cash is king—and without it, nothing else matters. We'll get through this, but only if we stay disciplined and focused."

As the meeting came to an end, Amit left with a newfound understanding of the delicate balance between innovation and financial survival. The team had worked tirelessly to develop a breakthrough product, but now they needed to be equally committed to financial discipline if Volt Motors was going to thrive in the competitive EV market.

Part 2: Securing Funds

The Electric Auto project was at a crucial stage. With production readiness in sight, there was an urgent need to secure a fresh round of funding to cover the costs of mass production, ensure product availability across key markets, and fund the marketing campaigns that would give Volt Motors the visibility it needed to compete against industry giants. The company needed a solid financial foundation for a confident launch—one that would not only produce the first batch of orders but also build momentum in the fiercely competitive EV sector.

Nisha, Suhani, and Amit had spent weeks preparing for a series of high-stakes meetings with investors, including private equity (PE) funds and the company's own promoters. Securing this round of funding would be critical—not just for the production of the Electric Auto but for ensuring that the company could execute its marketing plans and build brand presence in key markets. Without the additional capital, Volt Motors risked losing ground to its competitors.

The trio entered the investor meetings armed with presentations, financial projections, and a clear strategy for the future. But they knew that the investors would not be easy to convince. The stakes were high, and the questions they were about to face would be tough. Investors weren't just looking for innovation; they wanted proof that Volt Motors had the financial discipline, a clear business model, and a strategy to survive the long haul in a crowded market.

The Investor Meetings: Deep Drilling

The first meeting was with Kartik Sharma, a seasoned investor with decades of experience in funding start-ups. Kartik had seen countless companies pitch brilliant ideas, only to collapse under the weight of poor financial management. As Nisha, Suhani, and Amit took their seats across from Kartik and his team, they knew they had to present more than just a vision—they needed to prove Volt Motors had the ability to execute its plans.

Kartik wasted no time. "Let's talk about your business model," he began, leaning forward. "You're launching into a market that's already crowded with big names. What makes Volt Motors different? Why should we believe you'll succeed where others have struggled?"

Nisha, always calm under pressure, responded confidently. "What sets Volt Motors apart is our focus on the mass market—urban and semi-urban areas where electric vehicles are not just a novelty but a necessity. We've designed the Electric Auto with a clear target audience in mind: affordability, reliability, and eco-friendliness. Our goal isn't to compete directly with the high-end players but to dominate the market segment that needs cost-effective, environmentally friendly transportation solutions."

Kartik nodded but pressed further. "I understand that. But how are you going to fund this push into the market? You're asking for a substantial investment, and I want to know how you're going to manage that cash flow. What's your plan for balancing prudency in spending with the aggressive growth you're promising?"

Suhani stepped in, pulling up detailed financial projections on her tablet. "We're incredibly mindful of how we spend. Every rupee is accounted for, and we've made it a priority to focus on frugality while still ensuring quality. We've negotiated extended payment terms with our suppliers, which gives us more flexibility with our working capital. Additionally, we've mapped out a clear timeline for cash inflows from the anticipated sales of the first batch of Electric Autos. Our break- even point is within reach, and we've built contingencies into our budget to handle unexpected costs."

Amit, knowing the technical side was just as important, added, "We've also kept production costs down without compromising on quality by sourcing parts from reliable but cost-effective vendors. Our relationships with suppliers are strong, and we've designed the Electric Auto with modular components to make scaling production more manageable. Everything we've done so far has been about maintaining a balance between cost efficiency and scalability."

The conversation shifted toward the competitive landscape, with Kartik's team zeroing in on the presence of large players like Tesla, Tata, and Mahindra, who were already making strides in the EV market.

"How do you plan to stand out in such a crowded market?" asked one of Kartik's associates. "These companies have deeper pockets and established supply chains. What's your strategy to counter the competition?"

Nisha didn't hesitate. "We're not competing on the same terms as Tesla or Tata. Their focus is on premium electric vehicles, while ours is on mass transportation solutions. The Electric Auto is designed to meet the needs of the everyday commuter in cities and towns where EV adoption is growing but remains price sensitive. We've built a product that balances affordability, performance, and sustainability. Our strategy is to penetrate these markets first, establish a foothold, and then expand from there."

Amit added, "We've also ensured that our vehicle will have a first-mover advantage in certain semi-urban regions where larger players haven't focused yet. By targeting these areas, we can build brand loyalty and capture a significant share of the market before others even enter."

Kartik's eyes narrowed slightly. "And what about your future plans? You're asking for funding not just for production but also for marketing and distribution. How do you plan to balance all of that without running into cash flow problems again?"

Suhani was ready. "We've budgeted carefully for the launch. Our plan is to create product availability in key markets with strong ATL (Above the Line) and BTL (Below the Line) marketing activities. We'll focus our resources on the most promising markets first, ensuring that the Electric Auto is not just available but visible. We're leveraging digital marketing for cost-effective brand awareness while also working with local dealerships to create a strong presence in urban and semi-urban areas. Once we've secured a foothold, we'll scale our marketing efforts."

Nisha, sensing that they needed to close strong, added, "We're not here to make tall claims. Everything we've outlined today is based on solid planning and realistic projections. We've encountered challenges, but we've also proven that we can adapt and overcome them. Our focus is on long-term sustainability, and we believe that with the right financial backing, Volt Motors can become a leader in the mass-market EV segment."

Handling Tough Questions with Confidence

The conversations with Kartik and other investors that followed were tough, but authentic. Nisha, Suhani, and Amit didn't shy away from the hard truths. They addressed each question with honesty, acknowledging the risks but also laying out clear strategies for mitigating them. They didn't overpromise, but they did show that Volt Motors had a well-thought-out plan for the future.

Other investors echoed Kartik's concerns, focusing on Volt's ability to scale while maintaining financial discipline. They wanted to know how the company would handle cash burn during the expansion phase and what their contingency plans were if they didn't hit sales targets.

"Scaling up production is expensive," said another investor during one of the meetings. "How do you plan to manage cash flow once you start producing at higher volumes?"

Amit was prepared. "We've implemented a just-in-time inventory system to minimize holding costs. Our supply chain is flexible, allowing us to scale production based on demand without overextending ourselves. We also have a clear cost-reduction roadmap for our second and third production batches, where economies of scale will start to kick in. The first batch is always the most expensive, but as we move forward, our per-unit costs will decrease."

Suhani added, "Additionally, we've built conservative revenue estimates into our projections. Even if we don't hit our highest sales targets initially, we'll have enough liquidity to keep production running smoothly. Our focus is on profitable growth, not just growth for the sake of it."

The Outcome

After several rounds of tough questioning and deep dives into Volt Motors' business model, the investors were convinced. They appreciated the honesty and practical approach the team had taken. There were no unrealistic promises, only well-planned strategies backed by solid numbers. Volt Motors was granted the funding they needed to proceed with full-scale production, marketing, and distribution.

Back at the office, Nisha, Suhani, and Amit reflected on the journey that had led them to this point. The funding had secured the company's immediate future, but they knew that the real work was just beginning. The investors would be watching every move they made, and now they had to deliver on the promises they had made.

As they left the meeting room, Amit felt a mix of relief and determination. Volt Motors had the cash it needed to move forward, but every rupee would need to be carefully spent. The Electric Auto was on its way to market, but it was up to the entire team to ensure that the financial discipline they had promised would translate into long-term success.

Key learnings from Chapter 13: "Cash is King"

1. **Cash Flow is Critical:** Innovation alone cannot sustain a company. Financial health, specifically cash flow, is vital for survival. Volt Motors was a start-up dependent on external funding, which created immense financial pressure as cash reserves dwindled faster than expected.

2. **Every Decision Has Financial Consequences:** Unexpected costs, such as tooling rework, supplier delays, and problem-solving expenses, significantly impacted Volt's financial health. This highlights that all decisions, particularly in the production and supply chain, have financial implications that must be managed carefully.

3. **The Importance of Financial Discipline:** Nisha's message to the team emphasized the need for strict financial discipline. Every expense needed to be justified and essential to the business's immediate survival and goals. Discretionary spending had to be curtailed, with a focus only on what would help the company reach full-scale production and profitability.

4. **Managing the Cash-to-Cash Cycle:** Nisha explained the concept of the cash-to-cash cycle, illustrating that Volt Motors was operating with a negative cycle—spending more cash than it was bringing in. The team needed to shorten this cycle by negotiating better payment terms and speeding up revenue collection to improve financial liquidity.

5. **Delayed Payments and Stretching Cash:** One of the strategies was to negotiate better payment terms with suppliers and delay cash outflows. This was critical for extending the company's runway until revenue from Electric Auto sales began to flow in.

6. **Leadership's Role in Financial Survival:** Financial discipline wasn't just the responsibility of the finance team; it became everyone's responsibility. Leadership had to ensure the entire organization understood the importance of spending wisely and maintaining agility, especially in a resource-constrained environment.

7. **Building Investor Confidence:** Investors weren't just looking for a vision or innovation—they wanted proof of financial discipline and a sustainable business model. During the investor meetings, Volt Motors demonstrated how they were mindful of every rupee spent and had contingency plans to mitigate financial risks.

8. **Balancing Growth and Financial Prudence:** The team had to balance aggressive growth plans with financial prudence, ensuring they could scale production while managing costs. They introduced a just-in-time inventory system to keep holding costs low and planned for scaling production based on demand without overextending themselves.

9. **Transparency and Realism in Investor Discussions:** Volt Motors' leadership showed transparency in their meetings with investors. They addressed challenges openly and laid out clear strategies for

overcoming them, which helped them secure the funding needed for production and future growth.

10. **Execution Matters:** After securing the funding, the team knew the real challenge would be delivering on their promises to investors. Financial discipline and execution would be critical in ensuring the Electric Auto's success in the competitive EV market.

These lessons emphasize the critical balance between financial management and innovation, showing that even the most innovative products need strong financial backing and discipline to succeed.

Chapter 14

Discipline is Destiny

Introduction: The Final Push Toward Glory

The journey of developing the Electric Passenger Auto had been a long and arduous one for Volt Motors. Over the course of many months, the team had navigated setbacks, delays, and moments of doubt. What had begun as a daring vision to disrupt the electric vehicle market had transformed into a grueling marathon of overcoming technical challenges, securing funding, and keeping a fragile start-up afloat in a highly competitive industry.

Now, the finish line was in sight. The team had battled through every challenge thrown at them, and the product was ready to be unveiled to the world. But as the launch date approached, the atmosphere inside Volt Motors was one of heightened tension. The stakes had never been higher. The launch wasn't just the end of a project; it was the moment of truth that would decide the company's future. The Electric Auto had to succeed—it had to perform in the market, gain customer traction, and prove to the world that Volt Motors was a force to be reckoned with.

But in these final days, as the team prepared for the product's release, Amit knew that success wouldn't be determined by a stroke of luck or a last-minute stroke of brilliance. Discipline—the steady, methodical adherence to processes, principles, and planning—was what would carry them through. It had been discipline that allowed them to overcome the production delays, stay focused during financial struggles, and solve complex technical problems. And now, in the final push, it was discipline that would see them across the finish line.

Nisha Mehta, the CEO, had reminded Amit and the team throughout their journey that every detail mattered. There was no room for shortcuts. Every step they took now would set the stage for the company's performance in the market. And while they had proven their mettle many times over, the last few days before the launch were often the most unpredictable. It was during this time that many companies stumbled—rushed decisions, last-minute panic, and overlooked details could turn a near-success into a disaster.

Amit, with the weight of leadership on his shoulders, understood this better than anyone. Volt Motors had reached a critical juncture. The technical problems were behind them, the funding was in place, and the team was aligned. But now, as they approached the launch, they had to ensure that everything was executed flawlessly. They had been through the forming, storming, and norming stages of team development, and now it was time for them to perform.

In his quiet moments, Amit reflected on how far they had come. He thought about the long nights, the missed family time, and the sacrifices each member of the team had made to get to this point. The Electric Auto wasn't just a product—it was the culmination of their shared effort, their resilience, and their commitment to a vision that had often seemed out of reach.

The pressure was immense, but Amit knew that pressure could either forge greatness or cause cracks to appear. His job now was to keep his team grounded, focused, and disciplined. This launch was about more than proving they could create a successful product. It was about showing the world that Volt Motors was built on the solid foundation of teamwork, perseverance, and a disciplined approach to innovation.

With just days to go before the launch, Amit and his team gathered their final reserves of energy. They were tired, mentally and physically. Yet, they knew this was the moment that would define not just the project, but their careers, and the future of Volt Motors.

Discipline, not luck, would determine their destiny.

Part 1: Final Preparations

With the launch just days away, the atmosphere at Volt Motors was one of quiet intensity. The Electric Auto, after months of grueling development and testing, was finally ready for the world to see.

But Amit knew that the final preparations were just as critical as the months of hard work they had put in. In these final moments, the difference between success and failure would come down to discipline—following the processes they had built, maintaining focus, and resisting the temptation to rush or cut corners.

Amit had called for a core team meeting to ensure that every aspect of the launch was on track. This was a pivotal meeting, the last major review before they committed to the final rollout. He needed to be sure that there were no surprises lurking, no details that had been missed, and no last-minute crises that could derail the launch.

Seated around the table were the familiar faces that had been with Amit throughout the entire journey: Vivek, Suhani, Pooja, Asif, Pranav, Kiran and Rahul. Each of them looked both tired and determined. They had been through so much together—personal sacrifices, professional challenges, and moments of doubt—but they had also proven themselves resilient. Now, the finish line was in sight.

Amit began the meeting by laying out the agenda: they would review product readiness, ensuring that every component of the Electric Auto was launch-ready, before moving on to market preparation and production scheduling. He wanted to leave no stone unturned.

"Let's get started," Amit said, his voice calm but firm. "We've done a tremendous amount of work to get to this point, but now we need to be absolutely certain that everything is in place. We'll go through each area of the project, step by step, and make sure we're ready for launch. I know everyone's exhausted, but this is the final push. Let's make it count."

Engineering and Product Readiness

First up was Vivek, who had led the engineering team through countless iterations of the Electric Auto. His team had solved the

BMS issues, fine-tuned the powertrain, and ensured that the BIW structure was perfectly aligned after the tooling rework. Amit knew that Vivek had been pushing himself and his team hard, but he needed to hear the details first-hand.

"Vivek, how's the vehicle looking?" Amit asked.

Vivek nodded, pulling up the latest test reports on his tablet. "We've run the final series of road tests, and the results are solid. The BMS glitch we caught last week has been fully resolved. We've triple- checked the battery's thermal management system, and everything is performing within spec. Powertrain efficiency is where it needs to be, and we've run the range tests multiple times—we're hitting our targets."

Amit glanced over the numbers, impressed but not surprised. "And what about the BIW? Any issues with the structural integrity after the tooling rework?"

Vivek shook his head. "None. We've had zero issues with the new parts. The front and rear panels fit perfectly, and there's no misalignment anywhere. We've also stress-tested the chassis under heavy loads, and it's holding up perfectly. No signs of flexing or failure."

Amit felt a wave of relief but didn't let it show. "Good. And what about the software integration, Pranav?"

Pranav, who had been quietly reviewing his own reports, spoke up. "We've finalized the VCU and BMS communication protocols. The OTA updates are fully functional, and we've validated the software integration across the entire system. All error codes have been cleared, and we've simulated both urban and highway driving scenarios. There are no glitches— everything is stable."

Amit nodded, satisfied. "Great work, both of you. Let's move on to the production side."

Operations and Production Readiness

Asif, who had overseen the setup of the production line, was next. The transition from beta testing to full-scale production had been smooth so far, but there were still final preparations to confirm.

"Asif, where do we stand on production readiness?" Amit asked.

Asif, always precise, spoke with confidence. "The production line is ready. We've completed the final assembly station calibrations, and all the tooling is in place. The supply chain is flowing, and all parts are arriving on schedule. We've trained the production staff on the new processes, especially around the battery integration and chassis assembly. We're ready to hit our daily production targets as soon as we get the green light."

Amit leaned back in his chair, taking a moment to process the information. "And what about quality assurance?" he asked, turning to Jennifer.

Jennifer, who had been leading the charge on quality inspections, was well-prepared. "We've implemented the new three-stage quality checks—incoming, in-process, and final inspections. Every vehicle coming off the line will go through rigorous testing before it's cleared for shipment. We've run mock tests with the production team, and I'm confident we'll catch any issues early."

Amit felt a sense of calm wash over him. Everything was lining up, but there was still one more crucial area to cover.

Marketing and Sales Preparation

With the vehicle and production ready, Amit shifted the conversation to Kiran and Rahul, who were in charge of the launch marketing campaign and sales strategy, respectively. They needed to ensure that when the Electric Auto hit the market, it would make an immediate impact.

"Kiran, where are we on marketing preparations?" Amit asked.

Kiran pulled up the campaign timeline on the screen. "We're ready to go live with our ATL (Above the Line) and BTL (Below the Line) campaigns. The teaser ads have already generated significant interest online, and we've booked spots in all the major cities. Our dealerships are prepped with demo vehicles, and our sales team is trained to handle customer inquiries. We've created targeted campaigns for urban and semi-urban markets, and we're pushing hard on digital marketing to build brand awareness."

Amit nodded, appreciating the attention to detail. "And Rahul, how are we looking on the sales side?"

Rahul, who had been managing the financial projections and sales pipeline, responded confidently. "We've secured commitments from several key dealerships, and our early order volumes are strong. Based on our market analysis, we're expecting to hit our sales targets within the first two quarters. I've also ensured that we've budgeted for any unexpected marketing pushes if needed. Cash flow is stable, and we're well within our planned spending limits."

Amit sat back, taking a deep breath. The team had done an extraordinary job. Every aspect of the launch—from product readiness to production, marketing, and sales—was aligned. But he knew they couldn't afford to relax just yet.

Updating Nisha

After the meeting concluded, Amit headed to Nisha's office to give her the full update. Nisha had been following the progress closely, but with the launch so near, she needed to hear the final status directly from Amit.

"How are we looking?" Nisha asked as Amit sat down across from her desk.

Amit smiled, feeling a rare sense of optimism. "We're ready. Vivek's team has finished all the final tests—the vehicle is performing exactly as we need it to. Asif got the production line running, and we're ready to hit full capacity as soon as we launch. Marketing is set, and Suhani's confident in our financial position. There are no major red flags."

Nisha nodded, visibly relieved. "Good. I knew you'd get us here. But remember, Amit, the last stretch is often the hardest. We've come too far to let any detail slip now. Stay focused, and keep the team disciplined."

Amit agreed. "We've talked about that. We know these final days are critical, but the team is in the right mindset. Everyone knows how important this launch is—not just for the product, but for the company. Discipline will carry us through."

Nisha smiled. "That's what I like to hear. You've led the team well, Amit. Now let's make sure this launch is something the market will never forget."

As Amit left her office, he felt a sense of calm determination. The pieces were in place, the team was aligned, and Volt Motors was ready. Now, it was time to execute—and in the world of start-ups, execution was everything.

Part 2: Avoiding Last-Minute Panic

As the final countdown to the Electric Passenger Auto launch began, the team at Volt Motors found themselves in a familiar but tense situation—preparing for the unknown. While the product was technically ready, experience had taught Amit and his team that last- minute glitches were inevitable. This wasn't a new phenomenon; it was the reality of launching any complex product in a highly competitive market. But the stakes were higher now. Any misstep in these final hours could damage the company's reputation, delay production, and undermine months of hard work.

The pressure had mounted to a near-boiling point. The core team, exhausted after weeks of nonstop work, was showing signs of stress. It was in moments like these that human behaviour—the good and the bad—emerged most starkly. Everyone had their breaking point, and as launch day approached, cracks began to show.

The First Glitch: BMS Warning

It started with a seemingly small issue in one of the final BMS tests. During a routine check, the system had flashed a low voltage warning. In isolation, this might have been a minor hiccup—a quick recalibration issue or a sensor glitch. But with the weight of the impending launch pressing down on them, the team treated it like a full-blown crisis.

Vivek, who had led the engineering effort, was the first to spot the glitch. His initial reaction was one of frustration, evident in the way he banged his fist on the desk. "This shouldn't be happening now," he muttered under his breath. His team had run hundreds of tests, and everything had been stable. The pressure to ensure every single component was perfect was now taking a toll.

Pooja, seated next to him, picked up on the tension and reassured, "Vivek, it's just one warning. We've cleared the system before, right? Let's not panic."

But panic was already setting in. The room grew tense as more engineers gathered around the test bench, eager to identify the cause. Asif and Pranav arrived moments later, alerted by the internal communications chat that something was wrong.

"We can't afford any missteps now," Pranav said quietly to Amit, who had joined the growing crowd of engineers. "Everyone's jittery. A small issue feels like a major setback with the launch breathing down our necks."

Amit could feel the tension in the air. These were moments where leadership was tested, not by the size of the problem, but by how the team responded to it. He saw the anxiety building—people were speaking louder, cutting each other off, and tempers were flaring.

Vivek, now visibly stressed, started pacing around the room, muttering about the potential causes of the glitch. "If this is a power distribution issue, we're looking at a bigger problem. We might need to delay."

Asif cut in, trying to temper the panic. "We don't know that yet, Vivek. Let's isolate the issue before jumping to conclusions."

But the fear of a launch delay loomed large. For a brief moment, the tension threatened to boil over, with Vivek snapping at one of the junior engineers for suggesting a quick fix.

That's when Amit stepped in.

Stabilizing the Situation

"Everyone, calm down," Amit's voice cut through the noise like a knife. He had learned long ago that leadership in these moments wasn't about knowing the technical details better than anyone—it was about stabilizing the team.

He gestured for Vivek to take a seat. "Let's take a step back. We've been through tougher situations before, and we solved them because we didn't panic. Let's work through this the same way."

The team quieted down, and Amit continued. "Vivek, run a diagnostic on the BMS. Let's confirm whether this is a sensor fault or a deeper issue. Asif, I want you to check the power distribution system in the affected vehicle. Pranav, run a quick systems check on the software integration to rule out a communication error."

As they moved to their stations, Amit turned to the rest of the engineers who had gathered around. "The rest of you—stand by. No need to overcrowd this issue. We're running diagnostics, and we'll solve it like we always do. No rushed decisions, no panic."

Slowly, the tension in the room began to dissipate. With Amit's calm leadership in place, the team refocused on the task at hand. Vivek ran the diagnostics, and after an hour of testing and cross- referencing with Asif system checks, they identified the problem: it was a faulty sensor that had triggered the low voltage warning. A simple replacement of the sensor fixed the issue, and within hours, the BMS was back to running flawlessly.

Stakeholder Conversations

Later that evening, Amit knew he had to update Nisha on the situation. He had always been transparent with her, especially when problems arose. Even though the BMS issue had been resolved, it was important to keep her in the loop, especially with the launch so close.

He walked into her office, where Nisha was reviewing the final marketing plan with the head of sales, Rahul.

"Amit, what's the status?" Nisha asked as soon as she saw him.

"There was a small glitch with the BMS during testing—a faulty sensor triggered a low voltage warning," Amit explained. "We've isolated the issue and fixed it. It's nothing major, and we're still on track."

Nisha, ever the seasoned leader, didn't react with alarm. She trusted Amit's judgment. "Do we expect any more surprises?"

Amit shook his head. "I don't think so. The systems are stable, and we've run enough tests to know that everything else is performing as expected. But I wanted to bring it to your attention in case you hear any rumours."

Nisha nodded, appreciative of Amit's transparency. "Thanks for keeping me in the loop. We're so close now, Amit. I trust you to handle anything that comes up. But remember, we can't afford any last-minute disasters."

Amit took a deep breath, feeling the weight of her words. "I know, Nisha. But we've built a disciplined team, and I trust them. We'll be ready."

As Amit left Nisha's office, he caught a glimpse of the sales and marketing team finalizing the launch event logistics. The energy in the office was still tense, but Amit had faith in his team's ability to keep everything under control.

Reassuring the Team

The next morning, Amit gathered his core team for a final update.

The sensor glitch had rattled a few nerves, and he could sense that some team members were still anxious about the upcoming launch. They needed reassurance—and he knew exactly what to say.

"Look, I know these last-minute issues can be stressful," Amit began, looking around the room at the tired but focused faces of his team. "But we've been through worse. What got us through those challenges was discipline—our ability to stay calm, follow our processes, and trust the work we've done."

He turned to Vivek, Pooja, Kiran and the rest of the team. "We've prepared for this launch. We've tested everything. And yes, there may be a few hiccups, but that's normal. What matters is how we respond. And I know that every one of you will handle it with the same professionalism and focus that you've shown since day one."

The team visibly relaxed, reassured by Amit's confidence. There was still work to be done, but the panic had passed. Amit knew that the key to navigating these high-pressure moments wasn't to pretend that problems wouldn't arise—it was to face them head-on, with discipline and trust in each other.

As the team broke to get back to work, Amit felt a renewed sense of calm. The countdown to launch continued, but they were ready. Together, they had weathered the storms of uncertainty, and now they were on the cusp of success.

Part 3: Launch Success

The day of the Electric Passenger Auto launch had finally arrived. For months, the team at Volt Motors had poured their hearts and minds into developing a product that would disrupt the mass- transportation market. Now, the culmination of their efforts was about to be unveiled in front of a carefully selected audience of media personalities, top auto dealers, and influential vloggers from the automotive industry. It was a high-stakes moment, the kind that could make or break a product's reputation before it even hit the market.

The launch event was a glittering affair, hosted in one of the city's most iconic convention centres. The entire venue had been transformed to reflect Volt Motors' vision of the future—sleek, minimalist design, electric charging stations lining the entrance, and large LED displays showing images of bustling cities where the Electric Auto was poised to dominate. There was a palpable sense of anticipation in the air, and the pressure to deliver was intense.

Amit stood off to the side, overseeing the final preparations. He was proud but also nervous. He knew that today wasn't just about launching a product; it was about showcasing Volt Motors as a serious contender in the highly competitive electric vehicle market. Months of hard work, discipline, and perseverance had brought them to this moment, and now it was time to present it to the world.

The event began with Nisha Mehta, the CEO of Volt Motors, taking the stage. As always, Nisha exuded confidence, her presence commanding attention from the moment she walked to the podium. She began with a powerful opening statement that set the tone for the evening.

"Good evening, everyone. Thank you for being here to witness what we believe is the future of urban transportation. Today, we are not just unveiling a product—we are introducing a revolution in how people move in cities and towns across India. The Electric Passenger Auto is our answer to the growing need for sustainable, affordable, and efficient transportation. But this vehicle is more than just an EV. It's a statement of our commitment to innovation, environmental responsibility, and driving change."

The audience, made up of media honchos, top auto dealers, influential vloggers, and automotive enthusiasts, listened intently. The stage was set, and the excitement was building.

The Unveiling

As Nisha finished her introduction, the lights dimmed, and a dramatic hush fell over the room. A massive screen lit up, showcasing the journey of Volt Motors and the development of the Electric Auto. A slick video montage played, highlighting the technical prowess of the vehicle—its sleek design, eco-friendly features, and the intense testing it had undergone to ensure it was road-ready. The audience watched as the vehicle powered through rugged city streets, navigating tight urban spaces and showing off its cutting-edge battery technology and intelligent driving systems.

Finally, the screen faded to black, and a spotlight focused on the stage. There, covered in a futuristic silver cloth, was the Electric Auto. The tension in the room grew as the audience waited for the moment of the big reveal.

The Chairman of the company, Anant Malhotra, took the stage next. Anant had been the guiding force behind Volt Motors since its inception, and his presence lent an air of gravitas to the event. Known for his sharp business acumen and visionary leadership, Anant had a deep connection with the company, and his words carried weight.

"It gives me great pleasure to stand here today as we unveil a product that represents the future of transportation," Anant began, his voice measured and deliberate. "The Electric Passenger Auto is not just a vehicle—it's the embodiment of our belief that innovation and sustainability can drive real change. This product is a testament to the hard work, dedication, and brilliance of the team at Volt Motors. Today, we present to you a vehicle that is affordable, efficient, and designed with the needs of the urban and semi-urban commuter in mind."

With that, Anant gestured to the stage, and the silver cloth was pulled away in a dramatic flourish. The Electric Auto gleamed under the stage lights, its sleek body and futuristic design immediately drawing gasps of approval from the crowd. Cameras flashed, and the murmurs of excitement grew louder as the audience took in the vehicle's aesthetic and bold stance.

Amit stepped onto the stage next, taking his place beside the Electric Auto. This was his moment to explain the unique selling propositions (USPs) of the vehicle—to show the world what made the Electric Auto special. He looked out at the audience, a mixture of media heavyweights, influential auto bloggers, and top dealers, all eager to learn why this vehicle was different from anything else on the market.

Amit's Presentation: The USPs

"Good evening, everyone," Amit began, his voice steady but filled with energy. "This Electric Passenger Auto has been a long time in the making, and I am incredibly proud to stand here today and present it to you. Let me take a moment to walk you through what makes this vehicle truly revolutionary."

He gestured toward the Electric Auto, and a large screen behind him lit up with a detailed diagram of the vehicle. Amit's calm, methodical style of communication gave the audience confidence— they could see that this wasn't just a flashy launch. It was the result of months of disciplined engineering, design, and testing.

1. **Affordability:** Amit started with the core of the vehicle's market appeal. "Our goal from the beginning was to make electric transportation accessible to the mass market. We've achieved that with an incredibly competitive price point, making this Electric Auto affordable for urban and semi-urban commuters, as well as fleet operators. The total cost of ownership is significantly lower than traditional fuel-based autos, thanks to low running costs, minimal maintenance, and zero fuel expenses."

He explained how Volt Motors had worked to keep costs down through smart engineering, modular components, and efficient supply chains, allowing them to offer the vehicle at a price point that made it a compelling alternative to petrol and diesel autos.

2. **Battery Technology and Range:** "The heart of any electric vehicle is its battery, and we've designed this Electric Auto to go the distance," Amit continued. "Our advanced BMS ensures optimal energy usage, giving the vehicle an impressive range on a single charge."

   He highlighted the battery technology—lithium-ion, with fast-charging capabilities, and a range that would comfortably meet the needs of daily urban commuters. "With a range of up to 200kilometres on a single charge, drivers can go about their day without worrying about frequent recharging. And when it's time to recharge, our system supports fast charging, allowing the battery to go from zero to full in just a few hours."

3. **Eco-Friendliness:** Amit moved to one of the most important aspects of the Electric Auto—its environmental impact. "This vehicle is designed with sustainability at its core. With zero emissions, it offers an environmentally friendly solution for congested cities that are battling pollution. We believe this vehicle will play a major role in reducing urban carbon footprints, making our cities cleaner and greener."

   The audience, many of whom were media professionals with a keen interest in environmental issues, nodded approvingly. Amit had tapped into a growing concern, one that had helped push the demand for electric vehicles worldwide.

4. **Durability and Performance:** He then turned to the durability and reliability of the Electric Auto. "This vehicle is built to last. We've subjected it to some of the most rigorous testing possible—extreme heat, cold, and rain conditions—and it has performed beyond our expectations. The chassis and BIW are engineered for long-term durability, ensuring that this vehicle can handle the toughest urban and semi-urban conditions."

   Amit touched on the extensive field tests they had conducted, from crowded city streets to rough semi-urban terrains, and explained how the vehicle's suspension system, powertrain, and electronic controls had been fine-tuned for performance.

5. **Comfort and Space:** The Electric Auto wasn't just about performance—it was designed for both drivers and passengers. "We've paid close attention to comfort," Amit said, highlighting the spacious interior. "Our design offers extra legroom and a wider seating arrangement, ensuring that passengers and drivers alike have a comfortable experience, even during long rides."

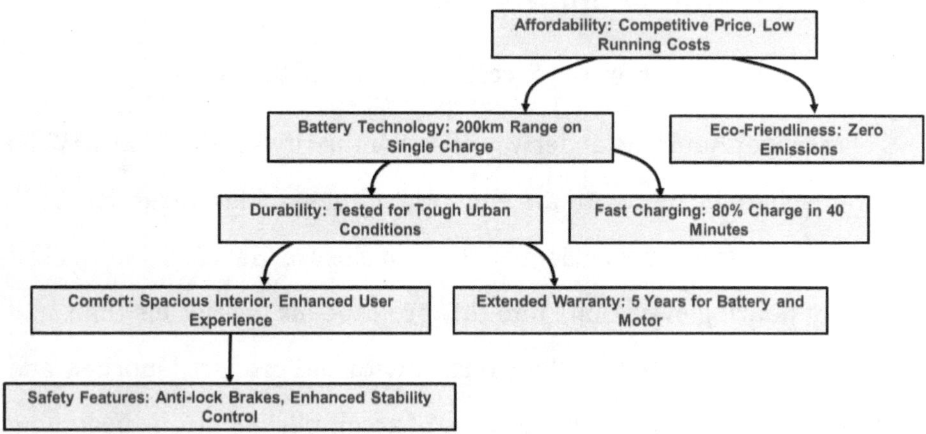

Fig 14.1

The Electric Auto also had increased luggage space, a feature Amit knew would be a selling point for fleet operators and drivers in crowded cities where space was a premium.

The Reaction

As Amit finished his presentation, the audience erupted into applause. It was clear that Volt Motors had not only created a product that was technically sound but also one that resonated deeply with the market's needs. The media, auto vloggers, and dealers in attendance could see the value in what had been created—and they were excited.

Auto influencers began live streaming their first impressions, praising the Electric Auto's design, eco-friendliness, and practicality. Top dealers were already engaging with Volt Motors' sales team, eager to place early orders. The positive buzz was palpable, and Amit could see that all the hard work was paying off.

Part 3: Celebration and Reflection

The celebratory dinner for the successful launch of the Electric

Passenger Auto was underway at one of the city's finest hotels. While the atmosphere buzzed with the euphoria of their achievement, for Amit, the evening carried an even deeper sense of closure. He had spent the last few years pouring everything into this project—his energy, his time, and sometimes even his health. Now, finally, with the product launched and well-received, the overwhelming sense of accomplishment was beginning to settle in.

Around the large banquet table, key members of Volt Motors were gathered. The soft glow of candle light illuminated the faces of his core team: Vivek, Pooja, Suhani, and Kiran. They sat together with their glasses raised, chatting, laughing, and soaking in the success they had worked so hard for. The head of the table was occupied by Nisha, who looked as composed as ever, and next to her sat Raghav, the ever-watchful strategist, who had quietly supported the project from day one.

As the evening began to wind down, Amit stood up, the room growing quiet. It wasn't planned, but he knew this was the right moment to speak from the heart. He cleared his throat, his emotions rising to the surface as he scanned the faces of the people who had been by his side throughout this monumental journey.

"I know it's late and we've all earned some rest," Amit began, his voice slightly hoarse, "but before we close this chapter, I wanted to say a few things. Tonight isn't just about the launch of the Electric Auto. It's about us, the journey we've all been through to get here."

He looked around the table, pausing on each person's face, as if he were silently acknowledging the individual battles they had all fought. "When this project began, none of us knew just how difficult it would be. There were times when we doubted ourselves, and there were moments when it felt like the weight of the world was on our shoulders. But what I've realized is that those moments didn't break us. They made us stronger."

Amit turned to Vivek, his face softening. "Vivek, I don't think I've ever met someone as committed to perfection as you are. I know we clashed—more times than I can count. But every time you pushed back, every time you refused to compromise on performance, you forced us all to be better. You held us to a higher standard, and I'm grateful for that. This Electric Auto wouldn't be what it is without your dedication to engineering excellence."

Vivek, who rarely showed emotion, gave a small nod, his expression one of quiet acknowledgment.

Next, Amit turned to Pooja. "Pooja, you've brought this vehicle to life. When we were all buried in numbers and specs, you reminded us that what we were building wasn't just a machine. You gave it soul, with your designs, your creativity, and your vision. I saw you grow into your own during this project, and I'm proud of the confidence you've found in yourself."

Pooja smiled, her eyes glistening with unshed tears. "Thank you, Amit. It means a lot."

Amit's gaze shifted to Suhani, the ever-calm force who had kept them grounded through the ups and downs. "Suhani, you've been the one who's made sure we didn't fly too close to the sun. You kept us all focused on what was feasible and reminded us that innovation doesn't mean losing sight of the bottom line. Your financial discipline ensured that this dream of ours didn't become a financial nightmare."

Suhani chuckled softly, raising her glass in acknowledgment.

"And Kiran," Amit continued, "You've been the voice of the customer in this room. Every time we got lost in technical discussions, you brought us back to the people we were building this for. Your understanding of the market, your connection to our audience—it's what's going to make this launch a success. You've made sure our product has a place in the real world."

Kiran smiled broadly, raising his glass in a gesture of thanks.

As Amit's voice grew softer, more emotional, he turned his attention to Nisha and Raghav, who sat side by side, watching him intently.

"Nisha, I don't think any of us would be here without your vision. You pushed us beyond what we thought we were capable of. Every time the project hit a wall, you showed us that there was always a way forward. I've learned so much from watching you lead, and I hope I've been able to inspire this team in the same way that you've inspired me."

Nisha, for the first time that night, allowed a small, warm smile to cross her face. "You've done more than that, Amit," she said. "You've proven that leadership isn't just about results—it's about guiding a team through the storm, and you've done that brilliantly."

Amit felt a lump rise in his throat as he turned to Raghav, whose quiet but constant presence had been a source of stability. "Raghav, you've been the one keeping the ship steady through all this. When everything felt chaotic, your calm and strategic mind kept us on course. I don't know if I've ever properly thanked you for that. You've been my sounding board, my guide, and the one who saw the big picture when I couldn't."

Raghav gave a slight smile, nodding appreciatively. "You led the team, Amit. I was just there to remind you of what you already knew."

The room was silent for a moment as Amit took a deep breath, allowing himself to feel the weight of the journey. "I want you all to know something," he said quietly. "This success—it isn't mine. It's ours. Every single one of you has poured your heart and soul into this project, and this win belongs to each of you."

He raised his glass, his voice growing stronger. "Here's to the sacrifices, the late nights, and the moments of doubt. Here's to the times when we thought we wouldn't make it, but we did. And here's to all of you—my team, my family. You've made this possible."

The team stood up, raising their glasses with him. The sound of clinking glasses echoed through the room as they toasted to their shared victory. There was no need for more words. They had all been through the same battle, and now they stood together, stronger than ever.

As the evening wound down, Amit found a quiet moment to himself, standing by the window overlooking the city lights. He reflected on the journey one last time. The project had tested him in ways he hadn't expected, but it had also shown him the power of resilience, teamwork, and trust.

The launch of the Electric Passenger Auto was just the beginning. There would be more challenges ahead, more battles to fight. But tonight, for the first time in a long while, Amit allowed himself to simply enjoy the moment. The journey had been long, but it had been worth it.

And as he stood there, gazing out into the night, he knew one thing for sure: this team, with their unwavering commitment and discipline, was ready for whatever came next.

Key Learnings from Chapter 14: Discipline is Destiny

1. **Discipline Determines Success:** The chapter emphasizes that discipline—not luck or last-minute brilliance—ensures the successful completion of high-stakes projects. Adhering to processes, principles, and planning was pivotal for Volt Motors to navigate challenges and bring the Electric Auto to market successfully.
2. **Leadership in Crisis:** Amit's ability to stay calm and composed in the face of last-minute glitches demonstrates the importance of stable leadership. By remaining focused and avoiding panic, a leader can guide the team through tense moments and keep everyone aligned with the ultimate goal.
3. **Stakeholder Management:** Through Transparency Open communication with stakeholders like Nisha and key team members kept trust intact and ensured that potential risks were managed proactively. Transparent discussions based on facts, rather than emotions, helped avoid rushed decisions.
4. **Team Collaboration Under Pressure:** In the final stages of the project, seamless collaboration across engineering, marketing, and

operations was critical. This teamwork enabled the resolution of last-minute issues, ensuring a flawless launch.

5. **Technical Readiness and Product Testing:** The chapter emphasizes the importance of thoroughly testing all aspects of the product—battery management, vehicle systems, production line quality, etc.—before the launch. Minor glitches are expected, but how they are handled can determine the overall outcome of the project.

6. **Human Behaviour in Pressure Situations:** Amit's role extended beyond technical challenges to managing the emotional strain on his team. Understanding and addressing human behavior under pressure ensured productivity and focus during the most critical moments.

7. **Celebrating Success as a Team:** Once the launch is successful, giving credit to the team for their hard work and sacrifices is essential. Amit's acknowledgment of his team's efforts shows the importance of recognizing the contributions of every individual involved.

8. **The Power of a United Vision:** Throughout the project, the team's shared vision and their collective commitment to discipline and excellence allowed them to overcome obstacles. A clear, unified goal helped align everyone's efforts, ensuring that each step contributed to the successful launch.

9. **The Balance Between Detail and the Bigger Picture:** While addressing last-minute technical details, the team never lost sight of the overarching goal: delivering a product ready for market success. Balancing granular focus with strategic thinking proved critical.

10. **Product Launch Impact:** The success of the Electric Passenger Auto's launch was not just about technical achievement but also about creating a powerful market presence. The product's USPs—affordability, eco-friendliness, durability, and comfort—resonated with the audience, demonstrating the importance of aligning product features with market needs.

These learnings highlight how **discipline, leadership, and teamwork** come together to overcome challenges and achieve success in both product development and corporate environments.

Glossary

EV - Electric Vehicle

Electric Vehicles are cars, bikes, or autos that run on electricity instead of petrol or diesel. They use a battery to store energy and an electric motor to move. In the novel, the team is working on an Electric Passenger Auto, which offers cleaner, cheaper transportation for city commuters.

BMS - Battery Management System

The Battery Management System is like a smart monitor for the EV's battery. It keeps an eye on the battery's health, how much charge is left, and prevents it from overheating. In the story, the BMS ensures that the auto's battery doesn't fail, even under tough conditions like Indian traffic and heat.

BIW - Body-in-White

This refers to the auto's bare metal frame before the seats, engine, or wheels are added. It's like the skeleton of the vehicle. In the novel, discussions around BIW focus on using materials that are strong but lightweight to ensure safety and energy efficiency.

BOM - Bill of Materials

A Bill of Materials (BOM) is like a recipe for making a product. It lists every single part, material, or component needed to build something, along with their quantities. For an Electric Passenger Auto, the BOM would include items like the battery, motor, wheels, chassis, and even screws and wires.

SOC – State of Charge

SOC tells you how much battery charge is left, like the fuel gauge in a petrol car. Drivers rely on SOC to know when to recharge. In the story, the team works to ensure the SOC readings are accurate, so drivers don't get stranded.

OTA – Over-the-Air (Updates)

Over-the-Air updates allow software changes to be sent to the vehicle without visiting a service centre. Think of it like updating an app on your phone. In the novel, OTA is mentioned as a feature that can keep the auto's systems updated with the latest improvements.

VCU – Vehicle Control Unit

The VCU is the brain of the EV. It controls everything—how the motor runs, how the battery works, and even how the brakes respond. In the story, the VCU ensures that all the parts of the auto work together smoothly.

ECU – Electronic Control Unit

The ECU is another critical controller, often managing specific systems like the battery or lights. Think of it as a mini-brain helping the main brain (VCU). The novel mentions ECU glitches as a challenge the team needs to overcome to ensure reliability.

MOSFET – Metal-Oxide-Semiconductor Field-Effect Transistor

A MOSFET is like a tiny electrical switch that controls the flow of electricity in the auto. It helps the motor run efficiently and prevents overheating.

In the novel, the team switches to better MOSFETs to fix issues with the battery chargers.

CAN - Controller Area Network

The CAN is a communication system that allows all parts of the auto to talk to each other—like a phone network within the vehicle. In the story, the team works to ensure smooth communication between the motor, battery, and other systems via CAN.

ATL - Above the Line (Marketing)

ATL marketing includes large-scale advertising like TV, billboards, or newspapers to reach a big audience. In the novel, this strategy is used to create awareness about the Electric Passenger Auto.

BTL - Below the Line (Marketing)

BTL marketing is more targeted, like running demos, offering test drives, or holding small events. It's used in the story to convince auto drivers directly about the benefits of the EV.

OEM - Original Equipment Manufacturer

An OEM is a company that makes parts or vehicles. In the novel, Volt Motors is the OEM developing the Electric Passenger Auto, while they depend on other OEMs for components like batteries or motors.

PE - Private Equity

Private Equity is money invested by firms or individuals in businesses like Volt Motors to help them grow. In the story, securing PE funding is crucial for scaling the project and launching the auto.

R&D – Research and Development

R&D is the process of creating and testing new ideas and technologies. In the novel, the team spends a lot of time in R&D to design a reliable, affordable, and durable auto.

CAPEX – Capital Expenditure

CAPEX refers to the money spent on big, long-term investments like setting up factories or buying expensive equipment. The story highlights how Volt Motors carefully manages its CAPEX to stay within budget.

TCO – Total Cost of Ownership

TCO includes everything a customer spends on the vehicle, from buying it to maintaining it over time. In the story, customers demand a low TCO, and the team designs the auto to save on fuel, repairs, and maintenance.

USP – Unique Selling Proposition

A USP is what makes a product special. For the Electric Passenger Auto, its USP is being affordable, reliable, and eco-friendly—perfect for urban drivers and fleet owners.

ROI – Return on Investment

ROI measures how much profit or benefit you get compared to the money you spend. In the novel, investors and fleet owners look at ROI to decide if the EV is worth their money.

CAGR – Compound Annual Growth Rate

CAGR shows how quickly a company or market is growing over time. The novel mentions CAGR to highlight the fast growth of the EV industry in India, encouraging investment.

KPI - Key Performance Indicator

KPIs are measurable goals that track success. For example, the team uses KPIs like battery reliability, customer satisfaction, and sales targets to judge their progress.

IRR - Internal Rate of Return

IRR is a calculation investors use to estimate how profitable an investment will be. In the story, securing a high IRR is key to attracting more funding for Volt Motors.

FEA - Finite Element Analysis

FEA is a computer simulation used to test how materials and designs will perform under stress. In the novel, the team uses FEA to ensure the auto's frame is strong enough for tough roads.

TMS - Thermal Management System

The TMS keeps the EV's battery and motor cool, preventing overheating. In the story, a reliable TMS is critical to ensure the auto runs well in India's hot climate.

Gratitude

As I bring this book to a close, I would like to extend my deepest gratitude to the people who have made this journey possible.

First and foremost, I owe an immense debt of gratitude to my father, N Divakaran Nair and mother, Radha D Nair whose unwavering support, love and blessings have been the foundation of all my endeavours. Their guidance and values have been my compass throughout life. They instilled in me the determination to pursue my dreams and the perseverance to see them through. I also want to sincerely thank my mentors, superiors, and colleagues, whose invaluable lessons, guidance, and insights into corporate life have shaped my understanding of the real-world dynamics that are reflected in this novel. Their collective wisdom and practical experience gave me the perspective to bring authenticity to the challenges, teamwork, and leadership portrayed in this story. The lessons I've learned from them, both personal and professional, have been pivotal in shaping my approach to this work.

Finally, I want to express my heartfelt thanks to my wonderful wife, Renju whose patience, understanding and constant encouragement have been invaluable during the writing of this book. Despite her own busy career, she graciously took the time to proofread each chapter, providing thoughtful insights and helping me fine-tune the details. Her keen eye for corrections and her willingness to support me in every possible way ensured that I was able to present my ideas with clarity and precision. I could not have done this without her.

To my family, mentors, and colleagues—thank you for your love, support, and for believing in this journey. Your blessings have been a constant source of strength.

www.ingramcontent.com/pod-product-compliance
Lightning Source LLC
LaVergne TN
LVHW091252150826
845673LV00006B/1392

* 9 7 9 8 8 9 6 9 9 5 1 6 6 *